MW00813021

"Judaism Disrupted sketches the foundational principles for a livable, vibrant Judaism, connected to the Jewish past yet open to being perpetually transformed. Strassfeld's open-hearted exploration of his own evolving relationship to Jewish tradition coupled with his rich and concrete discussion of how to root basic principles in ongoing practice makes this a book sure to interest and engage people with many different levels of Jewish knowledge and observance."
— **Judith Plaskow**, author, *Standing Again At Sinai: Judaism from a Feminist Perspective* and *Goddess and God in the World: Conversations in Embodied Theology*

"I can't remember the last time I felt pulled to underline a book constantly as I was reading it, but Judaism Disrupted is exactly that intellectual, spiritual and personal adventure. You will find yourself nodding, wrestling, and hoping to hold on to so many of its ideas and challenges. Rabbi Strassfeld reframes a Torah that demands breakage, reimagination, and ownership. Not only did I learn so much from Strassfeld's 11 principles; I was changed by them."
— **Abigail Pogrebin**, author, *My Jewish Year; 18 Holidays, One Wondering Jew*

"Judaism Disrupted is a book for our times. In it, Michael Strassfeld bares his soul as a lifelong struggler with the value and truth of Jewish existence. It is accessible, personal, but above all deeply honest. There are no holds barred in this bold encounter between a rich, well-informed Judaism and the demands of the present hour."
— **Rabbi Arthur Green**, author, *A Guide to the Zohar* and *Judaism for the World*

"In Judaism Disrupted, Michael Strassfeld once more reveals himself to be one of the most creative and spiritually sensitive teachers of our time. Drawing on his vast knowledge of traditional biblical, rabbinic, and Hasidic texts, and combining it with a keen sociological sensibility and sensitive psychological insights, he weaves a portrait of Jewish tradition that is relevant for our times. Strassfeld keenly understands the blessings of freedom and diversity inherent in Jewish tradition as well as present-day America to craft an aspirational vision of Judaism that speaks to the soul and stirs the mind."
— **Rabbi David Ellenson**, Chancellor Emeritus of Hebrew Union College-Jewish Institute of Religion

"Michael Strassfeld has 'traveled the distance,' from his Orthodox Day School upbringing, through the innovative, late 60s Havurat Shalom founding, to his training as a Reconstructionist rabbi, and through it all maintained a deep love of the Jewish tradition and a desire to transmit this love to others. Central to his reading of the tradition is that it has, does and will always change in response to the living needs of each generation. In this latest book, he offers a bold, honest, creative vision of a Judaism for this very moment in American society: one that challenges fundamental rabbinic views about God, prayer and the entire legal tradition. He argues that Jewish living should be based on core values and principles, not commandments given on high, and should serve to make us good people, not good Jews. In these pages he teaches a truly refreshing Torah replete with traditional wisdom and inspired practices to help us become the most just, compassionate, and awake human beings possible."

—**Rabbi Nancy Flam,** Co-founder of the *Institute for Jewish Spirituality* and *The National Center for Jewish Healing*

"JUDAISM DISRUPTED is a rare accomplishment! A book about Judaism that overflows with insight and wisdom for anyone seeking a meaningful, ethical, spiritual, and flourishing life! Drawing on a lifetime of studying, teaching, living, and loving Judaism, Strassfeld with imagination and awe wrestles, questions, and plays with an ancient inheritance uncovering and offering its life-affirming depths in a most accessible way.

"Strassfeld understands well that one can only preserve a religious tradition by fearlessly reconnecting it to its purpose—to enchant and elevate our life. With the best of today's innovators Strassfeld indeed disrupts... doing so in order to create anew."

—**Rabbi Irwin Kula,** President of Clal— The National Jewish Center for Learning and Leadership, author of *Yearnings: Embracing the Sacred Messiness of Life.*

"The great disrupter does it again. For half a century, Rabbi Michael Strassfeld has been a successful disrupter of religious laissez faire, insisting instead on being excruciatingly honest about the changing nature of the time and the need for Judaism to change along with it. In this, his latest book, he again challenges all our old bromides and emerges with an optimistic assessment of Judaism as a religion of deep awareness, of freedom and search, of holiness and helpfulness, and of uncertainty striving for wholeness."

—**Rabbi Lawrence A. Hoffman,** Professor Emeritus of Liturgy, Worship and Ritual, Hebrew Union College, NY

"JUDAISM DISRUPTED brought tears of relief to my eyes. Since 1973 Rabbi Michael Strassfeld has been the menschlichest voice of common sense talking about how to be an American Jew. Strassfeld recognizes that America and the world are in now a time of seismic shift and disruption, and within that disruption lies an opportunity for progress and healing that is uniquely Jewish. After his lifetime of writing and teaching, reading and singing, Michael Strassfeld can 'take the gloves off' to teach a fearlessly radical approach towards saving this disrupted world—an approach he securely roots in great teachings from millennia of Jewish history—and leave us feeling hopeful, inspired to work, and thrilled to be Jewish. Not scared about the future, thrilled.

"Reading this book brings the sensation of opening a sealed vessel from our ancient past to discover a scroll aglow with the Divine Spirit, prophecy for today that has always been true—Judaism is about freedom—but that needed Michael Strassfeld to give it voice in 2023. It's a guide for Jews to renew our covenant, and walk fearlessly with God into the unknowable future. It's a blueprint for all Americans on how to revere our Constitution as a document of our past that grants us the freedom to accept our present and to envision our future."

—**Rabbi Sharon Kleinbaum**, Rabbi of
Congregation Beit Simhat Torah in Manhattan

"Through his writings, chanting, communal leadership and personal example, Michael Strassfeld has long been an important guide for engaged, meaningful Jewish living. With JUDAISM DISRUPTED, he continues to forge a path toward transformation and interdependence grounded in Jewish wisdom and practice, offering a new paradigm for Judaism's relevance in the midst of seismic shifts.

"Beginning with the *Jewish Catalog,* Michael Strassfeld urged active practice of Judaism rather than passive participation, and his many following books deepened our knowledge toward this end. With JUDAISM DISRUPTED, Strassfeld distills 11 core principles for joyously and vibrantly taking up this challenge in a time of seismic change.

"In JUDAISM DISRUPTED, Michael Strassfeld seeks to re-invent the Torah for this moment. He draws on Hasidism, midrash, Reconstructionism, meditation practice and other sources to explain and interpret Jewish wisdom and practice and ultimately to empower contemporary Jews to make Judaism deeply relevant to our own lives."

—**Rabbi Deborah Waxman,**
President and CEO of Reconstructing Judaism

"Michael Strassfeld has created here a Judaism for our time, a faith that speaks to the realities and crises of 21st-century America and gives us ideas and practices to believe in and to do.

"Rabbi Strassfeld, an author of deep intellect and committed spirituality, proceeds to disrupt a Judaism that has become too hidebound and purposeless, disrupting because that is the necessary first step to rebuilding. In this amazing volume he proceeds to rebuild, to create, a Judaism with soul, passion and wisdom and a Judaism with practical guidance for what we each might do differently to find our own path to faith.

"Astoundingly, Rabbi Strassfeld offers us here, in a single volume, a new set of core principles, seeing our Torah as a torah of freedom, laying out the choices we have to use text, prayer, holidays and rituals in ways that meet our needs, connect us to forces beyond ourselves, open up new spiritual paths and make it possible for us to transform ourselves.

"Having wrestled with all the beliefs and practices of our faith Strassfeld is, powerfully, not afraid to let go and to move forward to a new set of truths.

"Michael Strassfeld makes the case for why we should bother with Judaism, explaining articulately and brilliantly that because it is about freedom and life it is precisely the faith that we need in these disruptive times. Our task is to disrupt it, to take it apart, and find those choices that give meaning to our lives."

—**Ruth Messinger**, Former Manhattan Borough President, Former Head of American Jewish World Service

"Michael Strassfeld has always been a disrupter, a holy disrupter for the sake of a Judaism that is honest, open, sensible, functional and meaningful. In this latest book, he draws from his knowledge of the traditional sources and his life experience as a seeker and a spiritual leader to reformulate Judaism for our time and for all who desire to encounter God, the world and themselves in depth and in truth."

—**Rabbi J. Rolando Matalon**, Rabbi of Congregation B'nai Jeshurun in NYC

"Michael Strassfeld brings a keen eye to contemporary Jewish life in JUDAISM DISRUPTED, honed through spiritual practice, professional experience, and a long engagement in Jewish thought and education. He has distilled his experience of the power and purpose of Jewish life into eleven guiding principles by which we might truly live with freedom, for connection and responsibility to each other; principles to guide spiritual practices meant to cultivate heart and mind to build a loving world. This is a clear-eyed statement of what Jewish life can and should be for a meaningful, livable future, beyond mitzvah to commitment, joy, social-justice, and love. May we all embrace such disruption."

—**Rabbi Jonathan Slater**, author, *A Partner in Holiness* and *Mindful Jewish Living: Compassionate Practice*

Judaism Disrupted

A Spiritual Manifesto for the 21st Century

Rabbi Michael Strassfeld

Ben Yehuda Press
Teaneck, New Jersey

Published by Ben Yehuda Press
122 Ayers Court #1B
Teaneck, NJ 07666
http://www.BenYehudaPress.com
To subscribe to our monthly book club and support independent Jewish publishing, visit https://www.patreon.com/BenYehudaPress

Ben Yehuda Press books may be purchased at a discount by synagogues, book clubs, and other institutions buying in bulk.

For information, please email markets@BenYehudaPress.com

Cover photograph by Nomi Ellenson. Cover art by Michael Strassfeld.

ISBN13 978-1-953829-37-5

22 23 24 / 10 9 8 7 6 5 4 3 2 1 20230201

Dedication

When the Israelites stood at Mt. Sinai waiting to receive the Torah, God asked them: Who will be your guarantors that you will keep it and then I will give it to you.

They replied our ancestors will be our guarantors.

God replied: I find fault with Abraham, Isaac and Jacob. Find me good guarantors.

The people replied: The prophets will be our guarantors.

God replied: I find fault with the prophets.

The Israelites said: Our children will be our guarantors.

God replied: Truly, these are good guarantors. I will give you the Torah.

—Midrash Rabbah on Song of Songs 1:4

The guarantors of Jewish tradition cannot be from the past or even from the present. Judaism can only be guaranteed by the future—those who will create the living Torah as it unrolls in their lives.

This book is dedicated to our children Max, Noam, Ben, Sara and Ruthie, along with their life partners, and our grandchildren, Sammy, Lainie, and Isaac. It is they who will create the Jewish future, each in their own way.

Contents

Foreword by Sylvia Boorstein

I had a phone call in the late 1990s from a journalist who said, "What do you think about the current trend of 'Salad Religions' where people pick and choose practices from a variety of religions and make up their own private religion? They say, 'I'm not religious, but I am spiritual.'"

Knowing full well that he was asking me because I was becoming more well known as a Mindfulness teacher at that time and people also knew I was a Jew involved with my synagogue community, I feigned surprise so I could figure out how to answer. He continued, "Well, do you think it is a good or a bad thing?"

"I suppose it might be good," I said. "Americans are thought of as having pioneer spirit, an ability to be innovative, to improvise new solutions."

"But how about having a private religion?" he asked.

"If people had totally private religions," I said, "They would have no one to cheer them on and no one to say that they were kidding themselves and that nothing was happening."

"What's supposed to happen?" he asked.

"What's supposed to happen," I continued, hearing myself rev up with enthusiasm as I answered, "is that spiritual practices are meant to sensitize us to the preciousness of life, to the sacredness of all life, to the vulnerability to loss and despair that we share with all other humans and to the potential for tenderizing our hearts so that we become genuinely compassionate people dedicated to the wellbeing of all beings and of the planet we all share! That's what is supposed to happen." I think the journalist was impressed.

I am, these many years later, heartened by what I see as the shift from thinking about one's religion as the name of the tribe we were born into, or chose to join, to expecting that the practices of a religious group—prayer and literature and ethical teachings and contemplative exercises—will transform the minds of practitioners to kindness. The book you have in your hands is a book about Judaism as a transformative spiritual practice.

The spiritual path that led me to meet Rabbi Michael Strassfeld began in 1973 at a workshop in Berkeley, California, on the Tanya, a classic Chassidic text. It was sponsored by The Aquarian Minyan and the teacher was Rabbi Zalman Schachter-Shalomi (z"l). The Minyan was known for its progressive orientation. My husband was interested in going. I went to keep him company.

It was a warm day in a crowded classroom and several hours into the teaching I was feeling sleepy when Reb Zalman (the honorific by which he was affectionately known) said, "It's time to *daven Mincha* (pray the afternoon prayer)." Everyone stood up. *Mincha* service is short and people said it out loud, by heart, all around me. Everyone was facing east, as is the custom. Reb Zalman had his back to us, but his voice rang out loudly and clearly and I watched how his arms, and indeed his whole body, seemed alive in his prayer. I had the distinct thought, "He really *means* this!" I not only thought that, I felt it in my body. That hadn't happened to me before, in the context of prayer. I felt awake, and alive, and happy to be there. It did not matter that I didn't believe the words, or believe that there was someone I was praying to. It mattered that I felt alive and connected to that moment and that community. It mattered that I admired that Reb Zalman, whom I respected as learned and intellectual and rational, could use those words to invoke in himself, and transmit to the roomful of people, a sense of expansiveness that felt divine.

Over the next twenty years, years in which I studied and practiced Mindfulness meditation and ultimately became a founding teacher at Spirit Rock Meditation Center in California, my practice life as a Jew became enlivened, meaningful and a pleasure. Reb Zalman and I became friends and, I am proud to say, colleagues. After Spirit Rock Center began to offer a full schedule of Mindfulness retreats, Reb. Zalman asked me, "What story are you telling the children of the meditators? It is important to have a story," he said, "because a practice without a story will only last one generation."

When I teach in Buddhist venues, I might say: In his many lifetimes before the one in which he was born as Siddhartha Gautama and was acknowledged as enlightened, the Buddha practiced and perfected all the virtues that would be the basis of his wisdom and that manifested as impartial kindness. When we teach children, we read them Jataka Tales, stories of early incarnations of the Buddha as a compassionate buffalo, or a self-sacrificing monkey-king. (Sometimes we tell those same stories to adults as well.)

At Congregation Rodef Sholom, in San Rafael, California where I am a congregant, I co-lead the Mindfulness class each Thursday morning using the Torah portion of the week as our text. Among my favorites is the story of the King Balak who insists that the prophet Balaam, skilled in cursing, curse the Israelites who are passing through his territory. After many failed attempts, it becomes clear that he has been so sustained by divine spirit that only exultation and blessing can come out of his mouth: "How lovely are your tents, O Jacob." When *my* mind feels at ease, steady and unconfused, it shifts from being preoccupied with what is happening in my particular life to the awareness of the miracle that the whole of creation is happening. From *what* is happening to *that* it is happening, and to awe that I am part of it.

It is clear to me that a story does not need to have happened in order to be true. Mostly, I do not believe the traditional stories I tell. But I consider myself a believer. I believe that individual minds can be changed from confused and impulsive to thoughtful, compassionate, and habituated to kindness.

My own spiritual life is one of evolution. I began my meditative practice of Mindfulness in the late 1970s, partly because it seemed that everyone I knew at that time was investigating meditative practices and partly because I hoped to find relief from my habits of fretful worrying.

I was not looking for an alternative to Judaism. I had always loved being a Jew and my family, the one I grew up in and the one I built with my husband and children, revolved around a Jewish calendar and practices. I had enjoyed being Jewish, but I had not expected it would soothe my anxieties or provide me with psychological insights. I had not imagined it could be a source of awakening to a more lively connection to the miracle and delight of being alive. It did, surprisingly, do both. In periods of meditation, I found that my mind, normally vulnerable to becoming frightened or irritated by thoughts that arose, was more expansive, more forgiving.

And, at times of experiencing a moment of peace of mind for which I was genuinely grateful, I was moved to say blessings, or prayers of thanksgiving that I had learned as a child and then abandoned. I met Rabbi Michael Strassfeld when I was invited to teach Mindfulness meditation in Jewish venues, and began to become more knowledgeable about Judaism.

I wrote a book about being a Jew whose experience of being Jewish was nourished and supported by my study and practice of Buddhism and Mindfulness. My Mindfulness teacher and friend and colleague Joseph Goldstein asked me this question one day as we took as walk together:

"Do you think, Sylvia, that Buddhism is a complete path to liberation?"

I replied, "I do think it is."

"Why then," he asked, "would you want to complicate it with Judaism?"

"The fact is," I replied, "that I am complicated with Judaism."

Michael Strassfeld's book is for people who are complicated with Judaism either by ancestry or by choice and would like it to be more alive to them, more central to their lives. It is for the people mentioned in the introduction whose Judaism is in their childhood memories or for those who remain connected but in a peripheral or rote way. This book is an invitation to take spirituality seriously by taking the structure and the literature of this sacred tradition and entering into it with the intention of becoming transformed by it. We are invited, via Torah study, or Sabbath observance, or holiday observance, or social activism, or contemplative practices, to become transformed and then to transform the world. I think about how, when I was younger, I thought of religious practices as something one did to qualify as observant rather than as a program one undertook to strengthen one's capacity to live with kindness and compassion in a complex and diverse world.

This wonderful book systematically, with warmth and humor and an abundance of scholarship, re-presents Judaism as a dynamic and transformative vehicle for creating wiser individuals who can be part of a wiser, kinder world.

Sylvia Boorstein
Author of *Pay Attention, for Goodness' Sake: The Buddhist Path of Kindness*; co-founder of Spirit Rock Mindfulness Center

Introduction: Why bother?

Dear reader,

I have met you many times. Sometimes it's at a party. Sometimes it's at a funeral. Once it was on an overnight train to St. Petersburg. The conversation is always a variation on the same theme.

It begins with the typical exchange of strangers with time together. Politeness encourages exchanging verbal resumes—name, where you are from, what do you do. Pleasantries. Perhaps it is a search for reassuring commonalities, particularly in a foreign country—are you an American? The tone changes when I reveal I am a rabbi (Helpful hint: When I want to be left alone, I tell people I work for the IRS).

Sometimes you tell me you have never met a rabbi. Or you have always been curious about Judaism. Sometimes, you tell me you belong to this synagogue or to a Jewish Community Center. Mostly, if you are Jewish, you tell me you have been busy in work which is why you haven't been in synagogue recently (usually meaning in many years). Or you wanted to go to High Holiday services but "your dog ate the tickets." I get a lot of excuses. Sometimes I get anger at Judaism or at a God who failed you. Then comes the real question: "Why would you want to be a rabbi?" you ask with a tone of incredulity in your voice.

I think what you are really asking is why would you care so much about Judaism as to actually devote your professional life to it?

You ask not because you are a self-hating Jew. On the contrary, you feel good about being Jewish. It is not a heritage that you deny. You attend a Passover Seder and eat latkes on Hanukkah. Your concern for social justice derives in part from Judaism's commitment to the poor and the stranger. Judaism is part, but only part, of who you are. It is to Jewishness, not Judaism as a religion, that you feel a connection.

Sometimes you say you attend synagogue services, but besides the community aspect, you are mostly unmoved by the experience. "Well, the truth is rabbi, I look around the world and I see religion as the source of a lot of the conflicts today. There's a lot of killing in the name of religion."

Or, "I think the case can be made that religion has overall had a negative effect on the world. Sure, there are saintly religious people but they seem to be the exception. A lot of the 'religious' people I know are not fanatics but I still get a sense of being judged by them for not being religious."

"Besides, you have to believe in all this stuff—heaven and hell, the resurrection of the dead, and God. C'mon rabbi—just between us, you look like a modern person; you don't really believe that stuff. You just pretend to because it is expected."

"And prayer—as a kid I prayed for my sick grandmother. I really loved her and prayed really hard for her to recover. She died. Look at the world; does God really reward the innocent and punish the wicked? I can't stand when people say God saved me from the tornado. What about their nice neighbors who were killed by the same tornado? Religion can be good or bad just like everything else in life, but I just don't get why I should bother. Every religion has ethical teachings but I don't need religion for that. What do all those rituals and prayers add to my life? If I like a Jewish holiday or value, I can incorporate it in my life but I can also focus on gratitude at Thanksgiving or use a teaching of the Dalai Lama to help enrich my life. The rules and rituals do not seem to have intrinsic value.

The evolution of understanding

This book is my attempt to answer the question under all these questions: Why bother? I write it from the perspective of someone who has had an evolving commitment to Judaism over the course of my life. I became a rabbi at the age of 41 but have always been involved in Jewish life. From the Orthodox (traditional) world in which I grew up, I now embrace a Judaism that draws upon the richness of the tradition as well as insights drawn from the contemporary moment.

"OK," you say, "how about a really short answer to why I should bother with Judaism?"

This may surprise you, but Judaism is actually about how to live a life of freedom. It asks us to take the most precious gift we have—life—and live it to the fullest.

Judaism urges us to strive for an awareness of our potential, not just our deficits. We are all imperfect people carrying those flaws into our daily interactions with the world. We are anxious and afraid. We are not naturally generous or patient or empathetic. We are simply overwhelmed with all we have to do to get through the week. We also frequently face real difficulties, caused by circumstances over which we have no control.

We are both mortal and immensely powerful. We will never achieve perfection, but we can do better to hold on to the vision of ourselves that we really want to be. Judaism calls us to live lives filled with purpose. How do we do this in the face of the many challenges we encounter? How do we find the strength to respond to setbacks and failures?

Judaism shows us how to live with purpose. Its wisdom helps me face the challenges of life. Wisdom, not answers—not answers about whether to stay in this job or relationship nor why my friend died so young. In fact, Judaism is more about questions than answers—especially questioning why the world is not a more just and compassionate place. Judaism's practices help give meaning to important moments in my life. It encourages awareness—awareness of the moment. It encourages gratefulness for the blessings in my life even as it helps me acknowledge the disappointments and losses that will inevitably be part of my experience. It enables me to embrace the universal aspect of existence but to do so grounded in a particular tradition—Judaism.

The ongoing conversation of Jews about a tradition that stretches over centuries serves as a rich resource as I move through the ups and downs of existence. That conversation responds to the existential aloneness of modern life, enabling me to feel connected both in the present and in the past to the Jewish people and the tradition. Judaism reminds me that the world is bigger than me, Michael; but at the same time it connects me to that universe, or, some would say, to the unity underlying the universe that can be called God.

If I am right, and Judaism is about freedom, awareness, and life, then how have we gone so wrong? How is it that a tradition that has so much to offer in this moment has failed to speak to so many of us?

How did we get here?

Until the modern era, Jews practiced rabbinic Judaism, created by a group of scholars in the first centuries of the Common Era. It was based on the notions that the Torah/Bible was revealed to the Jewish people at Mount Sinai. While the Bible contains stories and broad calls to behave in holy ways, these rabbis saw the Torah as essentially a book of law. Though the Torah does not describe itself that way nor does it clearly delineate what a law is, the rabbinic tradition found 613 commandments in the text of the Torah. These commandments were both positive (you shall eat matzah), and negative (you shall not eat bread during Passover) and divided into those that were ritual in nature and those that were ethical commandments. Every Jew was obligated to fulfill the commandments.

Along with the written text of the Torah, an oral tradition developed that the rabbis also believed was revealed to Moses at Sinai. They believed that both the written and oral Torah were literally the word of God and were therefore perfect and unchanging. The rabbis were the interpreters and authorities of the laws of Judaism called *halakha*, "the way" to walk in the world. The same scholars of the first centuries of the common era wrote down this oral tradition, known as the Talmud—the central text of religious study. These rabbis laid out in great detail how to fulfill each of the commandments in the Torah. While it is an oversimplification to claim that Judaism focuses on action and not belief, the rabbis did view behavior as essential.

Although the rabbis of the Talmud did not agree on one understanding of the nature of God, they shared certain principles. God is eternal, omniscient and omnipotent. God created the world. God is just and punishes the wicked and rewards the righteous. God has no form. God redeemed the Jews from Egypt and created a covenant between God and the Jewish people at Sinai. Jews are God's chosen people. There is an afterlife. God will bring about redemption at the end of days.

Beginning in the 19th century, many Jews challenged the validity of these beliefs. Scholars rejected the notion that the Bible had one author. Instead, they believed it was composed over centuries by a number of authors. Human authorship meant that the text was not infallible. There is also no reason that it couldn't be changed in response to new understandings and circumstances. Historians dismissed the notion that the Oral Torah was told to Moses at Sinai, claiming that it wasn't until centuries later that rabbis wrote it down. Recent scholarship even questions whether the Talmud is an accurate account of the statements of the rabbis found in its pages.

With its reliance on science and rationalism, modernity challenged the whole notion of a belief in God. Traditional notions of God rested on faith, not scientific proofs. Modernity, being this worldly in orientation, was skeptical of the existence of life after death. It questioned whether God intervened in the world, appeared at Sinai, commanded us, or cares whether we eat pork. Modernity is a challenge to Judaism and actually to all traditional religions.

The current moment

After two centuries of challenges, the future of Judaism is uncertain. We live in disruptive times. Major industries, from newspapers to trucking, are facing uncertain futures. Pandemics, terrorism and political discord are challenges to our sense of order in the world. Though the intensity of the disruptions is at a particularly heightened point, humans have lived in disruptive times for centuries. The modern world profoundly changed how humans thought of themselves and their relationship to everything else. Before modernity, God stood center stage and humans felt very mortal; Jewish tradition, along with other religions, preserved this notion. As the modern world placed humans at the center, God was relegated to the weekend. Moderns believed in their power to understand the world and, with that understanding, to shape it.

The rise of denominations—Reform, Conservative, Reconstructionist and even modern Orthodoxy, tried to bring religion in sync with the modern world. Each represented a communal desire to welcome modernity and preserve the tradition. Many Jews rejected religion altogether. Other *isms* came to the fore, ranging from nationalism to socialism. A secular identity became an option. Religion became a private option, particularly in America, with its separation of church and state.

While many of the denominational attempts to reform Judaism in the modern era achieved moderate success in the 20th century, the contemporary moment calls for something radically different. We need more than a tinkering around the edges because we are now at a moment of seismic shift. A new paradigm is now essential to respond to the profound challenges in understanding such issues as what it means to be a human being and what our relationship is to our world and to the cosmos. How does a particularistic tradition interact with an increasingly universal world?

An example of a past seismic change

We have been here before. This is not the first seismic shift to occur in Judaism. The transition from biblical Judaism to rabbinic Judaism must have felt like an earthquake to those who witnessed the destruction of the Second Temple in 70 C.E. While we have limited evidence of how Jews practiced their religion before the destruction of the Temple, we do know that the Temple in Jerusalem—with its sacrificial system and religious leadership of priests (*kohanim*)—was central to Jewish life. Synagogues existed in the last years of the Temple, but it is only with the destruction of the Temple that new forms of worship and religious authority emerged on a large scale. Rabbinic Judaism developed over the next centuries, creating prayer and synagogues, a system of commandments and the religious leadership of rabbis. For centuries, this approach has formed the core of Jewish life.

We are at such a seismic moment again, one that has also been unfolding for centuries, beginning with the Enlightenment. While there has been no cataclysmic event such as the fall of the Temple in Jerusalem, this disruption has been caused by modernity itself, with its emphasis on the individual, the multitude of choices of how to live, and the technology that has radically altered everything we do. Judaism requires radical change once again in order to respond to the needs of our times. This book sets out a framework for a new Judaism and offers practices that embody that framework. While it starts without an assumption that any specific aspect of rabbinic Judaism will be part of this new Judaism, this new Judaism is rooted in the values and texts of the Jewish past.

What is missing in today's Judaism?

What is the purpose of Judaism? The traditional answer is that there is a covenant between God and the Jewish people in which we are commanded to observe the 613 commandments and all the other elements of Jewish law (*halakha*). If we follow these rules, we will be rewarded in this world and in the world to come.

Today, the established Jewish community, both in its religious and secular spheres, asserts that Jewish continuity depends on enough Jews doing enough Jewish things, like lighting Shabbat candles or attending a Passover Seder. I disagree. Judaism isn't about doing the things that only Jews do, such as observing Jewish rituals or holidays. In truth, Judaism helps us to live lives of meaning, not to ensure Jewish continuity. Its purpose is not to fulfill the commandments in order to receive a Jewish merit badge from the Great Scoutmaster in the sky. Judaism does not exist to make God happy nor is it a method to get rewarded by God with a trouble-free life. The purpose of Judaism is to help us live our lives to the utmost. It is about bringing goodness into our lives and into the lives of everyone we encounter. It is about bringing justice to people we will never meet but with whom we share this planet. It is about being good caretakers of that planet. It is about constructing lives that enable us to be free.

This understanding has led me to reject the forms of rabbinic Judaism that make up the basic paradigm of Jewish life in the modern period. I no longer understand Judaism as a system of law and obligation. I have discarded the paradigm of dividing the world into dualities—men and women, permitted and forbidden, and Jew and non-Jew—which is a foundational understanding of rabbinic Judaism.

The future of liberal Judaism looks increasingly uncertain. It may be an act of chutzpah to say it, but it is time for a "new Judaism." Let me be clear: My purpose in writing this book isn't to save Judaism. It is to share with you the principles and values of Judaism that I have discovered over a lifelong engagement with the tradition, from the modern Orthodoxy in which I grew up to the radical traditionalism that now defines my practice. Radical traditionalism rejects much of the beliefs, paradigms, and practices of rabbinic Judaism, yet draws from both the rabbinic and mystical traditions in Judaism. This new Judaism is deeply connected to the past.

As I re-read rabbinic texts, I excavate the core meanings of practices that have been covered over by centuries of obfuscating accretions. Because I am rooted in the tradition, I look to sources in that tradition that support or even inspire the new principles and practices that I propose. I am particularly inspired by the teachings of Hasidism, a pietistic spiritual movement that arose in Eastern Europe in the 18th century, which has become an important source for texts on spirituality. Its emphasis on the potential in every person to grow and develop resonates with the optimistic view of human potential of much of contemporary psychology. Why and how my own Judaism changed is the story and the context for this book.

My Story

My father was born in Ukraine. His immediate family moved to Germany when he was a child and managed to immigrate to America in 1935. All the rest of the family was murdered by the Nazis. My mother's family had come to America in the first wave of eastern European immigration in the 1880s. My father was ordained as an Orthodox rabbi and his first pulpit was in Saratoga Springs in up-state New York, where I was born. We moved to Boston when I was three years old when my father was hired to be the rabbi of an Orthodox synagogue known as the Woodrow Avenue Shul. We lived in the ethnically Jewish neighborhood of Mattapan-Dorchester where you didn't need to observe any ritual practices to feel Jewish. None of the children I played with on our block went to synagogue on Shabbat. On High Holidays, Woodrow Avenue was closed to traffic; while the adults attended the three synagogues across from each other, the children hung out on the street playing with the horse chestnuts that had fallen from the trees. Later in the afternoon, teens would go to Franklin Field to flirt. Though Matta-pan-Dorchester was a nearly 100% Jewish neighborhood, there wasn't a single kosher restaurant.

We were Modern Orthodox. My parents were observant and were also interested in culture like theater and opera. Overall, we felt very much that we were Americans and Jews. Like many Modern Orthodox Jews in those days, we were also politically liberal. My father supported H. Stuart Hughes, an anti-nuke independent candidate, running for the U.S. Senate. I collected signatures to get him on the ballot (illegally, since I was only twelve at the time). The other two candidates were Henry Cabot Lodge, Jr. and Ted Kennedy (in his first campaign). Needless to say, Hughes lost badly.

My father marched in Selma with Martin Luther King, Jr. When he returned, he told us they practiced what to do in case they were attacked by police wielding clubs. They laid face down on the ground and covered the vulnerable back of their necks with their fingers as the organizers called them names while hitting them with rolled-up newspaper.

I attended Maimonides School in Boston, an Orthodox Jewish day school. Besides the secular curriculum, our Jewish studies focused on the classic Jewish texts: Torah, Prophets, Prayer and Talmud. We also studied Hebrew language and Jewish history. Typically, Jewish day schools did not teach many of these subjects. Rabbi Joseph Soloveitchik, the school's founder, felt that a broader Jewish curriculum was important and was part of the approach of modern Orthodoxy, of which he was a leading figure. Our general studies were given equal weight to our religious studies. Another unusual feature of Maimonides as a day school was that it was co-ed. Boys and girls studied together, including Talmud.

In those days, I believed the Torah was the unchanging word of God even as I was skeptical of "proofs" that were offered. I remember one of my classmates explaining to our history teacher, a descendant of one of the signers of the Declaration of Independence, that the revelation of the Torah on Mount Sinai really happened because 600,000 Jews witnessed it, unlike the resurrection of Jesus witnessed by only a few of his disciples. How could 600,000 people be wrong? I understood even then that this was about faith—believing in something that could not be proved. Either I believed the miracles in the Torah happened or I didn't. Explaining them as natural occurrences (it was really strong winds that parted the Sea of Reeds, allowing the Israelites to escape the Egyptian army), frankly seemed silly to me.

While prayer became an important part of my adult Jewish life, it was less so when I was young. I would often pretend to be asleep when my father was getting ready to go to synagogue Shabbat morning. Not wanting to wake me, he would let me sleep. The ruse soon failed. I would join him in a brisk fifteen-minute walk from our house to the synagogue where he served as rabbi. Since I attended a Hebrew day school, I had no problem following the services. I came to enjoy attending the services every week.

During those years, I prayed three times a day. I remember using a phone booth in North Station (a commuter train station) to recite the afternoon prayer while pretending to use the phone. One time, my sister banged on the glass of the booth to get my attention (to no avail) because Bill Russell, the great basketball player of the Boston Celtics, had just walked by on his way to the adjacent Boston Garden.

In my high school years, I was involved with NCSY—the National Conference of Synagogue Youth, an Orthodox youth group. A number of my classmates from Maimonides School and I would attend the regional conventions. We would lead the Hasidic style singing and dancing during the meals since this was a familiar practice in our Orthodox world. This spirited singing was an important influence on the way I would come to lead services later in my life.

My father decided to become the rabbi of a Conservative congregation in Marblehead on the North Shore of Boston. While my parents remained Orthodox in their own practice, there was no separation of men and women during services in the Conservative synagogue. I maintained that a service with mixed seating was not a "legitimate" service and prayed on my own before attending my father's service. It was a perfect adolescent rebellion—my parents were both annoyed with me and proud.

After graduating Maimonides, I attended Yeshiva University in order to continue my Jewish studies as well as attend college. That freshman year was a period of religious transition for me. I was attracted to a small group of Yeshiva University teachers that included Rabbis Yitz Greenberg and Shlomo Riskin, who were advocating for a left-wing Orthodoxy. It was 1967-68 and political turmoil was rife on college campuses. In that context, Yitz Greenberg posited a notion that one could take a position of civil disobedience to a Jewish law. Specifically, one could practice Judaism with a more egalitarian ritual role for women. By doing so, you recognized you were breaking the law but hoped that you could influence Jewish law to change. Initially, this was an attractive idea to me. Across campuses in America, students were performing acts of civil disobedience against the war in Vietnam. However, I soon realized that the whole notion of civil disobedience rested on the general acceptance of the law except in the one area you were questioning. In that area, you were appealing to a higher sense of morality to override observance of that law. As I came to feel that in more and more areas the traditional law was "wrong," I felt that civil disobedience was an inadequate response. It became clear to me that I actually had a problem with the whole system, not with just one or two aspects of it. Increasingly, I came to doubt the faith claims that underlay Orthodoxy.

The final moment of my break from Orthodoxy followed a talk given by one of the prominent teachers at Yeshiva University on the morality of the Vietnam War. After a long discourse on whether the war fell into the category of an optional or a mandatory war (the two categories of war in traditional Jewish law), the rabbi ended by saying the evidence was inconclusive. He suggested that in any case, we should remain at Yeshiva University studying Torah. It was not the uncertainty that was the most disturbing aspect of his talk. It was the implication that I should stay at Yeshiva University (and get a divinity student deferment from the draft), which meant that others (basically people who weren't Jewish) would go fight in Vietnam instead of me. The moral bankruptcy of his position, casually offered, convinced me that I no longer had a place in the Orthodox world. I transferred to Brandeis University.

As I entered the world of liberal Judaism at Brandeis, I began to struggle with observance and with my beliefs. The Bible courses I took convinced me that the Torah was not the unchanging word of God, but the product of a number of human authors. I was involved with the Jewish campus group, Hillel, and became the chair of the New England Student Struggle for Soviet Jewry. I was also the chair of Concerned Jewish Students, the student group that organized a demonstration at the General Assembly in Boston, the national convention of Jewish Federations, calling for more funding of Jewish education and culture. I believe that demonstration reflected two things: the emerging centrality of federations in American Jewish life and a shift in priorities of the organized Jewish community toward Jewish identity.

However, the event that more profoundly shaped my experience of Judaism during this chapter of my life was a Shabbat I spent at Havurat Shalom during my sophomore year. My father was friendly with Zalman Schachter-Shalomi (founder of the Jewish Renewal movement) and invited him to our synagogue in Marblehead. Over that Shabbat I got to know him and he invited me to spend a Shabbat with him at Havurat Shalom, an intentional community that was started in 1968 in Cambridge by Zalman, Arthur Green (the contemporary theologian and scholar of Hasidism), and others. It emphasized prayer, study and community that was both rooted in the Jewish tradition and also the contemporary moment. On the Shabbat that I was invited, Rabbi Shlomo Riskin, from Yeshiva University, was also a guest. That Shabbat afternoon there was a dialogue between Art Green and Shlomo Riskin about Orthodoxy and non-Orthodoxy. For me, it was a conversation between the world in which I had grown up and the world to which I was increasingly drawn. That weekend made it crystal clear to me that the eclectic Judaism being created in the havurah was my new Jewish home. I now had a community in which I could explore new ways of thinking that had been, until then, mostly going on in my head.

I got married and began graduate school in Jewish studies at Brandeis. We applied to join Havurat Shalom (as an intentional community, you couldn't just join) and were accepted. The next three years that we were members of Havurat Shalom profoundly shaped my Jewish identity. While I was in graduate school, the center of my life was at the Havurah, as it was for most of the 30 or so members. We studied at the Havurah, had regular talks by invited guests, and had a weekly communal meal. We held endless discussions about what we were doing. Each one seemed critically important at the time. Shabbat was central, especially Shabbat services. It was intense. Our Judaism was eclectic—drawing from a variety of texts and sources within Judaism, from other religions, and from the contemporary moment. Hasidism, the mystical, pietistic movement of the second half of the 18th century in eastern Europe, was a particularly important Jewish source for the spiritual life of the Havurah. Originally, I was somewhat resistant to mysticism. It was an aspect of Judaism that had not really been part of my day school education. But over the years, Hasidism and the spiritual aspects of Judaism have become central to my understanding of Judaism.

A word about Hasidism

As a mystical movement, one of the key concepts of Hasidism was the notion of *devekut*—cleaving or connecting to the Holy One. Prayer, rather than study, was the key spiritual practice for Hasidism. How was this sense of connection to be achieved? By striving for an ongoing awareness of life and of the deeper reality of the world. Intention/*kavanah* became even more important than just fulfilling the commandments. This led to a constellation of beliefs and practices in Hasidism. Prior to Hasidism, most mystical movements in Judaism were ascetic in orientation, emphasizing the spirit and the intangible. The material world was often seen as problematic, either as a distraction from the spiritual or as a temptation leading you away from the spiritual.

Hasidism emphasized that God is everywhere. No place is empty of God. God could be encountered in everything. Instead of seeing the world as a barrier to the spiritual, it provides countless doorways to find the spiritual. The popular picture of Hasidim eating, drinking, singing and dancing is rooted in this notion that the world can be a pathway to God rather than an obstacle course. Hasidism rejected the asceticism of earlier Jewish mysticism.

The rebbe—the spiritual master, was the central figure in Hasidism. The *hasid*—literally pious person—would become a follower of one of the masters. The connection of the *rebbe* to the *hasid*—the spiritual master to the follower— was critical to Hasidism. Hasidism was rooted in community. You couldn't be a hasid on your own. Nor could the *rebbe* be a *rebbe* without followers. The *rebbe* helped his followers experience blessings and holiness in the world. In a matter of decades, Hasidism captured the allegiance of much of eastern European Jewry. It allowed the average Jew to feel part of Jewish spiritual life through his connection to the *rebbe*. These ideas became important spiritual teachings for me and have remained an essential part of my religious life. I saw a path that would enable me to embrace the world and find holiness in it. Throughout my career, I have worked to make the spiritual accessible to everyone, not just to rabbinic scholars.

Discovering the holy in the activities of everyday existence became for me what Judaism is about. Hasidism's model for a Judaism that strove to be inclusive rather than elitist was a challenge for the Jewish life I was involved in creating. These reflect aspects of American culture in the 1960s and 70s. Most critical was Hasidism's psychological orientation, focusing on the inner life of the individual Jew. I am not suggesting that somehow the Hasidic masters knew Freud before Freud. What I am suggesting is that the move from the Middle Ages to modernity changed fundamental ways of thinking about the world and the place of humans in it. Humans moved to center stage in this modern world and Hasidism was part of that movement even as it also maintained a focus on God. Hasidism held that individuals had the power to shape their own lives. These ideas really resonated with me.

Increasingly, Hasidism has become an important source for many people in liberal Judaism. Why? First, it is an authentic Jewish tradition of spirituality that predates by centuries current trends in spirituality. Some Jews who are interested in spirituality feel uncomfortable with the idea of it all being borrowed from Eastern traditions such as Buddhism. It is true that the interest in meditation, yoga and spirituality is encouraged by the American form of Buddhism. Yet, Hasidism focuses on similar spiritual goals of being present in the moment and cultivating awareness.

You may wonder whether early Hasidism is similar to the contemporary world of Hasidism as it is lived in places like Boro Park in Brooklyn. Unfortunately, it is not. After the first few generations of Hasidic masters, the movement became very conservative. At its founding, it was on the cutting edge of traditional Jewish life, though in terms of Jewish practice it remained traditional in every significant way, even in its early years. In the 19th century the Enlightenment reached Eastern Europe and traditionalism became a target of modernity. Hasidism became a particular focus of attack by Jewish Enlightenment figures who saw the miracle-working *rebbe* as a benighted figure of traditional Judaism, keeping Jews enthralled to a superstition-laden past. Thousands of Jews began to leave traditional Judaism, attracted by the "isms" of the modern world, such as socialism or Zionism. Both Hasidism and traditional rabbinic Judaism circled the wagons in the face of the threat of modern culture. Hasidism moved from its original cutting edge approach to Judaism to the ultra-right wing of Orthodoxy. More than any other group of traditional Jews, it rejected modernity and its values as a threat to their way of life.

While today's Hasidim still follow a *rebbe*, they are as likely to study Talmud as the works of the early Hasidic masters. I believe that they have lost the spiritual outlook that I found so appealing. I am certain they would disagree with my interpretations of Hasidic texts or my view that early Hasidism was different than it is today. I do not believe I am misreading these texts but is clear to me that Hasidim today read those same texts as though they were still living in 18th-century Poland.

Not all aspects of early Hasidism resonate for me. Its inclusiveness did not extend to women, who were marginalized in a Hasidic world that valued male bonding. Reflecting views from earlier Jewish mysticism and historical experience, non-Jews were seen as completely *other*. Finally, while the model of the spiritual master and the follower has some appeal to me, I ultimately find it more problematic than helpful. Too often, it turns out that the spiritual master has clay feet.

Back to my story.

We felt that Havurat Shalom was on the cutting edge of a new Judaism that we shared with similar groups around the country. The idea emerged to publish a book about that Judaism. *The Jewish Catalog*, edited by Richard Siegel, Sharon Strassfeld and me, was the expression of that Judaism. In a critique of existing Jewish life, it urged Jews to actively practice Judaism in a way that resonated with them, rather than being passive participants. It made no claims on how to be a "good Jew." Rather it laid out our Jewish lives and invited the reader to take from the *Catalog* what appealed to them. It provided information on how to observe various Jewish practices, whether it was how to tie the fringes for a prayer shawl or baking challah. Its style was eclectic, informal and contemporary. It was a huge success, appealing to many looking for a vibrant, joyous Judaism rooted in the moment.

We left Havurat Shalom for Manhattan where my wife had a job and settled in the Upper West Side. I edited a Passover Haggadah for the Conservative movement and then wrote a book entitled *The Jewish Holidays* (Harper & Row). Shabbat services became the focus of my Jewish life. I was on a quest to find the perfect service. I was involved in starting the West Side Minyan and then starting Minyan M'at, both lay-led Havurah-style services. I was involved in the revitalization of Ansche Chesed, a dying Conservative congregation that a number of minyanim joined to help bring it back to life.

I began working at Ansche Chesed, running its educational and social programs. Eventually, I decided I didn't want to be organizing events where other people taught and led. Though I had resisted the idea for years, I decided to become a rabbi. I commuted to the Reconstructionist Rabbinical College in Philadelphia.

Reconstructionism was founded in America by Mordecai Kaplan, who described Judaism as an evolving religious civilization, seeing Judaism as always changing from one generation to the next. Reconstructionism did not have a traditional notion of God. It also understood that culture, not just religious texts, is an intrinsic part of that civilization. Having been basically non-denominational since my havurah days, Reconstructionism seemed the best choice for me. I became a rabbi at the age of 41 and was hired to be the rabbi at Ansche Chesed.

The next turning point in my life revolved around spirituality. I was invited by a friend, Rachel Cowan (spirituality teacher 1941-2018), to attend a silent meditation retreat led by Sylvia Boorstein (contemporary meditation teacher) for a small group of rabbis. I realized that there were many Jewish practices that I observed because I grew up doing them, yet they did not feel like a spiritual discipline. It became clearer to me that Judaism wasn't about performing rituals, but was meant to give purpose to our lives. Out of that retreat and other events the Institute for Jewish Spirituality emerged, offering programs and retreats for Jewish clergy and laypeople that focused on a Judaism centered on cultivating awareness.

Encouraged to write a new *Jewish Catalog* 25 years after it first was published, I wrote *A Book of Life: Embracing Judaism as a Spiritual Practice*. Spirituality became for me the way I experienced Judaism. For a number of years, I was adjunct faculty for the Institute for Jewish Spirituality and led services at some of its retreats. I remarried and became the rabbi of the Society for the Advancement of Judaism, a Reconstructionist synagogue in Manhattan.

I retired in 2015 and began to examine my life and what I had learned about Judaism over the course of my career as a rabbi. The world had changed a lot since *The Jewish Catalog* was published in 1973. As I began to write this book, I realized I had changed a lot as well. I had moved farther away from the traditional observance of my childhood. I felt that Judaism was facing unprecedented challenges and needed to engage in a process of serious reflection and change. Some things had become clear to me in my last years as a congregational rabbi. I had increasingly felt that traditional prayer didn't work for many people. The problem wasn't just the length of the three-hour Shabbat morning services or the Hebrew prayers. It needed a radical reconstruction. The more I tried to set down on paper what I thought Judaism was about for our time, the clearer it became that I was talking about a new vision of Judaism. I tried to make the case for why the other forms of liberal Judaism, as well as Orthodox Judaism, were not the answers. I wrote a manuscript of 450 double-spaced pages and asked a variety of people what they thought of it. I realized that I had tried to say too much. In doing that, the most important points were getting lost. I began a major rewrite of the book. I tried to go straight to the core of what I was trying to say. In the process of studying and doing research, I also discovered some powerful texts that made me change my ways of thinking about Judaism. As you will see in a few pages, one text stated that the Torah is all about one thing—freedom. In this notion, Judaism is about teachings and practices to live your life fully/freely. I rewrote the book focusing on that idea and what I believe are the core principles of 21st-century Judaism. Even in the seventh decade of my life, I discovered new truths about Judaism and new truths about myself, which form the core of this book. And that is a really good place to begin.

What is the Contemporary Challenge?

Rejecting the paradigms of rabbinic Judaism

Central to rabbinic Judaism has been defining Judaism around the observance of the commandments/*mitzvot*. Critical to my process is reconstructing observance—*halakha*. Contemporary Jews have raised many questions about traditional *halakha*/Jewish law. What is the authority of *halakha* if we no longer believe in a God who commands specific actions? Is there some way we can take the tradition upon ourselves as a commitment to the Jewish people or to the Jewish past? Since Jews have for centuries observed Shabbat, should we continue this practice? Do we distinguish between ethical commandments and ritual commandments? After all, we all can see the purpose of treating the ethical commandments seriously v it is wrong to lie or embarrass someone publicly. Is it really wrong not to keep kosher or not pray three times a day? Even if the ritual might be a beneficial thing to do (such as resting on Shabbat), do we really think not resting is wrong in the same way that we know lying is wrong? On the other hand, if Judaism is only a system of ethics, what distinguishes it from every other system of ethics?

The starting point for a reconstruction of *halakha* is acknowledging it is no longer law. We are bound by the laws of the country in which we live. If we are caught violating those laws we will be punished. There is no real enforcement of Jewish law. If we don't observe Shabbat or we eat bread on Passover, nothing happens to us. Even in Israel, *halakha* is not enforced by Israeli courts.

While the traditional *halakha* deals with business transactions in addition to ritual practice, the reality is that economic matters are regulated by the American legal system. There are religious courts that Orthodox Jews occasionally use even in business matters, but both sides have to agree to participate in their proceedings. In many ways they function like binding arbitration proceedings in the American legal system. In Orthodox communities there can be communal pressure to conform to the observance of *halakha*. This is only effective if the person wants to be an accepted member of that community. For the most part Orthodox Jews observe *halakha* because they feel committed to the practice.

There is a benefit to feeling obligated to obey Jewish law. Otherwise, it is only up to me whether to observe the practice or not. Facing an important work deadline, it could be hard to resist the pressure of saying to myself: I will skip Shabbat this week in order to get my work done. For those who are strict Shabbat observers, the idea of skipping Shabbat for the week is not a possibility to be considered. There is certainly something lost when observance is done only out of self-motivation. Yet, I believe that is in fact how most Jews outside the traditional world approach Jewish practice. What to observe and what not is a personal decision. It is also a personal decision when to skip that observance. Ultimately, it is my decision whether to gossip or not, pray or not, observe Shabbat in some fashion, give to charity, or volunteer regularly for a social justice project. While there may be encouragement or discouragement from the people who are part of my life, it is really my choice.

A reimagined *halakha* also rejects the notion that fulfillment is the key element of *halakha*. There is a discussion in rabbinic Judaism about whether you need to have *kavanah*—the correct intention—in order to fulfill a commandment/ *mitzvah*. In other words, if you are lighting Hanukah candles and all you can think about are the presents you expect to receive, have you fulfilled the commandment? While the rabbis set out very specific instructions for the correct way to light the candles, they don't stipulate that you need to have the correct intention. Of course, the rabbis likely thought that having the correct intention was a good thing, but they rarely required intention in order to fulfill the commandment. I wonder whether, having adopted a system of commandment and fulfillment, the rabbis thought also requiring intention was too difficult. Performing commandments could have become like filming a movie—take #73 on candle lighting—if every time your mind wandered, you had to do it over again. Staying focused for a few minutes is no easy task for our busy minds. If the average person was going to be able to succeed at all with the *halakhic* system, then relatively simple and tangible requirements for fulfilling the commandments were essential. On the other hand, without intention/*kavanah*, the danger exists that commandments could become rote ritual, divorced from their spiritual meaning. Hasidism critiqued the rote performance of ritual and stressed the importance of intention/*kavanah*. It is ultimately a debate between the relative importance of doing the act and of the meaning of the act.

What is the purpose?

Let's begin by exploring the purpose of *halakha*. There are a number of traditional understandings about why we should fulfill the commandments. The first is that God commanded them, and we should obey God. God punishes us with afflictions if we don't fulfill the commandments and rewards us with blessings if we do. A corollary of this notion is that even if we don't feel rewarded in this world, we will be rewarded in heaven. These notions are not compelling if we don't believe in a God who commands and who rewards and punishes us either in this world or in the next.

A second reason for observing the commandments is in order to help ensure the continuity of the Jewish people. We have been both a people and a religion right from the beginning. That has made Judaism different from many religions, which were based essentially on specific religious doctrines. While it is true that there was an ethnic and even national component in the Catholicism of Irish Catholics, they also knew that there were plenty of other people throughout the world who were also Catholics. In other religions, you converted to the religion. In Judaism you converted to a religion, but you also joined a people. While the peoplehood component was present in Judaism throughout history, it became a more important element in the modern period with the rise of nationalism and the lessening of faith in God and religion. Beginning in the 19th century, various forms of Judaism advocating for Jewish nationalism and secularism arose.

All the contemporary talk in the established Jewish community about continuity leaves unanswered the core question: For what purpose are we preserving Judaism? Just to preserve it for its own sake is not compelling to me. If Jews no longer find Judaism meaningful or if it turns out Judaism can only flourish when we are being persecuted or by withdrawing from the world into separatist enclaves, then I am not sure Judaism can or will survive. The argument for observance for continuity's sake seems to me wrongheaded and one that I think people will increasingly find unconvincing.

The most compelling argument for observance is that it helps us become better human beings:

> "As for God, God's word is purifying" (Ps. 18:31). Rav said: Precepts were given only so that mortals might be purified by them. For of what concern can it be to the Holy One whether, in [preparing meat] a person slaughters an animal at the windpipe or at the gullet? Or of what concern is it to God whether a person eats animals that are unclean or animals that are clean? Hence, precepts were given only so that mortals might be purified by them. (*Genesis Rabbah* 44:1; *Tanhuma*, Shemini, 8)

This rabbinic text gives voice to our concern as moderns. Does God really care whether I keep kosher or not? This text teaches that the purpose of the commandments is not for God; it is for us. Just as God doesn't need sacrifices because God likes barbecued meat, so God doesn't need us to fulfill the commandments to demonstrate our loyalty and commitment. The *mitzvot* are to help make us better people. This notion, found in a rabbinic Midrash, expresses what I believe is Judaism's purpose. The question remains whether the current system and specific commandments are effective in this purpose. For me, the answer is no, or not often enough.

A vision for a new halakha

Halakha is a spiritual path, related to the original meaning of its root, "to go." Each of us is on our life's journey. *Halakha* suggests that there is wisdom and awareness that can help us on our way. It is the spiritual practice of the Jewish people honed over centuries of discussions and developments. Like any practice, it requires a regular commitment. You cannot get the benefits of working out if you only go to your gym three times a year. For our lives, we can imagine a system that does not focus on fulfilling a commandment, yet which still appreciates the importance of actually performing *mitzvot*. Something happens in the doing that is different from just thinking about the values underlying the commandment. Judaism would remain a practice of doing, not just thinking or believing. This would be a system without an emphasis on sin. The obligation is a self-commitment because you believe that a spiritual life requires both practice and discipline. Therefore, there will be times to do a *mitzvah* despite your lack of interest or intention because, like any discipline, you need to practice on a regular basis. This is true even as you strive to make this a habit of the heart—a practice of opening the heart, of awareness of the moment and of the Holy. It is *kavanah*, the intention of the heart and mind, which gives these precepts meaning.

Yet *halakha* as a practice is different than gym workouts or learning to play an instrument. Those practices are done for a desired self-benefit. *Halakha* is a practice that can make you better or more satisfied or happier, but its focus is not only on you. Its focus is also on the other people in your life, as well as social justice around the world and the health of this planet. For some, it echoes the Kabbalistic myth of restoring the universe and God to wholeness.

In response to such classic *halakhic* questions as how much matzah you need to eat to fulfill the commandment, the answer would be—it is not an important question. For example, if you like matzah, eat a lot; if matzah is not your favorite, then eat less. The point, after all, is to eat matzah in order to remember that we were slaves in Egypt. What if we don't eat matzah? This would not be a betrayal of God or the Jewish people. It would be a loss to our spiritual life not to remember the story of the Jewish people. It is a story that we were born out of slavery and became free. Remembering that story, we are called to act on behalf of those in this world who lack freedom and live under oppression. *Halakha* enriches our lives so that we can live those lives fully enhanced with purpose and meaning. Besides emphasizing *kavanah* and being less concerned about fulfillment, we need a fundamental reexamination of some of the categories of *mitzvot* as well as new practices. We will look within the tradition for ideas that can support these new practices as well as discard some ideas and practices of the past.

One problematic legacy of rabbinic Judaism is its emphasis on dualities. In particular, it seems to be organized around distinctions—between kosher and non-kosher; weekday and Shabbat; pure and impure; permitted and forbidden. Isn't much of traditional *halakha*—Jewish law and practice—about differentiating between the good and the bad?

Doesn't that reflect a dualistic notion of the world—a world of distinctions? It certainly can be useful to categorize things by groups as a way of organizing our universe. It is useful to have the word "chair," which can be used for a variety of objects on which we sit. The problematic nature of distinction occurs when it is no longer neutral but has values attached to it.

If there is any doubt about the hierarchy found in distinctions, one need only look at the daily morning blessings. In the traditional liturgy, a man thanks God for not making him a non-Jew, a slave, or a woman. There is of course a blessing to be recited by women. Unfortunately, it doesn't give thanks to God for not making her a man. If it did, then these two blessings about men and women would be offering thanks for who we are. Instead, the version for women thanks God for "making me according to God's will." These blessings make clear the problem with the categorization that underlies rabbinic Judaism's understanding of the world. There are the good or better categories: Jews, free people and men. There are at best the lesser categories: people who are not Jewish, slaves and women. The liberal movements have changed these blessings to express only positive values, thanking God for making us Jews, free, and in God's image. It softens but doesn't really address the central issue.

We see the idea of distinction clearly in the ceremony marking the end of Shabbat. *Havdalah*, as its name suggests, is about differentiation. It distinguishes between *kodesh* and *hol*—the holy and the profane, light and darkness, and between the seventh day and the six days of creation. Light and darkness may be neutral, though certainly darkness can be seen as scary while light may be seen as good or beautiful. More clearly, the distinction between the sacred and the profane, between Shabbat and the six workdays, could be expressing a hierarchy of values. In the traditional liturgy, a fourth distinction is made at *Havdalah*—between Israel and the nations. This latter distinction could be understood as factual just as we refer to Jews and non-Jews or the young and old or renters and owners. Yet the traditional understanding of *Havdalah* is that these distinctions have an assigned value. The notion that Jews are the chosen people is traditionally understood to mean that Jews are more special than others. Similarly, holiness is preferred over the profane. By distinguishing Jew from non-Jew, it is impossible not to read a preference on the part of the rabbis.

For rabbinic Judaism, the text of *Havdalah* as we have it was a deliberate choice. We have ancient versions of *Havdalah* that have other distinctions, for example, between the dry land and the sea. That distinction or similar ones such as earth and sky could have been used in the authoritative version of *Havdalah* had the rabbis wanted to make a statement about the importance of distinguishing between one thing and another without an attribution of value. Why distinguish without value? Perhaps to appreciate the myriad blessings of this world. Perhaps to appreciate the individuality of people. Perhaps even to be able to use the element of choice, of distinguishing, when we need to—when it is a choice between good and bad or wisdom and foolishness.

Why then does rabbinic Judaism set up a hierarchical vision of these distinctions? One possibility is that early on in rabbinic Judaism the rabbis understood that they were creating a Judaism for a people living in exile. Living as a minority in an often hostile world, it was useful, even helpful, to create a world of distinctions between us and them. It was useful, even helpful, to create separation from the vast outside world ready to engulf us and the precious interior world, to see the world as divided between light and darkness and for Jews to be the bearers of the light in a darkening world.

Across the ancient world there was often a sense of insiders and outsiders—you were either a citizen of Rome or a barbarian. The notion of cherishing diversity as a value was rare. Yet, the desire for categories goes deeper than that in the ancient world. In Genesis, the world begins in chaos and moves toward structure. The animals are divided by their species. Order is important because the ancient world was often a place of chaos. There was the human-created chaos of wars and conflicts. There was the chaos of nature bringing droughts and floods. There were the unexplained deaths due to the mystery of disease. Ancients tried to bring order to that world by placating the gods. Rituals helped "convince" the gods to give humans a good harvest. It was a world in which a sense of order was laid over the chaos because humans didn't feel they could control what would happen. Disorder was seen as dangerous, even demonic. Things that didn't fit into the created categories of society were seen as problematic.

There was halakhic significance to these categorizations. Hence there is one category: adult males with all the responsibilities and privileges of Judaism. Then there were those of a different and, I would argue, lesser category, such as children, women and slaves. These were bound by some aspects of Jewish law (especially the prohibitions), but had a different status than Jewish men. Strikingly, of the three categories, male children would become adults and slaves could be freed; women could never change their status. It is the essentialist definition of these categories that is the real problem. It suggests that women are essentially different than men and that they cannot change. Some have tried to argue that women are separate but equal, that they have a role different than but equally important as that of Jewish men. Others have argued that women are not obligated to fulfill certain commandments because they are inherently more spiritual and don't need them. Yet, isn't this another version of essentialism? Such statements deny the central teaching of the biblical text, which is that we are all created in the image of God. Essentially, we are the same. Stereotypes of categories of people, whether positive or negative, are just not true. What is true is that most stereotypes end up being negative.

Doesn't the notion of distinction in Judaism precede rabbinic Judaism? The story of humanity, it can be argued, really begins when Adam and Eve eat of the Tree of Knowledge of good and evil. We need structure. We need to distinguish between being helpful or hurtful. Isn't being able to distinguish between good and bad and making choices what Judaism is all about?

Maybe not. If the journey is to bring us back to wholeness, if our greatest dream is to strive for *shalom*/peace—maybe distinctions are not the basic substructure of the universe, but only temporary constructions. *Shalom*/peace and *shalem*/whole are from the same Hebrew root. The mystics certainly see that the overall arc of humanity is to move from separation to restoring the world to its original oneness.

The point isn't that we should live in a world without distinctions. Distinctions are inevitable and necessary. The problem is rabbinic Judaism's decision to divide the world into categories that are hierarchical and unchanging. Today, we live in a world very different from the ancient past. To give a contrasting example from rabbinic Judaism, let's look at how we regard bread on Passover. Fifty-one weeks a year, it is perfectly acceptable to eat bread. In fact, as in many other cultures, bread is the staff of life. Yet for one week a year, during Passover, bread and other leavened foods are strictly forbidden. Whatever the purpose of the prohibition, it is clear that there is nothing intrinsically bad about bread. We forgo bread to remind us of the unleavened bread we ate as we left Egypt. Perhaps the leavening process reminds us to be careful not to get too puffed up about ourselves. Maybe the intention of *Pesach* is to help us focus on one basic aspect of our lives—food and eating—that at other times of the year we ignore. Focusing on it one week a year is then the purpose of the ban on leavened food. Yet all those possible reasons are not about the essential nature of bread.

We live in an open society. The ghetto walls, both literal and metaphorical, are gone. The challenge for much of world Jewry is not how to live in a hostile surrounding environment but rather how to live in a boundaryless environment. Modernity and its values are a challenge to Judaism because, in fact, we embrace those values so deeply.

Ultimately, the real problem with dualism and other distinctions is that over and over again it was used to say category A is better than category B. This was true about men and women, about whites and people of color, and many ethnic or religious groups. Those in Category B often seemed like a secondary class of humans. They were not as smart as the people of Category A. They were like children who needed to be coddled. They were beastlike and needed to be controlled. The attitude toward these others was almost always a mixture of contempt and fear. At times it was used to support the status quo. Distinctions don't have to lead to stereotyping and hierarchies, but it is too easy to do that.

The story of America over the last century is one of expanding inclusivity. Women were given the right to vote, segregation was ended, and marriage equality became the law of the land. This inclusivity came through struggle and there is still much to be done. However, the arc has been clear. This has been echoed in the Jewish world as well, especially regarding the role of women. It is in our best natures to move away from exclusion and toward inclusion.

If this is true, then should the traditional paradigm of distinction remain the basic way we understand Judaism? I am not suggesting a Judaism without boundaries. There is a difference between right and wrong and between caring and indifference. But those distinctions are based on moral differences, not on people's identity. I am asking us to think about the fundamental way we structure our world and how Judaism should reflect that thinking. This is a greater challenge than just eliminating the hierarchical distinctions. There is a more fundamental question than even what is the nature of *halakha*—Jewish law—and in what ways, if any, is it binding. It asks whether the paradigm that was so helpful to rabbinic Judaism, that paradigm of dividing the world into two categories of good and bad (and an occasional third category of *pareve*—neutral) is the paradigm that will help us create our Jewish identity in this modern world. Today, do we need to shift our paradigm away from distinction?

The organized Jewish community is worried about its future. How can it survive in an open society? Obviously, these are real concerns; but for Jews who embrace the open society, the answers cannot lie in a decision to stand at the border to guard our Judaism. We have tried that tactic for over a century and it has failed, and not because we haven't said it well or clearly. It has failed because we can't create effective boundaries that are not just invisible but that are counter to the way we live our lives. We embrace American society. We reject any notion that we are different from our fellow Americans. We don't want ghetto walls except when we want Jews to marry Jews. Perhaps we need a Judaism based on something other than distinctions in order to give structure and expression to Jewish life in this open and fluid 21st century.

Advancing the holy

Let me make a beginning suggestion. In his three-volume commentary on the Book of Leviticus, Jacob Milgrom (20th-century Bible scholar) talks about the distinctions that are so much a part of Leviticus. He sets out that there are two pairs discussed throughout the book: pure/impure and sacred/common. In diagramming them, he places a broken line between the pure and impure and between the sacred and the common. He writes: "There is no fixed boundary. Israel by its behavior can move the boundaries—either way. But it is enjoined to move in one direction only: *to advance the holy* into the realm of the common and *to diminish the impure* and thereby enlarge the realm of the pure."

The category of holy and common seems particularly fruitful for this discussion. It is striking that Milgrom translates *hol* not as *profane*, but as *common*. He does this because, according to biblical law, it is not wrong to change the holy into the common. There are acceptable ways to desanctify things. I like the word *common* instead of *profane* for other reasons. For me, common is a much less hierarchical category than profane. Life is about sanctifying all things, but their initial quality is common, not profane. The work week is common, not profane, in comparison to the holiness of Shabbat. We live most of our lives in the commonplace. It is not Judaism's expectation that we should spend the whole week observing Shabbat. We are to live in real life. The work of Judaism is to find holiness amidst the common. It is to strive for the awareness that allows us to celebrate the simple ordinary things. It is to help make the world a better place so more people can experience the blessings that life can offer. Extraordinary moments are extraordinary in part because they don't happen all the time.

In this new paradigm, we would still strive to live lives of holiness and to make this world more sacred, more extraordinary, more holy. We do this not so much by categorization and differentiation but by following the words of Abraham Joshua Heschel (20th-century theologian): Live as though the redemption of all people is dependent on the devotion of one's life.

This new paradigm would be more attuned to this modern world. We would accept the unitive nature of this world. We live in an America that accepts differences and strives to expand the circle of who is inside as much as possible. It is an America that no longer sees women as second class; it is an America that is moving to accept people regardless of sexual orientation or of race. It is an America that has moved closer to the ideal of our founders that all men are created equal or, in our version, that all people are created in the divine image—*be-tzelem elohim*.

One cutting edge of this issue today is about gender. There are those who say that gender is not co-equal to our sexual organs or the body into which we were born. Increasingly transgender people seek to be welcomed rather than feared in our society. The traditional way to look at this issue is that the primary human distinction in the story of creation in Genesis is God creating humans as male and female. Each to their kind is echoed through the other creatures in this world.

Yet there is another way to read that central verse: And God created human (*adam*) in God's image, in the image of God, God created human, male and female God created them. (Gen. 1:27). The word "*adam*" appears only in the singular. There is no plural form in Hebrew the way there is for man and men. *Adam*/human is created in the image of God and is created male and female. Clearly, both males and females are created in God's image for it says, "God created them." What if the verse is also saying that *adam*/human is created with male and female within that one body? What if that suggests that there is a spectrum of maleness and female-ness within *adam*/human who ultimately only exists in a singular form? We are to understand that rather than seeing x or y as a better model, we should see the world as a spectrum. The colors of the rainbow of the covenant with Noah remind us that it is not useful to see the world as white and black but to understand that nuance and complexity are actually closer to the image of a God who created the world and all the diversity it contains.

We need to respond to the new challenges of this world just as our ancestors had to respond to the world in which they found themselves. I think the old answers and paradigms will not satisfy those asking questions. We must reframe the question, and in so doing reset the agenda. The old questions—who are you, who is your mother, who is your spouse, how committed are you—will not be effective in a world that increasingly rejects arbitrary boundaries.

Our central questions today ought to be: How can we help you create a meaningful Jewish life? How can we be a sustaining community to you? How can we be a setting that assists you in your inner spiritual work? How can we help you live a life committed to social justice?

Re-inventing the notion of Torah

What is God asking of us?

If I no longer believe in the traditional notions of the revelation at Sinai, what do I believe happened at Sinai and what is its significance? Rather than preserving the Jewish tradition as unchanged, I believe our task is to re-invent the Torah for this moment. The following sources from the tradition suggest more dynamic ways of thinking about Torah.

What did the people hear at Sinai? The Talmud answers: They heard the Ten Commandments. Another opinion is they heard the first two commandments only (Makkot 24a). Or perhaps it was only the first word anokhi—I—meaning that it was not the content but the experience of being in the presence of the Divine that mattered. Menahem Mendel of Rymanov (Hasidic master 1745-1815) says that it was only the aleph of the first word anokhi that was heard, which is paradoxical because aleph is a silent letter. Gershom Scholem, (20th-century scholar of Jewish mysticism) wrote, "To hear the aleph is to hear next to nothing, it is the preparation for all audible language, but in itself conveys no determinate, specific meaning … Rabbi Mendel transformed the revelation on Mount Sinai into a mystical revelation, pregnant with infinite meaning, but without specific meaning" (*On the Kabbalah and its Symbolism*, p. 30). This suggests it is not 613 commandments that were given at Sinai, but rather it was an encounter calling us to respond to God seeking partners in taking care of this world.

Or to use traditional language, Torah is an answer to the question, "What do we think God is asking of us?" The prophet Micah says, "God has told you what is good/*tov* and what God asks of you: to act justly and to love kindness and to walk humbly with your God" (Micah 6:8). Can we translate that sense of Godliness into a practice that will make us better human beings and will remind and encourage us to make the world a better place? Torah is the Jewish people's response to the encounter at Sinai. Whether Moses composed that response in forty days or it took centuries and a number of authors and editors to give us the text we have makes no difference. It is all out of an impulse to respond to the call of Sinai. The authority of the text rests in the ongoing conversation that the Jewish people have had for centuries over that text and its meanings.

It is a mistake to think that this process has stopped with Sinai. Our understanding changes. The world changes. It is not just that the Torah was written in ancient times and therefore has nothing directly to say about our contemporary reality of computers or cloning. More significantly, I can't believe that the word of God, which is to be eternal and true, would say that slavery is okay, homosexuality is an abomination and women should have a second-class status. That just can't be the word of God. If it is not the word of God, then it is the word of men (and as far as we know it is literally the word of men, not women). It is subjective and flawed, which is why it is our task to constantly ask what it meant and what it should mean today.

The value of ancient wisdom

Why then not throw it all out and start again? For 3,000 years these texts and their commentaries have been studied and debated. The Jewish people have tried to apply these texts to new situations, sometimes successfully, sometimes mistakenly. It is not simple. It is a challenging process. You cannot be sure you are correct. Figuring out what the Torah has to say is just like all the hard questions in life. If it were simple, you would know the answer before the question was even asked. What I do find in the three-thousand-year discussion is wisdom and texts that give expression to values with which I want to shape my life.

The account of the revelation at Sinai in the Torah is found in chapters 19-20 of the Book of Exodus. The account is confusing—I think deliberately—as it tries to depict a moment that is beyond a describable experience. It is also a split screen: God is giving instructions and the people are gathering. In print, simultaneous actions can only be described sequentially. What is clear in the text is that the people move a distance away out of fear and ask Moses to act on their behalf, believing that if God speaks to them, they will die. Moses reassures them but the people still remain at a distance. In Art Green's (contemporary theologian and scholar of Hasidism) felicitous description, we are the people who fled Sinai. Given the opportunity to hear directly the word of God, we found it too intense. We said in effect, "Moses, you go and tell us what God said."

In life, we want so much to hear the word of God. For some it is to know what to do. Or it is a desire for certainty. Or it is the hope to remove all the veils of confusion and finally know the real truth. Yet we spend our lives fleeing the truth. One modern form of revelation as truth-seeking is psychotherapy. We seek a better understanding of our issues and ourselves. For many people therapy is rediscovering the truths about ourselves that we actually already know. In successful therapy, we don't just rediscover those truths in a moment of great insight; we rediscover them bit by bit and over and over again. Over time, perhaps the understanding is a little deeper. Perhaps the truths that we flee need to be met over and over again if they are to be more than just talk therapy and actually find their way deep into our hearts. Real change comes about through a long process.

Timelessness of Torah

The Torah can be such a pathway to holiness and to wholeness. It is why each year in synagogue we read the Torah from the beginning of Genesis through the end of Deuteronomy. As we finish that reading, we begin again. Torah does not have a "The End." We read the Torah again and again because the world changes. We change. Therefore, we hear the Torah differently because we are different or because this contemporary moment is different. Saying the Torah is the word of God means for me that it is a text that is rich with multiple meanings. Even the traditional understanding of the Torah texts suggests that there are multiple meanings. The tradition states there are four methods for understanding Torah:

- *Pshat*—the simple meaning of the text
- *Remez*—allegory
- *Drash*—imaginative interpretations
- *Sod*—secret, mystical meanings

The four methods are collectively called PaRDeS, taken from the first letter of each method. Put simply, the sage Ben Bag Bag described the Torah in this way: "Turn it this way and turn it that way for it includes everything" (*Pirke Avot/ Ethics of our Ancestors* 5:24).

It is noteworthy that the tradition claims that every word of Torah is literally the word of God when all of it (except perhaps the Ten Commandments) had to be transmitted to Moses. Right from the beginning we start a game of telephone as one teacher passes it down to his students and one generation passes it on to the next. How could no word be changed in that act of transmission, which occurs over and over again?

What makes Torah timeless is not that it is the unchanging word of God, but rather that it helps shape our response to the issues and challenges of our time. Some of those challenges have been with humans from the beginning. Others are unprecedented or feel unprecedented, which is almost the same thing. For instance, how are our brains being changed by our increasingly digital world? The traditional view of Torah suggests that it should be preserved and carefully transmitted from one generation to the next. I suggest that our task as Jews is to look into it and use it as a blueprint for our life and for our world.

Such notions of a more dynamic sense of Torah can be found even in traditional sources. *Seder Eliyahu Zuta* (a midrashic work) tells the following parable:

> Once there was a king who loved two servants. To each he gave a measure of wheat and flax. The wise servant took the flax and

spun it into a cloth. He took the wheat and made a loaf of bread, which he covered with the cloth. The silly servant did nothing. When the king returned, he praised the wise servant and scorned the silly one. So too when God gave the Torah to Israel, God gave it as wheat from which flour should be extracted, as flax from which clothing should be made.

Hands-on revelation?

This parable suggests that we are to transform the Torah, not just carefully preserve it in the form in which we received it. We start with the Torah as the raw material. Our life's work is to make the Torah ours by reworking it. It is to be the clothing and the food of our life. We are to engage in Torah. It is a process both conservative and radical. We don't start from scratch but with the text of the Jewish people for the last 3,000 years. Yet we take the Torah and, like the wheat, we transform it, all the while still recognizing its origin.

The Talmud tells the following story:

> When Moses ascended on high at Mount Sinai, he found the Holy One affixing crowns to letters. [Certain letters in the Torah scroll have marks above them called crowns]. Moses asked, "Lord of the universe who stays your hand?" [i.e., is there anything lacking in Torah so that additions are necessary?] God replied, "At the end of many generations there will arise a person, Akiva ben Joseph by name, who will infer heaps and heaps of laws from each tittle on these crowns." "Lord of the universe," said Moses, "permit me to see him." God replied, "Turn around." Moses went and sat down behind eight rows of R. Akiva's disciples, and listened to their discourses on law. Not being able to follow what they were saying, he was so distressed that he grew faint. But when they came to a certain subject and the disciples asked R. Akiva, "Master, where did you learn this?" and R. Akiva replied, "It is a law given to Moses at Sinai," Moses was reassured. (Menahot 29b)

Since in fact no one, including Akiva, has derived any laws from the crowns on the Torah letters, this tale has gone out of its way to make a point. Regarded as the greatest master of the Talmudic period, Akiva is teaching a class. Sitting in that class, Moses cannot understand what is going on. Clearly, the rabbinic tradition, as exemplified by Akiva, is vastly different from Moses' world. This is despite the traditional claim that Moses received both the written and oral Torah at Sinai and that no student would ever say anything not already revealed at Sinai. Moses is lost and very upset until Akiva states that the source for a particular law is that it was given to Moses at Sinai. Instead of jumping up and calling Akiva a liar, since Moses had not heard before anything in Akiva's discourse, Moses is reassured by Akiva's "lie." Why? Because by that statement Akiva has placed himself in the tradition of the Torah of Sinai. Akiva is not advocating a new Torah but rather is teaching Torah, as he understands it both as a tradition handed down beginning with Moses and as understood by its contemporary teachers. Akiva's understanding of Torah is dynamic.

Change is the only constant

For the Torah of Sinai to be the covenant between God and Israel, it can't be the unchanging word of God. If the covenant is going to be a real partnership, the Jewish people must have the authority to change the terms of the contract. Otherwise, it is a contract imposed on us by an all-powerful God rather than a contract that we accepted willingly. The text tells us the Israelite people gathered at Sinai said *na'aseh ve-nishma*—literally we will do and we will listen (Ex. 24:7). It really meant they would fulfill the terms of the contract. Yet, as much as the biblical text portrays this as a willing acceptance, the rabbis understood that the story is not so simple. After all, this was the God who brought ten plagues in Egypt and wiped out the Egyptian army at the sea. When God offers you a contract, isn't there only one right answer to One who is far more powerful than you? The rabbis give expression to this notion by picking up a phrase in Ex. 19:17, which says the Israelites were gathered *tahtit*—at the foot of the mountain. The word *tahtit* often means underneath. The rabbis imagined God holding Mount Sinai over the assembled Israelites, proclaiming to them that if they don't accept the contract, God will drop the mountain and bury the people underneath. Needless to say, the people accepted an offer they just couldn't refuse. The rabbis were disturbed by this idea and note the obvious problem. A contract that you accept under duress is not a valid contract. They wondered when the Jewish people actually accepted the covenant of Sinai willingly. They found their answer in the book of Esther, read on Purim, where it is written (9:27): they fulfilled what they received (*kiymu ve-kiblu*). For the rabbis, these two words indicated that the Jews of Esther's time agreed to fulfill what they had received at Sinai (Shabbat 88a).

Why does this willing embrace of Torah finally take place at Purim? It is striking that Purim is a story of redemption that is carried out solely by human action. There is no divine intervention. In fact, God's name does not appear in the Book of Esther—unusual for a book of the Torah. How appropriate that a story where the Jews take their salvation into their own hands becomes the moment when they can accept the covenant freely. There is no mountain hanging over their heads. The Torah becomes ours when we internalize its message, which is to stand up against oppression. We are not to follow the Torah because God commands us but rather because we understand that God's way of righteousness and justice is the way to be in the world.

One way to view the Jewish calendar is that we begin with the month of Nisan during which the Exodus from Egypt is celebrated at Passover. From the Exodus we come to Sinai to receive the Torah once again. Yet for us to really receive the Torah, we must pass through the whole festival cycle until we get to Purim, which occurs in the last month of the year. No sooner do we freely accept the Torah by recommitting to live by it, then we begin the whole cycle once again, starting with slavery and freedom.

The journey continues

From these texts we learn that Torah and tradition change. It is not an unchanging truth. Rather it is a truth that we need to strive for over and over again; it is shaped both by the Jewish tradition and by the contemporary moment. The revelation of the truth is an ongoing process that began at Sinai and continues into our time and beyond. Upon reflection, it seems obvious that the Torah at Sinai is not the final word of revelation. The rabbinic tradition states the Torah speaks in the language of people. This means that it spoke to the people of its time. It didn't abolish slavery. Yet, the rabbinic tradition also says that the Voice of Sinai calls out every day. Our task is to hear that Voice and figure out what it is saying at this particular moment. It is a fundamental mistake to fix the Torah in one time and place.

Maimonides, 12th-century philosopher and rabbinic scholar, describes the unfolding nature of revelation when it comes to the sacrificial cult. He says that much of the Torah is a reaction to what was happening in ancient times. The people surrounding the Israelites were worshipping gods through sacrifices. God doesn't need sacrifices. In fact, sacrifices are problematic since people could mistakenly come to believe, as their idolatrous neighbors did, that God eats the sacrifices. However, God knew that it would be too radical a change to do away with sacrifices immediately—cold turkey, if you will—and so the Torah lays out a whole sacrificial cult. Maimonides suggests that prayer is a more elevated way to worship God, but prayer could be instituted only centuries later. Maimonides had a sense of a progression in Judaism.

What does all this mean for liberal Jews? Does Jewish law have any significance if its authority doesn't rest on its being the word of God? Can it still be a tradition if it is rooted only in the subjective contemporary "truth"? Ultimately, the Torah is subjective and complex for liberal Jews. Yet, it is not just the reality of Torah that has changed over time. Judaism is our opportunity and our challenge to try to continue to improve our understanding of Torah. For me, *halakha* remains rooted to its original meaning of a path. *Halakha* is the Jewish path through life. Beginning with Abraham we are told *Lekh lekha*—go forth. We are all to go on the journey of life; *halakha* is that journey infused with the wisdom and practice of Judaism.

Abraham: spiritual trailblazer

If you think about it, the model is Abraham. He is told to go forth on that journey. We know that Abraham offers welcome to travelers. The only ritual we know he observes is that of circumcision. In fact, when he offers food to the travelers, he seems to offer them milk and meat together, which would be a violation of the laws of keeping kosher. We have no idea whether he observed Shabbat. This question of what Jewish life was like before the laws were given at Sinai is a provocative one for the Talmudic rabbis. On the one hand, how could the patriarchs observe the Torah before it was given? How could they celebrate Passover and the rest of the "historical" holidays before those events occurred? On the other hand, it was unimaginable to them that Abraham had not practiced Judaism by keeping kosher and observing Shabbat. The Talmud answers that Abraham observed the whole Torah, even minor rabbinic enactments. (See *Yoma* 28b).

How is that possible? Is the Torah a form of natural law that can be discovered through logic and observing the world? Yet, among the traditional categories of law there are those whose reason we do not know (*hukkim*). Presumably these cannot be discovered by the use of logic. According to some of the Hasidic masters, the 613 commandments are paralleled by 613 limbs and sinews of the body. In other words, the Torah is embodied in us. The commandments can be discovered by paying attention to our body or perhaps to the spiritual equivalent of our body. Abraham knew the Torah because of his spiritual greatness and insight. Perhaps he observed it on a totally spiritual level. He didn't eat matzah to celebrate freedom but he connected to the idea of freedom as a defining Jewish principle. For the Hasidic masters, this discussion resonated with their emphasis on the importance of *kavanah*—intention. For them, paying attention to the intention of the commandments, not merely observing them, was central.

This Hasidic model of Abraham as a pious Jew before there was a revelation at Sinai is an important one for liberal Jews. It suggests that the purpose of Torah is to live a life of holiness. It is not about fulfilling the commandments but about living a life filled with meaning and purpose. A great spiritual master might be able to live such a life because of their unusual ability to maintain a level of awareness and clarity of vision. Abraham, even though an imperfect person, could maintain such a life without the Torah of Sinai. Yet, we need the Torah of Sinai for two reasons. First, most of us are not spiritual masters. Second, if the Jewish people is to be a people, we need to have a commonly held tradition. The Torah is that commonly held tradition—even if we don't agree completely on its interpretation and practical application.

Incorporating all that is Torah

There are also many different Torahs. There is the written Torah, the text that we have held as sacred for many generations. There is a midrash that says the Torah is the blueprint for the world (Genesis Rabbah 1:1). It is that ur-Torah that God looks into and uses to create the world; it is Torah at its most universal. There is also the Torah that predates Sinai, which the patriarchs observed, according to tradition. It is the *derekh Adonai*—the way of God. Abraham and others can intuit from the broad principles of compassion and justice how to apply those principles to the challenges of life.

And what of the Torah after Sinai? Some of the Hasidic masters of the late 18th century and 19th century had a more dynamic understanding of Torah than that of the rabbis who preceded them. For instance, the Sefat Emet (19th century, in his commentary on Bereishit) redefined the notion of the Oral Law. While the Written Torah was the text that we have in the Torah scroll, the Sefat Emet held that the Oral Law was no longer just the additional details given to Moses on Mt. Sinai, but comprised all of the deeds of the righteous. The Sefat Emet explains that this is why the Torah doesn't begin with the revelation at Sinai or the Exodus from Egypt. The book of Genesis recounts the stories of the patriarchs and matriarchs. Those stories are the Oral Torah. The Sefat Emet states this more explicitly in a second teaching when he says that it is the responsibility of the Jews to add to the Written Torah (Teaching for Shavuot). This would suggest that the Torah continues to evolve, change and grow with each generation. The Sefat Emet takes this one step further by suggesting that we should be committed to contributing to the ongoing creation of the Oral Torah.

A teaching of another Hasidic master, the Degel Mahaneh Ephraim (18th century), frames this dynamic quality of Torah in a different way. Focusing on the phrase *darosh darash* taken from Lev. 10:16, which could be translated as "you shall surely interpret," the Degel believes that the Written Torah cannot be understood without the interpretations of the rabbis. He emphasizes that the Torah requires both the Written and Oral Torah; whoever denies even a single statement of the Oral Torah is as though they denied the whole Torah. Here he is quoting a rabbinic statement from the Talmud. However, he concludes his teaching by saying:

> Thus, in every generation, its expounders complete the Torah. Because the Torah is expounded in each generation according to what is necessary in that generation, and what is the root of the soul of that generation. Therefore, God opens the eyes of the wise of each generation to God's holy Torah. One who denies this is also like one who denies the whole Torah. (Teaching on Bereishit)

The Degel suggests that the teachers of each generation must respond to the needs of that generation. Each generation's Torah is different. Clearly the Degel is reserving the authority to interpret the tradition only to the teachers of that generation, the Hasidic masters. Yet it is clear to me that he is saying each generation's Torah differs from the one that preceded it. Perhaps in the context of history, he wanted to make claims on the authenticity of the changes that Hasidism made from the normative rabbinic Judaism of his time. Even so, it remains a teaching that supports the notion that Judaism must be responsive to the changing needs of the moment. I would take one more step and say that all those who are committed to the Jewish enterprise, not just the spiritual masters, can be engaged in creating the Torah of our time.

One last Hasidic teaching is by Rabbi Levi Isaac of Berditchev (19th-century Hasidic master). In the Talmud, there are a number of arguments that are left unresolved. The Talmud concludes these arguments with the word *Tayku*. A traditional explanation of the word is that it is an abbreviation for *Tishbi Yitareitz Kushyot U-bayot*, meaning that Elijah the prophet will answer all the questions and difficulties. Levi Isaac asks why it is that Elijah will, at the end of days, come and answer all the unanswered questions. Since at the end of days, all the righteous will be resurrected, shouldn't it be Moses—who heard the whole Torah directly from God and therefore knows it better and more directly than anyone else? Levi Isaac answers by saying that what is unique about Elijah is that he never died. He rose alive to heaven in a fiery chariot. In order to successfully interpret *halakha*, you have to understand the contemporary moment:

> Only someone who is alive and in this world. Such a person can know what aspect is necessary. One who is dead really can't know what aspect is necessary. Elijah is alive. He never tasted death. He is always in this world. Therefore, it is Elijah who

will explicate all the questions and difficulties for he knows
which aspect is necessary for the world.... (From Likutim in
Kedushat Levi)

Once again there is a sense that *halakha* needs to respond to the contemporary needs of the moment. The authoritative reading of the law is not what it
meant when told to Moses, but rather what it means today. While these teachings
of Hasidism reflect a desire to respond to the needs of its followers, it must be
acknowledged that these same Hasidic masters did not advocate changing traditional Jewish law. Whatever changes Hasidism made from the traditional Jewish
law of their time were relatively minor. Yet, they were aware that Hasidism was a
critique of the existing traditional Judaism of their time. It was a revival movement
that also wanted to make spiritual experiences accessible to a wider circle of Jews.
In other words, their religious life was an innovation even as they remained deeply
committed to the tradition.

From a very different perspective, Rabbi Mordecai Kaplan (20th-century
theologian) came to a similar conclusion centuries later when he posited Judaism as an evolving religious civilization. The term he used for the movement he
started, Reconstructionism, didn't mean that we should change the things in the
tradition that needed reforming. It wasn't only about fixing the tradition we had
inherited. Rather he saw each generation's task as both a challenge and opportunity to reconstruct Judaism. This could involve rejecting parts of the tradition,
re-interpreting other parts and inventing new parts. Kaplan believed that the
tradition had a vote, not a veto. Kaplan's notion of a dynamic tradition is the one
that best expresses what I think our relationship to Torah should be. It also echoes
the notion we saw in the Hasidic texts, that each generation has unique needs and
understandings of Torah.

The Torah is traditionally referred to as a tree of life/an *eitz hayyim*. Trees
need to continue growing. Sometimes they also need pruning to enable them to
thrive. As a tree of life, the Torah is what we need to embrace to enrich our lives.

Minhag America:
The emerging practice of American Judaism

In the late 19th century a leading Reform rabbi, Isaac Mayer Wise, believed that a new way of practicing Judaism was emerging in America, which he would call *Minhag America*, the custom of American Jews. At the time, it did look like Reform Judaism would become the only form of Judaism in America, but history turned out more complicated than he imagined. A few decades later, Conservative Judaism emerged and became the largest denomination of Judaism. By the beginning of the 21st century, Conservative Judaism declined and once again Reform Judaism became the largest denomination. Orthodoxy, once thought to be on the verge of extinction in Isaac Mayer Wise's time, has instead increased its numbers significantly. Reform, Conservative, and the newer Reconstructionist Judaism were all attempts to respond to modernity and have succeeded in attracting some Jews to be active members in Jewish communities. Yet, many Jews affiliated with these denominations have been only sporadic participants in Jewish life. The number of Jews belonging to synagogues in the non-Orthodox world has decreased over time in the United States and the number of unaffiliated Jews has increased. I believe that the major factor causing this decline is the growing sense that Judaism is fairly peripheral to the big issues of life—purpose, loss, success and failure, relationships, and connection.

A new *minhag*

A new *Minhag America* began to emerge in the second half of the 20th century and the beginning of the 21st century among liberal religious Jews. It takes the form of a common set of practices in certain areas that are based not on Jewish law but on a combination of values and desires. This *Minhag America* includes some major principles, such as a commitment to egalitarianism and the inclusion of LGBTQ Jews. It includes a more open attitude toward sex before marriage. It includes a notion of Talmud Torah, the study of Torah, as a spiritual as well as an intellectual practice. It values informality and community. It has made social justice a central aspect of Judaism. There is no group of rabbis or of lay people who met and agreed upon the definition of *Minhag America*. It is simply that over time, liberal Jews have come to understand Judaism in a new way.

To explicate one example: Liberal Jews who observe traditional kashrut will not eat forbidden animals like pig or shellfish, and will only eat chicken and beef slaughtered in a traditional ritual manner. However, nearly all of them will eat in any restaurant regardless of whether it is under rabbinic supervision. According to tradition, this is forbidden. Even if a person is only eating fish or dairy in a restaurant (and the food itself therefore is kosher), it is forbidden because the restaurant's oven was also used to cook non-kosher meat. The truth is that there is no real justification in the traditional sources for eating in a restaurant that is not rabbinically supervised. Why then do many Jews like myself eat in such restaurants? It is not only that eating in restaurants is one of the pleasures of modern life. It also reflects a desire by many Jews to be fully a part of American society, which means being able to socialize with colleagues and friends over meals. For people like me, not eating meat (or shellfish) in restaurants is kosher enough.

Similarly, there have been other changes from Jewish law based on changing values. For instance, it has become the practice of liberal Jews to engage in sex before marriage (and also not to be celibate following a divorce). Traditional religious authorities prohibit any sexual intimacy outside of marriage. Why do liberal Jews engage in premarital sex? Sexuality is a very powerful and attractive impulse. It is also true that American Jews are mirroring the practice of non-Jewish Americans, most of whom think sex before marriage is acceptable behavior. The notion of an unmarried couple living together has become commonplace. Many believe that this is actually healthier and may be beneficial to couples in developing their relationships.

Women in Judaism

Another area that has shifted is the role of women in Judaism. This clearly reflects the influence of feminism in American society. All of the liberal denominations have become egalitarian, where women have roles in religious life equal to those of men. Ordaining women rabbis has changed the face of Judaism. While there existed within Jewish sources some support for such changes as calling women up to the Torah for an *aliyah*, there were other changes, such as counting women in the minyan, that lacked any real basis in traditional sources. Yet when the Conservative movement made these decisions in favor of egalitarianism there was little opposition to counting women for a minyan, since it made getting the quorum of ten easier. On the other hand, there was more opposition to calling women to the Torah despite textual support. Why? Because the visual of women on the *bimah* felt unnerving to men who saw that as masculine space. This supports the notion that, in the end, the debate was less about Jewish law and more about societal sensibilities. The truth is that the discussion about the role of women in services was always about the role of women in society. It was not about what *halakha* had to say but about how people felt about such a change. Is this a change to be embraced, accepted reluctantly, or resisted?

While the majority of Orthodox Jews decry changes such as an equal role for women or welcoming LGBTQ Jews into Jewish life, in fact, Judaism has always been influenced by and open to the world around it. Scholars have suggested that the broad methods of Talmudic study were borrowed from the Greeks. Maimonides (12th-century philosopher) was clearly influenced by the ancient Greek philosophers. We also have examples of Jewish law adapting to a changing sense of morality. While the biblical text sets out a circumstance where parents could condemn to death a rebellious son, the rabbinic tradition clearly felt uncomfortable with this biblical law and basically defined it out of existence. They did so by making it impossible to meet the rules of when it would apply.

Always adapting

Judaism has always interacted with and adapted to the larger world around it. Sometimes Jewish law rejected practices just because they were practices of Christians or Muslims. Other times Jewish practice and beliefs were influenced by broader trends in society. The challenge has always been whether a broad trend adds to the Jewish tradition, is a passing fad, or is a negative phenomenon.

These societal trends can influence even the most traditional Orthodox communities. While the medieval world was ascetic in its orientation, the modern world is more embracing of the pleasures of life. While the ultra-Orthodox world values expressions of piety above and beyond Jewish law, it is striking that in at least in some areas, this community may be less observant of stringencies (*humrot*). One area has to do with fast days. There are a number of fast days besides Yom Kippur on the Jewish calendar that many Orthodox Jews observe today. There were many more fast days of an optional nature that some people observed in the Middle Ages. They included three fast days after the pilgrimage festivals and a weekly fast day during the winter months. I suggest that these fasts are not observed today because even the most traditional elements of the Jewish community have adapted a more accepting attitude toward the pleasures of life and thereby have rejected the asceticism that was prevalent in pre-modern times. One could argue that the challenge to Judaism today is not asceticism but consumerism. Have we moderns embraced the pleasures of the world too much? Should Judaism encourage us to live simpler lives? Is this part of the environmental challenge of our time?

Contemporary insights

My understanding of Judaism is rooted in the contemporary moment. It is influenced by contemporary American spirituality even as I seek traditional Jewish sources to give expression to that spirituality. While I acknowledge the danger of just embracing the latest new idea, I believe that our task is to reveal new insights into how to live a life of meaning. We are to continually unroll the Torah, seeking new meanings hidden in its black letters and in the white spaces between the letters. Much still remains to be revealed.

This is why I think using the term *Minhag America* seems appropriate. Outside the traditional community, we are living in a post-halakhic world. Jews don't feel obligated by a God who commands them to keep kosher. While some changes made from traditional Jewish law can be defended on moral principles, such as egalitarian roles for women and men, other changes, such as eating pizza in a regular pizza parlor, have no morally compelling purpose. There is a Talmudic principle that states, "go out and see what the people are doing." When it comes to living together before marriage or the acceptance of homosexuality, the people are changing how the liberal Jewish community behaves despite clear traditional prohibitions by Jewish law.

Minhag/custom is a traditional category in Jewish law. Some customs are old, such as breaking a glass at a wedding. Some are new, such as the observance of Holocaust Memorial Day. Customs do not have the obligatory status of *halakha*/ Jewish law; nevertheless, many customs are widely observed. I believe *minhag*/ custom is a better term not just because we don't feel bound by the commandments. We are in a time of great flux. I hope the coming decades will see much experimentation in terms of practice. Those differences will be more than those that currently separate Conservative, Reconstructionist and Reform from each other. Perhaps decades from now, there will emerge a consensus about what a 21st-century Judaism should look like. It is also possible that part of the form of this new Judaism will be an acceptance of a broad diversity of observance as an important principle. People will observe Shabbat in very different ways and will figure out a way to accommodate each other at communal gatherings.

Notice I don't call this *Minhagei America*/the customs of America, set in the plural. Why? Because I hope we will feel that we are part of one community even if people practice very differently. We will all strive to live out our understanding of what it means to live a life imbued with the values and wisdom of Torah. It will be challenging to accept ideas and practices at variance with our own. Yet, instead of thinking of other Jews as doing too little or as doing too much, we will appreciate each of our unique approaches to Judaism. We will celebrate the differences and try to make accommodations for those practicing differently.

In my synagogue, we had lengthy discussions about what the synagogue's Shabbat practice should be. Initially, it was fairly traditional: not allowing writing, banning the use of cell phones anywhere in the building, and a prohibition on photography. One Shabbat a couple with young children came to services. During the service they gave their children coloring books and crayons. At the next ritual committee meeting, one member was furious that the children were allowed to color in services on Shabbat. He said: Someone needs to be authorized to make sure our policies are enforced. I replied: There is another way to look at this. How great that this couple wanted to bring their young children to services. We had very few children present regularly at our services. How amazing that they were so thoughtful as to bring coloring books to services so their young children wouldn't be restless and disruptive to the members sitting near them!

A person coloring or writing has no legal impact on your Shabbat. You are not complicit in her "sin" by sitting near her. It is only a problem if you are asked to participate in an activity that violates your Shabbat practice. Why does someone speaking on his phone in the hallway on Shabbat violate or ruin your Shabbat experience? What if we accepted a diversity of Shabbat practice as our norm? What if that was broadly true of practices related to ritual? There are, of course, limits. Talking on your cell phone in the sanctuary during services would be prohibited whether the service was on Shabbat or on a weekday, because it is disruptive. But, in the spirit of Abraham and his open tent, you also want to be reasonably accommodating to people. Imagine if you invited someone to dinner who is a vegetarian and you told them, "Tough luck; we are only serving meat."

Minhag America, the practice of Judaism here in North America, begins with important principles and values. These are drawn from tradition as well as from trends in our society. How we take these principles and create *mitzvot* and practices to encourage us to live by them is the focus of the next chapters.

What is Judaism Disrupted?
Judaism is about Freedom

> The amount of happiness that you have depends on the amount
> of freedom you have in your heart.
> —Thich Nhat Hanh

The book of Exodus tells us the Jewish people's origin story. Origin stories offer important insights into how a people sees itself. Exodus begins by recapitulating the narrative of the patriarch Jacob, who journeys to Egypt with his family to escape a famine and reunite with his son Joseph, the viceroy of the land. Years later, a new Pharaoh comes to power and decides the Israelites are a threat and therefore need to be persecuted and enslaved. Awkwardly, the Jewish story does not begin with a mighty hero or a great victory over our enemies. Our story begins not in triumph but with oppression.

Yes, it will end in liberation as the Israelites leave Egypt. Despite this triumph, the Torah tells us repeatedly to remember that we were slaves in Egypt. We are to remember our inglorious past even as we celebrate our journey into freedom. That memory of persecution is intended to affect how we live our lives. We are to treat the stranger with compassion because we were strangers in the land of Egypt. What it means to be a Jew is to remember the oppression and therefore respond to those in need. This is the lesson of our origin story. We are never to forget where we came from—slavery. No matter how successful or how far we have journeyed, we must remember how our story began.

Humility is not a popular concept in the modern world. It can be understood as an excuse to accept the status quo. It is often dismissed as false. Most importantly it runs counter to the modern sense of the empowerment of individuals to shape their destiny. Giving people agency is a good thing and yet part of the purpose of religion is to remind us that no matter how powerful or successful we are, there is something larger than us in the world. Ultimately, each of us is a tiny speck in the universe and our lives are a brief moment in history. We can and should still strive to shape our world. Yet even as we do so, our memory of slavery calls us to act on behalf of those who are on the margins of our society, those who are not powerful, and those whose path to success has been strewn with obstacles. We are called to act on behalf of those who are what we once were.

The story of Egypt is the particular story of the Jewish people, but it demands of us to engage in a universal challenge—to continue the work of God's creation by building a better world. This is the work for each of us as individuals—but it is also the responsibility of the collective whether that collective is a neighborhood, a people, or a nation.

Be the change

This challenge to us to improve the world rests on the belief that everything can change. When Moses meets God at the burning bush and is told to go tell Pharaoh to let the Israelites go, Moses asks God: *Who should I say sent me? What is your name?* God does not give the expected answer—*I am the God of Abraham, Isaac and Jacob,* thereby reconnecting God and the people to a (hopefully) remembered past. Instead, God answers: *ehyeh asher ehyeh*—I will be what I will be. (Ex. 3:14).

Religious people often mistakenly think of God as unchanging. In the past, it was a reassuring notion, distinguishing monotheism from the myriad pagan gods who were perceived to be fickle and unpredictable. For some it is still an anchor to hold onto in a rapidly changing world. Yet, the God of the Exodus tells Moses not to think that there is one fixed notion that describes God. The God of Exodus is the God of freedom, which by definition requires an understanding of God as ever-changing. Thus, God says: *Don't think that someone whose parents are slaves will inevitably also be a slave.* God says: *I will be what I will be*—and so can you. The world is a world of possibility and change. Judaism is at its heart a revolutionary tradition that seeks to change rather than uphold or preserve the status quo. Despite how Judaism is sometimes presented, its purpose is not to preserve the Jewish past. It is a call for change. It questions what is. It reminds us that Jews were slaves and were liberated and that is the beginning of our story. We are to make our story every person's story; that is, a story of the freedom to exercise choice.

The beginning of the Amidah—the central prayer of Jewish services—describes God as the God of Abraham, the God of Isaac and the God of Jacob. Why doesn't it more simply say the God of Abraham, Isaac and Jacob? Why the need to repeat the name of God three times? One answer is that each of the patriarchs had his own relationship to God. In that sense the God of Abraham was not the same as the God of Isaac. This point is made in a story told of a man who complained that his new *rebbe*/religious leader was doing things differently than the *rebbe's* deceased father. The new *rebbe* replied, "I am following exactly the traditions of my father." When the follower looked at him quizzically, he replied: "My father didn't imitate his father, and I don't imitate my father." While we are rooted in the Jewish past, we must find our own path, creating new ways to be Jewish. This too is part of the message of freedom that we carry with us upon leaving Egypt.

The centrality of the Exodus goes beyond the repeated notion that we must remember that we were slaves and therefore treat other people with compassion. As important as the commitment to social justice is, there is something even more central to Judaism that we learn from this story. The people of Israel appear to be free, having left the bondage of Egypt behind. The former slaves quickly discover it is hard to be free. During their 40-year journey to the Promised Land, they constantly express a yearning to return to Egypt. With freedom comes responsibility and the need to make difficult choices. We move from Egypt to the giving of the Torah at Mt. Sinai because the Torah is about freedom. If we think that we remember the Exodus only so that we help those who are in need, we miss the most fundamental teaching of this story. We need to constantly free ourselves. Life is full of obstacles and illusions that keep us stuck. The 19th-century Hasidic master known as the Sefat Emet teaches:

> The purpose of all the commandments, both positive and negative, that were given to Israel, is so that every person in Israel shall be free. That is why the liberation from Egypt comes first [before the giving of the Torah]. Torah then teaches the soul how to maintain its freedom, by not becoming attached to material things.
>
> These are its 613 counsels. Every mitzvah/commandment in which the liberation from Egypt is mentioned tells us yet again that by the means of this mitzvah one may cling to freedom. In the commandment regarding the [gifts to the poor of] leftover gleanings, the corners of the field, and forgotten sheaves, Torah says: "Remember you were a slave" (Deut. 24:22). In this way your food will have no waste, and you will not become overly attached to wealth.... A Jew has to be free in soul, in body, and in all he or she has...This is the purpose of the entire Torah.
>
> That is why they (the rabbis) read "engraved (harut) on the tablets [Ex. 32:16], as though it said "freedom (herut) on the tablets." "The only free person," they added, "is the one who is engaged in Torah," for Torah teaches a person the way of freedom. (Comment on the Torah portion Ki Tetze, from *The Language of Truth* by Arthur Green)

This teaching suggests that we can easily be enslaved without ever being literally in bondage. Most people are not physically enslaved and yet they live a life in which they are not really free. In Erich Fromm's phrase (20th-century psychologist), we often want to "escape from freedom." The responsibility that comes with freedom can be a heavy burden. We can live a life of slavery to our fears and insecurities. We can live a life bounded by the limitations of our expectations, or a life circumscribed by the lack of faith in our abilities. Most of all we can be enslaved to the needs of the everyday—making a living, errands, relationships and all the mundane tasks of life. Who has the time to reflect on whether we are serving our vision for ourselves or just being a slave to Pharaoh—the unending taskmaster calling us to build the treasure cities of our existence?

Be free

In this understanding, Torah is first and foremost about freedom. Torah is not, as commonly believed, about 613 commandments. Rather it is 613 counsels that teach us how to escape to freedom. Our biggest challenge is to take the precious gift of life and do as much as we can with it. We live our life with the consciousness that we are limited by our mortality. Torah reminds us of our potential, for we are also created in the image of God. Torah can free us from the grind of everyday life where day follows day, week follows week and year follows year—picture the way calendar pages fly off the wall in old movies to illustrate the passing of time. Freedom is an awareness of what life is and can be. As the Sefat Emet suggests, the Torah reminds us to strive for non-attachment. Real living means not holding on to what we possess in the face of the ever-encroaching final night. Torah is meant to be an ongoing pointer to the precious blessing of life. It is hard to cherish each moment of life amidst our busyness. The Sefat Emet returns elsewhere in his commentary to this theme of freedom through Torah when he expresses that Torah allows us to rise above nature. I think he means that the most basic fact of our life is that we are mortal. We cannot escape our death. Yet, Torah suggests that our mortality doesn't have to define our existence. We have the ability and the freedom to create, to think, and to feel. Those abilities can shape our lives.

In another teaching, the Sefat Emet says that some people look to the creation of the world presumably to be in wonder of the vastness and variety of this planet. Instead, he suggests that Sinai is the moment that we should always place before our consciousness. Why? When the world was created sparks of holiness were scattered throughout the world. Every human being has a spark of holiness within them. All of these sparks are covered or hidden by a material surface. It is our task to seek out and redeem all these sparks of the divine. This is the reason that the Israelites had to go down to Egypt—to receive the sparks that were there. This is an important point. Life is about engaging with the brokenness of the world. This act of redemption enabled the Israelites to leave the slavery of Egypt and journey into freedom. This is not a one-time event. The Israelites quickly fall back on old patterns and want to return to Egypt. *Mitzrayim*/Egypt is always calling to us. The opposite is also true: Sinai is also always calling us—to be free. We are to remember the Exodus from Egypt because its story is repeated every day. We are "enslaved" by the things that constrict us—that either prevent us from reaching our potential or that lead us down pathways of hurt to ourselves or to others. In the face of such challenges, we can respond with openheartedness. We can move forward instead of sliding backward. We can, to use the Sefat Emet's language, redeem the sparks in that moment. The Sefat Emet deeply believed in the possibility of renewal. He taught that every day the world and each of us are/ can be created anew.

Judaism is not a vision of a return to a perfect past. Our journey is a forward one—to a promised land that no one has yet seen. Despite our flaws, and the limitations of being human, even despite our mortality, Judaism says we can still shape our lives in freedom. At the burning bush, God claimed the name of *I will be what I will be* and we have that same potential for ongoing renewal.

In the face of all the negative voices that we constantly hear, some real and some only in our head, Judaism believes we are free to make choices not just between good and bad but whether to live a life that is conscious of our power and freedom. Will we escape from freedom and return to Egypt, no matter how cleverly disguised as anything other than a pyramid? That is our question. For after all, no matter how magnificent the pyramids are, they are only tombs—monuments to death. We are not here to spend our lives building pyramids so that we are remembered after we are gone. Instead, we are here to devote our time to living. The purpose of Torah is to encourage us and remind us to strive to live a life of compassion, loving relationships, and devotion to our ideals. The Jewish tradition does that by suggesting ways to focus on important themes in life—such as openheartedness, gratitude, and awareness. There are daily practices to aid us in cultivating these qualities. There are the annual festivals that encourage us to reflect on home and shelter; on food; on change. There is Shabbat, a weekly practice calling us to stop our work week and take a deep breath. The Torah understands the lure of Egypt and how easy it is to become enslaved. How past patterns can keep us chained to unwise or even harmful behavior. Just the weight of the past can increasingly impede our journey forward. Yet, we are reminded that as a people we were once slaves, and we became free. Each of us can be free again. This is the real inheritance of the Jewish people leaving Egypt—the experience of freedom. The practices of Judaism, some ancient and some new, are aids in that striving for freedom. The first step is to gain insight into the ways that we are enslaved. Then we begin the process of breaking those chains. Finally, we try to repair the mistakes we made or hurt we did to others and to ourselves. Freedom begins on the individual level, but needs to spread outward into society, for the world needs to be redeemed.

How does freedom come about in Egypt? God asserts that redemption will come about through God's *yad hazakah* and *zeroa netuyah*—a strong hand and an outstretched arm. Usually, these words are understood as synonyms—metaphors for God's power that will bring the plagues and eventually cause Pharaoh to relent and let the Israelites go. It is true that every struggle for freedom requires a steadfast commitment to the cause. Even non-violent causes like the civil rights movement needed people who not only were willing to work for freedom but were willing to be arrested and even to risk their lives by protesting the injustice of segregation. It requires a *yad hazakah*—a willingness to stand up and protest and to keep standing up. It also requires a *zeroa netuyah*—an outstretched arm. An outstretched arm doesn't have to be another metaphor for a hand of power. It can also be a hand extended to help someone to get up off the ground. It is a hand of welcome, a hand of connection and support. Those hands are just as important as the hand of powerful resistance to injustice. Standing together while marching for freedom is how freedom comes about. This origin story of slavery and freedom and its lessons are so important to Judaism that we tell the story every year at the Passover Seder.

> "The Exodus from Egypt occurs in every human being, in every era, in every year, and in every day."
> —Rebbe Nahman of Bratslav (Hasidic master 1772-1810)

Core principles

If Judaism is all about freedom, then what are the major principles that help us keep our eyes on the prize of that freedom? I suggest that there are eleven core principles:

1) Since humans are created in the image of God, we have within us a spark of the divine that cannot be extinguished. This leads to the freedom to realize we are all equal.

2) We live in a moral universe. Therefore, our task is to continue the work of creation by bringing goodness into the world. This leads to the freedom to make the world a better place.

3) We need to strive to live with awareness of the true nature of existence. Unawareness leads to slavery. Awareness leads to the freedom to see clearly.

4) Focusing on our own freedom isn't enough. We need to help as many people as possible to be free—hence the importance of social justice. This leads to the freedom to help free others.

5) Holiness is an essential aspect of Judaism. It is not just what makes human beings special. It is not just extraordinary moments in life. Holiness can be found in our everyday interactions. Judaism also uses holiness to create special times such as Shabbat and holidays. This leads to the freedom to discover the holiness all around us.

6) Taking care of our planet has become an essential task if there is to be a future for God's creation. This leads to the freedom and responsibility to protect our planet.

7) God, or the sense that there is something larger than ourselves, is a notion that defines our place in the universe. This leads to the freedom to deeply understand who we are and who we are not.

8) Critical to being free is for us to work on our inner characteristics. This leads to the freedom to live up to our potential.

9) It is inevitable that we will make mistakes. We need to engage in the process of reflection and change/*teshuvah*. The ability to change is an essential aspect of freedom.

10) Being a lifelong student of Torah helps us to continue to grow and refine our insights into our lives. This leads to the freedom of growth and renewal.

Ten is a big number in Jewish tradition, echoing, of course, the Ten Commandments. How nice it would be to have ten core principles. But in a Judaism disrupted, one more is essential.

Only after I finished writing this book did I realize that there is an eleventh core principle that is necessary for a Judaism of the 21st century. It is the universal context in which we live. Rabbinic Judaism was meant to be portable; it could be carried wherever Jews traveled in the world. Now, we need a Judaism that is permeable, allowing the outside world to easily interact with the inner world of Jewish life. How do we live in an open society?

11) The last core principle is to use the previous ten to create a Judaism without borders leading to the freedom to be really connected to others.

The next chapters will explicate each of these principles in depth and connect them to practices in order to incorporate them in our busy lives. Part of this approach will be making explicit the connection between many of these principles and the major holidays in the Jewish calendar.

Core Principle #1:
Created in the Image of God

The rabbis debated which of Judaism's many principles was the most important.

"You shall love your neighbor as yourself" (Lev. 19:18). R. Akiva said: "This is a great principle of the Torah."

Ben Azzai said: The verse (Gen. 5:1) "This is the book of the descendants of Adam. When God made Adam, God made the human in God's likeness" utters a principle even greater (Sifra Kedoshim 4:12).

While the commandment to love your neighbor as yourself is often considered the single most important principle in the Torah, Ben Azzai instead chooses the idea that humans are created in God's image as the most important. Why? Because the notion that we are all created in God's likeness means every human is of equal worth. This is the starting point for all human relationships. To deny this is to deny the truth about humanity. Everything flows from this notion that places the source of human equality not in a human ideal but in the origin of the world's creation. All the ethical teachings of the Torah, including *love your neighbor as yourself*, derive from this belief.

The Hebrew word for honor or respect is *kavod*. It is a key word in the Torah because it tells us what the fundamental attitude toward all our fellow human beings should be. One of the Ten Commandments tells us to honor our parents—those who gave us life (Ex. 20:12). This principle is translated into practice through the notion that all people must be respected because they are created in God's image.

To understand this principle further we need to examine how the Torah understood the nature of human beings. The best source for the answer is the story of creation: "And God said: 'Let us make human in our image, after our likeness ...' And God created the human in God's own image, in the image of God, God created the human; male and female God created them" (Gen. 1:26-27).

What is the nature of this human being? The human is created in God's image. What does that mean? On the face of it, it is a puzzling description to state that humans are in the image of a God who in Jewish tradition has no image! The text doesn't explicitly answer this paradox. It suggests that we, like God, are unique. Yet we are also like every human being, and we share features with all living beings that breathe, eat, and reproduce. Ultimately, we are connected to all of creation, making us both particular and universal. We have the ability to speak and, with words, we continue to create. Our task is not just to survive or reproduce like other animals. We will build with our hands; we will create art and music; we will think and invent. In all these ways we are created in the image of God who spoke the world into being.

The Garden of Eden

God places the human in the Garden of Eden. God then says: "It is not good for the human to be alone; I will make a help meet for the human" (Gen. 2:18). The Garden of Eden seems very paradise-like. Yet we get our first sense that everything is not perfect. If at the end of each day of creation, God looks at the world and says it is *tov*/good, we now see what is not good. "It is not good (*lo tov*) for humans to be alone." God decides to create an *ezer*—another. She will be an independent being and yet be in a relationship with him. While usually *ezer* is translated as helper, it can be better understood as a person in relationship rather than a subordinate. The point is not just to have other humans in the world. It is to have relationships based on caring, because that will help mitigate the sense of existential aloneness that humans will experience. Real relationships of connection are the essence of the human experience. Human beings are social creatures, which is one way that human beings are not like God—after all, there is only one God.

God understands that for a human, aloneness is *lo tov*—not good. Therefore, another person is created—a woman who is both the same and different. Humans are created to help each other. They can find other humans with whom to be partners or friends. Loving relationships between human beings are part of the *tov*—good—of this world.

Eating of the Tree of Knowledge:
Paradise lost or real life found?

> Human history begins with man's act of disobedience which is at the very same time the beginning of his freedom and development of his reason.
> —Erich Fromm (20th century psychologist)

The Torah begins with God creating the world and human beings. God placed the humans in a garden. God's first words to humans set out one rule:

> "Of every tree of the garden you are free to eat; but as for the tree of knowledge of good and evil, you must not eat of it; for as soon as you eat of it, you shall die." (Gen. 2:16-17)

At first, it seems Adam and Eve are living in paradise where all their needs are met. Food is provided. Apparently, the temperature doesn't require them to wear clothes. Their only task is to name all the plants and creatures in the garden. Adam and Eve name everything, an imitation of God who names the dry land Earth and the waters Sea. Creation comes about through language. Unlike God, humans can not actually create things by speech, yet their naming of everything in the world demonstrates that Adam and Eve are continuing the work of creation.

Where is the moral good in the Garden of Eden? How could Adam and Eve be able to know whether at the end of a day they can say, as God did during creation, that today was good (*tov*)? God gives them only one rule. They cannot eat of the tree at the center of the garden. What is that tree? The Tree of Knowledge of Good and Evil—*tov ve-ra*. If *lo tov*, not good, suggests an absence of goodness, *ra*-evil is the opposite of good. Whether the translation of *ra* is bad or evil, it suggests doing something wrong.

What is going on in this essential biblical text? It does seem to be about knowledge and innocence. It particularly seems to focus on sexuality. In the preceding verse we are told that Adam and Eve are naked and yet felt no shame. One of the consequences of eating of the tree will be a self-consciousness of their nakedness, and so they make themselves clothes. For some commentators, this text is about the fall of man tempted by woman or the phallic snake.

In that interpretation, this story is about desire and the human relationship to the pleasures of the world. It suggests that the pleasures of this world, especially sex, are a temptation that should be avoided. It becomes the justification for an ascetic strand in biblical religions. The human story begins with failure. While Judaism doesn't have a concept of original sin, this story is traditionally understood to be about the humans breaking the one rule they have. Its consequences are severe. They are exiled from the Garden of Eden. Outside the Garden, humans will have to work hard to earn a living. Women will give birth in pain. In other words, there is a disharmony with nature, exemplified in the struggle to grow crops and to give birth. Nothing will come as easily as it did in the Garden of Eden.

Let me suggest another way to read the story, which begins with this exercise. Imagine that Adam and Eve had never eaten of the Tree. They would have remained unaware of their sexuality and presumably would never have had children. They wouldn't have faced any challenges related to survival because their food was provided for them in the Garden. They wouldn't have had any real sense of *tov*/goodness because they would have no idea of what *ra*/evil is. Would they have really been alive in a way that was so different than the animals? There was one difference: they could speak, and they had the ability to name the animals. What would they have done with the rest of their lives when they had finished naming everything?

Didn't they have to eat of the Tree of Knowledge of Good and Evil in order to live a life of blacks and whites and greys? If they were to be held responsible, didn't they need the ability to make unwise choices as well as wise ones?

What was special about the fruit of the Tree of Knowledge? The Torah says: "When the woman saw that the tree was good for eating and a delight to the eyes, and the tree was desirable as a source of wisdom, she took of its fruit and she ate. She also gave some to her husband and he ate" (Gen. 3:6).

Eve says three things about the fruit: it is good to eat; it is a delight to the eyes; and it is desirable as a source of wisdom. Earlier (Gen. 2:9), God is described as creating the world and then creating a garden in Eden. "And from the ground, God caused to grow every tree that was pleasing to the sight and good for food." In other words, the fruit of all the trees in the Garden were described like the fruit of the Tree of Knowledge. The only difference is that the fruit of the Tree of Knowledge had a third characteristic—"it is desirable as a source of wisdom." Isn't wisdom a good thing—something to be desired rather than avoided?

Why then does God tell them they are not allowed to eat of the Tree of Knowledge? One way to understand the Book of Genesis is that God is figuring out how to create a world with human beings. The God of Genesis doesn't seem to be all-knowing. God doesn't figure out in advance that Adam is going to be lonely and is going to want a partner. God doesn't anticipate the flood and the need to wipe out the world and start over again. Or perhaps a different perspective on the same stories is that the author/s of Genesis were trying to figure out the Divine/human relationship. It seemed to make sense to have the humans live in an idyllic garden. Who wouldn't want to live in Paradise? However, it would have meant that they could not be real human beings. Initially, it seemed a good idea to have humans not know or be capable of doing evil; but then the world couldn't really be a moral universe and would remain instead a mechanical one. Humans needed to know good *and* evil, and be able to choose. Then humans would be powerful like God in their capacity to have an impact on the world.

Yet, the conclusion of the story makes clear how humans are also fundamentally different from God. For it turns out there are two special trees in the garden—the Tree of Knowledge of Good and Evil and the Tree of Life. In the end, humans are expelled from the garden to prevent them from eating of the tree of eternal life. Humans, unlike God, have limitations most profoundly exemplified by their mortality.

I would argue that humans must eat of the Tree of Knowledge in order to be human, and must not eat of the Tree of Life. To do otherwise would profoundly change the fundamental nature of human beings. Like children leaving their sheltered parental home, humans must leave that garden in order to face the challenges and opportunities of life. Humans are powerful; yet death is the limitation on every single human being's power. The garden was a place of certainty and limited choices. The world is a place of uncertainty because of nearly limitless choices.

The Tree of Knowledge of Good and Evil allows for perception. If before the world was all just natural, now it is differentiated. Those eyes which enjoyed looking at the fruit are now open. They become self-conscious. They know they are naked. Humans immediately make clothes. The world is now filled with good and bad things. There are things to be revealed and covered. Decision making has come into the world. Humans and nature are not one. Along with the ability to distinguish between good and bad comes the consequences of those choices. Yet without the ability to choose and live with those consequences Adam and Eve would have remained naked in the garden, lacking any sense of self-awareness. "How do I look?" is now a key concern. Self-perception versus how others perceive us becomes central to the internal dialogues of our lives.

While often understood as a story about sexuality, it really is a story about being in the world with all its pleasures. If we are to be human, then we need the wisdom to see what is good and bad. Eve understood the need to eat of the tree and therefore wanted Adam to eat as well. Otherwise, we don't have the ability to say at the end of a day of our creating, *ki tov*—it is good.

However, they both missed the lesson that accompanied their newfound wisdom. With choice comes responsibility. Knowing they had broken the one rule God had given them, they hid. God asked, "Where are you?" (Gen. 3:9). Neither answered *Here I am—hineni*. Neither admitted what they did. Adam said: "I was afraid because I was naked, so I hid" (Gen. 3:10). This is the first example of humans lying and making excuses. We know Adam wasn't naked; he had just made clothes. However, he felt naked, embarrassed because he had disobeyed God and thought God would be angry. It is the first psychologically revealing moment in the Torah. Adam experiences what is going on as different from reality. He is wearing clothes and yet he feels naked. Guilt has created a separation between the actual and the perceived. This is the state of life outside the Garden. Humans can both create and distort their reality.

Instead of admitting responsibility, Adam blames Eve, who blames the snake. Blame and shame instead of accepting responsibility and apologizing mean the garden of nature and connection is completely shattered. Now humans will have to work at making a living and work at being in relationships. Before, Adam and Eve were as one body; now they experience life as existentially unconnected. They experience the world in exile and alone. The way back to the garden is blocked. They need to work at finding a way forward.

The central myth of exile

My understanding of this story is that its emphasis is on exile. The human condition is not original sin, but that we live in exile. We don't live in the Garden of Eden; we live in the world—a world of struggle and complexity. Exile is the actual historical experience of the Jewish people for most of its existence. Even after the founding of the modern state of Israel, many Jews live in exile. I would posit that the condition of exile is true for all Jews—and, for that matter, all people. Exile is not just living in an imperfect world. It is a sense of alienation from your own self and from others.

The kabbalists of Safed (16th-century Jewish mystics) describe the creation of the world coming about in a cosmic explosion that scattered pieces of the Divine throughout the world. In their understanding, the Divine is in exile from itself. Our task is to restore all the pieces to make the Divine whole again. Exile began before the Garden—even before humans were created.

While this understanding of the world being in exile can seem overwhelming, it is important to remember that the human begins in wholeness or in the perfection of the Garden of Eden. Knowing that, we are meant to be optimistic that the world can be restored to its original state of oneness. Ultimately, it is the most powerful statement of our role as the ongoing creators (or restorers) of the world.

Genesis as a guide to how not to act in the world

Genesis is traditionally understood as presenting models for how to live our lives, especially when we get to the stories of the patriarchs and matriarchs. In truth, Genesis is also showing us classic mistakes that humans make (and mistakes that God makes as well). It specifically highlights the dangers of religion. Why does the text do that? People are imperfect, and so is their understanding of religious truth. Within every principle is the seed of its own misuse. Genesis both suggests how to live in the real world, and also how to watch for common mistakes. The first story after the Garden is the story of two brothers, Cain and Abel. It is a catastrophe.

In chapter four of Genesis, Adam and Eve give birth to two children. Abel was a shepherd and Cain was a farmer. They both offered a sacrifice to God. Cain offered his crop. Abel offered an animal. God paid heed only to Abel's sacrifice. Upset, Cain kills Abel. God asks: "Where is your brother, Abel? Cain says: I do not know. Am I my brother's keeper?" (Gen. 4:9). God curses Cain to be a wanderer on the earth.

It is pretty depressing to begin the human story with fratricide. Is the Bible suggesting that the basic human condition is that we kill each other? Or is it a warning that this is the way it could be? God, seeing Cain is upset, says: "Sin crouches at the door, its urge is toward you, yet you can be its master" (Gen. 4:7). You are not helpless. You can make a choice. Cain chooses to kill his brother. The story we have is very brief, but there is no suggestion that Abel in any way provoked the attack. Disappointed by God's rejection of his sacrifice, Cain turns that emotion into rage at his brother. When confronted by God, he lies and says he doesn't know where Abel is. And then he adds: *Am I my brother's keeper?* He rejects any responsibility, not just for the killing but for his brother altogether. If the Torah says it is not good for a person to be alone, Cain embraces that aloneness.

And what about God's role in this story? We don't know why God chose a sacrifice of sheep over vegetables. Was one a more generous sacrifice? Did it have to do with the intention of Abel compared to Cain? It is possible that there was no explanatory reason for choosing one sacrifice over the other. In a world of choice, we have the ability to choose. Yet that choice is not unlimited. We are human. A world of choice means some things will be chosen and some things will not. It is not just that hard decisions need to be made—the hiring of one person for a job but not another. We cannot choose everything. We will be friends with some people and not with others. We will fall in love with this person and not that person. Feelings will be hurt no matter how much we try to be kind to people. It is the nature of our world. The story teaches us that choices have consequences; that hurting people is an inevitable by-product of living. The fact that hurt is inevitable doesn't free us from trying as best we can to be our brother's keeper. Choice necessitates responsibility. So far no one in our story, not Adam and Eve, not Cain, and seemingly not even God, takes responsibility for their choices. How will each of us answer Cain's question: *Am I my brother's keeper?*

The other consequence of giving humans choice means that God does not protect Abel. Humans can choose to hurt or kill innocent people. The only protection is when people understand that they are their brother's keeper. Cain stands as a warning to us of the path to be avoided. It would be a mistake to read this story as being literally about fratricide. The vast majority of people would not murder their siblings or anyone else for that matter. Yet, we frequently hurt people. Too often, we do it on purpose out of anger or annoyance. Other times, we do it unintentionally. We go on and on about how great our children are, forgetting the person we are talking to has a difficult relationship with their child. We can hurt people innocently because we don't know that they are in the middle of a personal crisis. Each of these kinds of situations command a different degree of our responsibility. They range from our being fully responsible when we choose to hurt to being innocent when we have no idea that what we are saying touches a sore point for that person.

The story of Cain and Abel encourages us to be aware of the potential consequences of our words and deeds. Instead of striking out in anger, we might pause and wonder, why am I angry? How many times have I become irritated with my spouse/partner because I can't get the "smart" TV to work? Or why does this issue seem to push such an emotional button for me? Why does this feel like a situation I have experienced many times before?

The story of Cain and Abel comes at the beginning of life outside of the Garden to teach us that life in the real world is challenging. We will struggle to earn a living. Humans will plant crops but grow "thorns and thistles." We may think that our killing someone is unlikely and yet humans killing each other is an essential part of the story of humankind. Our real daily struggle is to avoid offering expressions made of thorns to those with whom we interact at work and at play, on the road and at home. Instead, we are to offer words of kindness. Our ability to choose is fundamental to being human. Yet its consequences are also fundamental. We can use choice to bring more goodness into the world; or at our worst, we can damage or destroy another image of God.

There is one more point from the story of Cain and Abel. While it is true that we cannot choose everything or everyone, couldn't God have chosen Abel *and* Cain's offerings? This mistake is repeated over and over again in Genesis where one son is chosen over another: Isaac over Ishmael, Jacob over Esau, Joseph over all his brothers. Isn't the first rule of parenting to *not* have a favorite child? Why can no one in Genesis love all their children equally? It is an obvious mistake, and yet one we all make. Some make it with their children; some make it with other relationships. That's why Genesis repeats the mistake over and over again—to demonstrate to us how easy it is to make it. The consequences are dire. The book begins with fratricide and ends with the near-killing of Joseph by his brothers and then their selling him into slavery, a fate of a living death. In between, there is exile or hatred between brothers. No family should be like those of Genesis. Yet only at the end of the book will Joseph and his brothers be an example of reconciliation.

This core principle's primary teaching is that we should treat other people with respect/*kavod*. The rabbinic tradition called this principle *kavod ha-beriot*— respect for all living creatures. The Talmud (*Berakhot* 19b) says this principle of respect for all human beings even overrules negative prohibitions. On the surface this seems to be a radical statement. It suggests that dishonoring a person is to be avoided even if that means violating a negative commandment. The Talmudic discussion of this principle goes on to limit its application in ways that I think contradict the obvious and radical meaning of the text. Yet, it still remains a legal principle in Jewish law focused on this concern for not embarrassing people. For instance, Rabbi Joseph Soloveitchik (20th-century Modern Orthodox theologian), applied this principle to the question of whether a Torah reader should be corrected if he is making a mistake while reading Torah during services. He ruled they should not be corrected if you have a sense that the reader would be sensitive about it. The principle of honoring every person broadly translates to an attitude of concern for all human beings.

Being created in the image of God is our first core principle. All the other core principles rest on this fundamental notion of who we humans are. As an image of God, we are to continue the work of creation. We also have the ability to choose. While we are unlike God because we are mortal, we also have aspects of being without limits—such as our ability to deeply love others. We are like all other human beings even as we are unique beings. Therefore, we are existentially alone and strive to be deeply connected. We will more fully explore the aspect of humans continuing the work of creation in the next core principle.

Core Principle #2:
Living in a Moral Universe

> To love our neighbor as ourselves is such a truth for regulating
> human society, that by that alone one might determine all the
> cases in social morality.
> —John Locke (17th-century English philosopher)

The second core principle is also found in the creation story. "In the beginning God created the heaven and the earth…God said: 'Let there be light'; and there was light. God saw that the light was good…" (Gen. 1:1).

At the end of the first day of creation, God reviews what has been accomplished and says: *ki tov*/it was good. God could have said *it's finished*, or even *well done*. Instead, God uses the word good. Good is a value. It is not objective in the way that complete or incomplete can be. By calling it good, God introduces values into the world. This universe is not just a mechanical world run by the laws of nature. It is a world where morality is critical.

As much as finishing the things on our to-do list each day is important, of overarching importance is to be able to look at our day and say that what I did for myself, for others and for the world was good. God's statement tells us we are not here just to be successful or even to enjoy life. We are here to make the world good. The world is not just neutral. As we shall see, humans are meant to continue the work of creation and thereby be co-creators of the world. God's response to creation is *tov*—it is good. If I had to choose one word to summarize what Judaism is about it is that word—*tov*/goodness.

Ethics alone could call upon us to act in caring ways. Some might suggest that being ethical is utilitarian. We are good to others in order for them to reciprocate. Here the Torah is making a faith claim that cannot be proved. The universe has a moral purpose. We are meant to effectuate that purpose. The purpose of life is to strive to bring goodness into the world. Being human, we will often fail, but goodness remains our purpose.

God doesn't call just the first day good. In this first week of creation, we see the unfolding of that creation each day. Judaism believes that unfolding continues beyond the first week of creation. In the prayer book, we say "in God's goodness, God renews each day the work of creation." Not only do new plants reach for the sun each day. Not only are new animals and human beings born each day. Each of us is renewed each day. Just as some cells of our body die and new cells develop to replace them each day, so each day we are like a new being. The world changes, reminding us that we too have the potential to change. This too is part of the goodness of God's creation of the world.

The call to do good by imitating God is found at the end of each day of creation when God declares *ki tov*/it is good. Actually, because *tov*/goodness is so important to God, we come to understand the importance of human beings. What does goodness mean in a world that is simply natural? Are animals good? Is wind good? Without humans to make choices the category of goodness is not really applicable to a universe run by the laws of nature. God's declaration of the world's goodness is a statement about the potential that exists in the world. The potential for goodness was waiting for the creation of human beings who could actualize that possibility—or its opposite, evil.

The importance of goodness is given explicit expression in a commandment found in Deut. 6:18: "Do what is right and good in the sight of God that it may go well with you." It is worth quoting the Ramban's (13th-century Bible commentator), interpretation of this verse:

> At first Moses stated that you are to keep God's statutes and tes-
> timonies that God commanded you, and now Moses is stating
> that even where God has not commanded you, give thought, as
> well, to do what is right and good in God's eyes, for God loves
> the right and the good. Now this is a great principle, for it is im-
> possible to mention in the Torah all aspects of people's conduct
> with their neighbors and friends ... But since God mentioned
> many of them, such as "do not go about as a talebearer among
> your fellows" (Lev. 19:16) .... and the like—Moses reverted to
> state in a general way that, in all matters, one should do what is
> right and good, including even compromise and going beyond
> the requirements of the law. Other examples are... that one's
> conversation with people be pleasant. Thus, people should seek
> to refine their behavior in every form of activity, until they are
> worthy of being called "right and good." (Excerpted from *Ram-
> ban: Commentary on the Torah* translated by Charles Chavel,
> Shilo 1976)

This commandment is the everything commandment. This is the one that includes everything not covered by the other 612 commandments. As the Ramban says, it is impossible to mention in the Torah every aspect of people's relations with each other. Even if there is no specific commandment, the general principle is you should always do what is right and good. Nowhere is there a commandment that your conversation should be pleasant, but that is an essential activity of human beings and is critical to a caring society. The central operating principle of Jewish practice is to do good. Our job is to continue the work of creation each and every week of our lives, to strive to be able to echo God's words from that first week by saying today I helped make it *tov*—a day of goodness.

There are no limitations on what the Torah asks of us. It is not just about eating kosher food or praying. All activity, all life, is part of Torah. In each moment, we should strive to do what is right and good. If we do, the verse goes on to tell us it will be good for us. In the tradition, this was understood to mean God will reward the righteous. For me, it means that *tov* is the reward for *tov*, that is, good is its own reward. By doing good, we are not guaranteed to win the lottery, but we are "guaranteed" to live a life of harmony and peace rather than discord and anger. We create our own spiritual environment. It can be an environment so polluted with negativity that it is hard to breathe or an environment redolent with the scent of the Garden of Eden.

Building a good society practice

Many of the most important ethical commandments of the Torah are found in Leviticus chapter 19. The most famous is "Love your neighbor as yourself." The commandments in Lev. 19 are about creating a society of caring for those around us in the everyday interactions of life. It is a remarkable vision, which of course no community lives up to, but it remains a vision for us to strive for every day of our lives. It begins with negative attitudes to avoid and climaxes with the injunction to love your neighbor as yourself. Let's examine together these few verses. This process of interpretation is an example of the way the Torah text can guide us in ways to bring *tov*/goodness into the world.

> **You shall not insult the deaf or place a stumbling block before the blind. (Lev. 19:14)**

The rabbis understood this verse more broadly than just about someone who is literally blind. They saw it as an injunction against manipulating people by playing on their emotional weaknesses. In rabbinic Judaism, the deaf were seen as a vulnerable category of people because society hadn't discovered ways of communicating with and teaching them. Whether someone has an obvious physical vulnerability or a subtler emotional one, we should not exploit those vulnerabilities. The rabbis understood this verse to apply to everyone. Therefore, they taught that this verse prohibits selling an object whose flaws are hidden. You need to fully disclose any flaws for it to be considered a legitimate sale. Even if the vulnerability is only a lack of knowledge, this verse was understood to prohibit taking advantage.

Do not go about as a talebearer among your countrymen. (Lev. 19:16a)

The rabbis interpreted this verse as a prohibition on gossip. They understood how gossip can tear at the fabric of a community. Talking negatively behind a person's back is destructive to relationships. For this reason, the rabbis prohibited gossip, even if it was true. The person who is the focus of gossip doesn't have the chance to contextualize the accusation nor to try and make amends. Because gossip is destructive, the motivation of the gossiper is considered negative. There is a different equation in the case of saying something negative about a person only to find them standing behind you. Or in the modern version of that, hitting "reply all" on your email instead of being careful not to send it to the person you were talking about.

It can be argued that information shared to be helpful is in a different category. A performance evaluation at work would be an example of criticism whose purpose is both to help the person being evaluated and to protect the company. The lines are not always clear-cut. Information about public figures published by news media could also be seen as different from negative information about private people. Motivation and purpose are key factors in separating gossip from legitimate criticism. The question we must ask is, why are we saying this about the person? What is the purpose of this piece of gossip? Am I trying to be helpful by sharing a valid critique of the person—*My experience is that John takes things on but doesn't really come through in the end.* Or is it just negativity for its own sake—*Where did she get that outfit? It's another sterling example from her collection of the wardrobe of poor choices.*

Do not stand idly by the blood of your fellow. (Lev. 19:16b)

The second half of this verse is understood by the rabbis to call us to speak out when others are in trouble. We move from not manipulating other people or gossiping about others to a positive action on their behalf. This is not just what we should refrain from doing, but also what we should actively pursue. Our response to seeing someone being hurt by another person must not be to say that is none of our business. In a healthy society, each of us needs to act on behalf of those who need help. This can be an injustice in the workplace, acting out at home, or oppression in society. As important as speaking out about injustices in our society, it is also important to call out family and friends. The hurtful comment, whether made deliberately or accidentally, is as much a part of creating a caring society as addressing issues of social injustice. This vision of a caring society comes to a climax with the last two verses.

You shall not hate your kinsfolk in your heart.
(Lev. 19:17a)

This is a challenging commandment, asking us not to hate others. The commentators point out that the verse says, "in your heart." Lest you think only hateful action, such as hitting someone or verbally abusing them, is forbidden, the verse says that even if it is only in your heart that you hate, you have violated this commandment. You don't have to gossip or share your hatred with others. Even if no one knows how you feel, you have violated the commandment. One could argue that hatred corrodes a society even when it is not openly expressed. It is hard to imagine that it won't affect how you relate to the person you hate. Isn't it next to impossible to contain your hate in your heart? What does it do to your heart to carry that hatred with you? This leads to the second part of the verse.

Reprove your kinsman. (Lev. 19:17b)

It is our obligation to give reproof to those who have done wrong or spoken hurtfully. If someone has hurt you, it is not enough for you to tell yourself that you are moving on and that you do not carry hatred in your heart for this person. As admirable as that would be, it is not just about you. The person who hurt you hasn't changed. Our obligation is not just to ourselves but to those who hurt us, and thereby to our society. The rabbis stress that we are supposed to rebuke someone in such a manner that he or she can hear the reproof. A nasty comment about someone's obnoxious behavior will surely not be effective in helping that person become a better human being.

Reproof may reveal that you misunderstood what was being said or done. In response to the reproof, the person could explain what happened in a way that makes you realize that this is all a misunderstanding. In that circumstance it is easy for both of you to move on. Even if it was a deliberate slight, a reproof may enable an apology and reconciliation to take place. That is also why it isn't enough to just move on by forgiving the hurt yourself.

Incur no guilt because of him or her. (Lev. 19:17c)

The end of this verse has been understood in three ways by the rabbis. First, it enjoins us not to incur guilt by hating a person; therefore, engage in reproof. Second, it requires that we not stand idly by; if you see wrongdoing, you must speak out or you will be complicit in the wrongdoing. There is a debate by the rabbinic authorities whether this commandment of reproof only applies to someone who has wronged you or also if you see a stranger being wronged. Those who think it should apply only when you are the wronged party believe that for reproof to be effective (really heard by the person being reproved) there needs to be some relationship between the people. It is certainly true that where there is some existing trust or history it is more likely the reproof can be heard as coming from a place of caring rather than just criticism. Other commentators believe that we must speak out even if the wrongdoing affected others or even people we don't know personally. Reproof then is linked to the commandment to not stand idly by.

The third interpretation of the rabbis of the phrase "Incur no guilt" is that it is strongly forbidden to publicly shame a person. As much as you are supposed to reprove, you are also not supposed to humiliate the person. The rabbis teach that to embarrass someone publicly is like spilling their blood (*Bava Metzia* 58b). They explain that when someone is humiliated, the blood drains from their face; hence it is like killing. The rabbis are not suggesting that humiliating another is a capital crime; rather, they are using hyperbole to point out how hurtful such speech can be, even though it is a common occurrence.

The various principles here are not easily balanced. You need to process your feelings of hate or anger by reproving the person who hurt you or hurt others. The purpose is for that person to hear the criticism as valid and for them to change their behavior. Therefore, it needs to be said in a way that will be effective. Telling someone he is a jerk is not reproof. The reproof is for everyone's benefit, not just so you can get these feelings off your chest. It is supposed to be effective but not embarrassing.

The Talmud acknowledges the difficulty of the process of reproof:

> Rabbi Tarfon said: I wonder if there is anyone in this generation capable of giving reproof. For if anyone says to another: "Take the chip from between your teeth," the other retorts, "Take the beam from between your eyes."
>
> Rabbi Eleazar ben Azariah said: I wonder whether there is anyone in this generation capable of accepting reproof.
>
> Rabbi Akiva said: I wonder whether there is anyone in this

generation that knows how to give reproof without humiliating the one reproved." (*Arakhin* 16b)

You shall not take vengeance or bear a grudge against your countrymen. (Lev.19:18a)

The Talmud, commenting on the verse, says the following:

> It was taught: Which is vengeance and which is bearing a grudge? If she said to him: Lend me your scythe, and she was refused; and the next day he said to her: Lend me your spade— If she replied: I will not lend it to you, just as you did not lend it to me—this is vengeance; and if she replied: Here it is—I am not like you, who do not lend—this is bearing a grudge." (*Yoma* 23a)

Vengeance is being caught in a cycle of tit for tat. Since you weren't nice to me, I won't be nice to you. In vengeance, you justify your ungenerous response because that is how that person treated you. There is an implied superior quality in this "vengeance." I normally would have been happy to lend you the tool you needed, but since yesterday you didn't lend me a tool then today it seems only fair to treat you the same way. In other words, you brought this on yourself.

The moral superiority in bearing a grudge is even clearer. I will lend you the tool even though out of fairness I shouldn't, but I'm not like you. I am magnanimous—here's the tool. It comes with a generous serving of humble pie. This verse urges us not to be a grievance collector despite how this person has treated you in the past.

Love your fellow as yourself. (Lev. 19:18b)

This is the ultimate positive expression of these commandments. What does it mean in practice to love your neighbor? The questions about fulfillment of this *mitzvah* are immediately obvious—what is love? I may like my neighbor but he is not in my top ten list of friends. When do I have to love him—all the time? If I thought a nice thought about him this morning, is that enough for the whole day, or a lifetime? Does love involve some action? Can you really command emotions? How do I know when I have fulfilled the commandment? This kind of commandment stands outside the structure of fulfillment that is so fundamental to traditional Jewish law. Despite this, it is one of the 613 commandments. This is true of all the ethical commandments of Leviticus chapter 19.

Couldn't these commandments serve as models for a different way to think about Judaism as a practice? We commit to observe them not because God commands them or in order to receive a reward from heaven. Rather we commit to observing them because that is how we want to live our lives. We think the world would be a better place if we love our neighbor. We would be in a better space if we didn't hate people, even if only in our hearts. We can choose to live in a neighborhood constructed of envy, anger and hatred. Or we can live in a neighborhood constructed of compassion, forbearance, and love. Where would we rather live—where we think the worst of everyone, or the best? In which neighborhood would we be happier—a place of locked doors and locked hearts, or a place of openheartedness? Americans have an image of themselves pulling together in times of crisis. What if we did that not only on 9/11 or at natural disasters? What if that was the ongoing nature of our neighborhoods? What if we could stretch ourselves beyond our neighbors to the people who live across town or across the country? They seem different in their race, religion, beliefs and values. Yet we are all citizens wanting the same thing—to live a good life with family and friends.

Loving your neighbor certainly doesn't fit the usual understanding of commandments, because loving can't be clearly defined. It is a mindset, not something you do for a moment. It is why these commandments serve as a good model for rethinking how we understand the *mitzvot*/commandments. It does not say love your neighbor in your heart. While mindset is the foundation for practicing this commandment, it is expressed through deeds of lovingkindness. Maimonides understood loving one's neighbor to mean doing such specific acts as visiting the sick or comforting mourners. Unlike other traditional commandments that have a *shiur*—a measurement of what is required, such as how much matzah to eat, these acts have no minimum requirements. They are open-ended. You do as much as your heart desires in response to the needs of others. Whether rejoicing with them at joyous occasions, mourning with them at tragic ones, or helping those in need, the requirement to love your neighbor means treating everyone in the way you would like to be treated. Hence the phrase: Love your neighbor *as yourself*. As an example: the way you would want to be treated when visiting an unfamiliar place should guide you when encountering strangers. Do you go out of your way to give them directions to their destination?

Instead of commandments in the traditional sense, *mitzvot* become guidelines for behavior and the embodiment of values. These verses in Leviticus 19 express a vision of a compassionate society. They encourage a society where you love your neighbor enough to gently reprove them. Instead of holding on to every hurt, you are encouraged to move on to forgiveness. The other ethical commandments could also fit under this rubric of guiding principles. It is an ambitious vision of a compassionate society, yet it is clearly at the heart of what it means to be a holy people.

We began with the foundational value of every human as an image of God. This translated in this chapter to our greatest challenge: to build a world of compassion and justice. In the next chapter we will begin exploring how to cultivate qualities that will enable us to bring goodness into the world.

Core Principle #3:
Living With Awareness

We began with the most fundamental of Jewish values: that we are all images of God and our purpose is to do good. How might that happen in the busyness of our everyday existence? We know that how we think about what we do is critical. In Jewish tradition, this is called *kavanah*/intention. In 21st-century spirituality, it is called awareness. Practices like meditation or yoga are essential aspects of contemporary American spirituality. Can we find sources for awareness practices in the Jewish tradition?

Ritual Commandments

In fact, Judaism has many awareness practices that are rarely described as such. Everyone can understand why ethical commandments, such as the commandment to love your neighbor, are of value. The observance of rituals, however, can seem disconnected from such values. What larger purpose is served by not turning on electrical appliances on Shabbat or not mixing milk and meat together? Let me suggest that the purpose of rituals is to remind us of our values and goals. They are no different than paying attention to our breath during silent meditation. For example, when we pause before we eat to recite words of blessing, we remind ourselves that we should be grateful for food and the gift of life. The purpose isn't found in reciting the blessing itself; rather we say the blessing to heighten our awareness of gratitude. A daily meditation practice is meant to help train us to pay attention not only while meditating but to be more aware throughout the day. Judaism's awareness practice is a little different than meditation because it focuses on cultivating a specific aspect such as gratitude, compassion, or equanimity.

Broadly, the intent of ritual is to help remind us of the life that we want to live. It once was a challenge to live that life because of the necessity to work for the basics—food, shelter, clothing, and safety. For many of us today, however, our experience is that if we work hard enough, we will have at least those necessities, if not much more. We may still be concerned about earning a living but for many it is not the major concern of our lives. Instead, we struggle with unhappiness, loneliness, and anxiety. We can have 200 Facebook friends and still feel that no one cares about us. We find that the lives we thought we would be living have slipped away over the years. What happened to the values we cherished and the dreams we had? Why do so many of us wonder about the meaning of our lives rather than delight in everything we have experienced? The anxiety of worrying about having enough food has been replaced by the anxieties of our inner landscapes.

Ironically, eating too much food has become a source of anxiety for many people.

The busyness of our daily lives makes it easy to take for granted the values that in fact elevate our lives. We love our family and care about our friends. We want to make our world a better place. Yet, we too often forget to say or demonstrate that love and caring. We are too busy to take the time to do the real work to make our society more caring. In many ways, technology has robbed us of the downtime that might enable us to notice the beauty of the day or realize we wanted to be in touch with a friend who is going through a hard time. We all have things we would like to spend more time doing, whether it is going to concerts or being in contact with distant family members. Yet, most often we don't change our daily routines despite our best intentions.

Do Jewish rituals really help us to live a life of awareness? Unfortunately, too often they do not. That is partly because of the emphasis on the tradition of fulfilling the commandment, rather than on its purpose. It is essential for the Judaism of the 21st century that we shift the emphasis to purpose and intention. Rituals are training tools for becoming a better and more aware human being.

A central question about the nature of ritual revolves around its capacity to become so rote as to render it meaningless. How do we create a method of being consciously aware of the moment even as we are busy with the everyday tasks and interactions of life? Without regular awareness practices, it is too easy to put off to some never-reached future time a focus on these essential aspects of life. Routine matters; awareness of that routine matters more.

If one of the purposes of Judaism is to help us focus on what we want to do and be, ritual becomes the structured method to remind us of what is important. Its purpose is not to reprimand us about our failures, but to help us be our best selves. *Practice* might be a better, more contemporary term for *ritual*. A practice is something we do on a regular basis for a particular purpose. We acknowledge the purpose can only be achieved by doing it regularly.

An example of an awareness practice:

The *Sefer Ha-Hinukh* is a medieval work that gives a brief explanation of each of the 613 commandments in the order in which they appear in the Torah. Mitzvah #16 is the mezuzah. Once hung on the doorpost, the mezuzah remains there. Every time you move from one room to the next, the mezuzah serves as a continual reminder to live a life committed to Jewish practice and principles. Today we would describe that practice as helping us to live a life of awareness. Awareness brings our wandering minds back in focus, paying attention to the moment and literally re-minding ourselves of what is important.

Of course, as with all such symbols, its very prevalence makes it disappear from consciousness. A traditional practice is to touch the mezuzah with our hand, which we then kiss, as we pass by it. This too can become a rote practice. Here is an alternative suggestion: consider touching the mezuzah when you leave your home in order to acknowledge the transition from the home to the outside world. Transitions in many cultures are seen as a time of danger. Demons or the dark forces were thought to lurk in the liminal spaces. While we are no longer worried about demons, taking a moment to mark the transition from home to the outside world as we leave in the morning can be a good practice. While home is not without its challenges, there is a comfortable familiarity and a sense of safety at home. The outside world has both opportunities and challenges. Acknowledging this with a simple ritual can help navigate this transition with awareness. Similarly, it could be a good practice when you return home at the end of the day to wipe off the distress of the day in order to greet loved ones with pleasantness or to just slip into the comfort of your own space. Since it is impossible to be aware at every single moment or even every transition, choosing this transition as the one to ritualize as a moment of awareness may be helpful. Remember to take your keys, your cellphone and a moment of awareness as you leave for the day.

Non-ritual awareness practice

The Sefer Ha-Hinukh views the mezuzah as one of the constant commandments (*mitzvot temidiyot*). The author is referring to a special category of *mitzvah* that has no action associated with it and whose sole purpose is to focus on matters of belief. Traditionally, these *mitzvot* are referred to as the constant commandments because they apply all the time. Maimonides (12th-century philosopher and rabbinic scholar) lists six: to believe in God; not to believe in any other god; to believe in the oneness of God; to love God; to fear God; not to be misled by your heart and eyes. The Sefer Ha-Hinukh adds the mezuzah to the list.

These mitzvot could be seen as examples of a different kind of an awareness practice in that they don't really involve an action such as lighting candles or even saying a blessing, but rather require cultivating fundamental beliefs. As I delved more deeply into this category of *mitzvot*, I wondered whether in fact they would be helpful to us. Five were related to a belief in God, which in traditional Judaism is, of course, central. But how shall people who do not share that belief in God still develop an awareness practice? For those who don't believe in God, a sense of the oneness underlying all creation can be an important counter reality to an anxiety about our existential aloneness. To cultivate a sense that love is the basic animating force of the world could be a powerful practice. Finally, living with a sense of awe (rather than fear) reminds us of the truth that we are a small part of a very large universe.

The last of Maimonides' traditional constant commandments is actually different from the rest. What does it mean to not be misled by your heart and eyes? It seems to be related to action and traditionally refers to avoiding the desire for forbidden things. The midrash talks about those senses over which we have no control, like seeing, hearing and smell, which cannot be filtered out. These senses are distinct from those over which we have choice, such as touch and taste. For the former, not being misled can be an ongoing challenge (Genesis Rabbah 67:3). This last of the six constant commandments can be understood as reminding us to avoid behavior that is detrimental to our well-being.

There is another traditional commandment to add to the category of constant commandments that can serve as a model for having an ongoing awareness of an important value—in this case, the value of freedom. As we have discussed, moving from slavery to freedom shaped our experience as a people and is an essential aspect of Judaism. It is an ongoing experience, both for us as individuals and as a society. As the Torah repeats over and over again, we are instructed to treat the stranger and those on the margins of society with compassion because we were strangers and we were slaves in Egypt. We are supposed to remember the slavery and the Exodus every day, not only at Passover.

This is a major principle of Judaism. It is one of the 613 commandments and certainly should be understood as one of the *mitzvot* of awareness. It also demonstrates how the *mitzvot* of awareness are supposed to shape how we act in the world. We don't just intellectually remember the experience of Egypt— this *mitzvah* is meant to guide how we treat other people, especially the more vulnerable among us. While there isn't a specific ritual or action attached to it, this commandment encourages an awareness and a sensitivity that demands we engage in the world to help those in need of assistance or protection. There may be other such principles by which you want to live your life. Bringing them to consciousness in a regular (ritual) way can make them more present for you.

In my imagination, *Minhag America* Judaism has several types of awareness practices. One focuses on basic beliefs and principles, such as that everyone is created in the image of God or that there is a oneness underlying the universe. A second type of awareness practice involves rituals that encourage an awareness of the natural world around us, such as offering blessings for beautiful smells or vistas. A third type reflects an acknowledgment that it is difficult to always be aware. Judaism creates particular times to concentrate our awareness on a specific value, whether it is a glimpse of perfection and peace on Shabbat or repentance on Yom Kippur. We live with imperfection, but this last type encourages us not to lose sight of the ideal. On that level, all commandments are constant commandments, helping to shape us beyond just this moment.

In the next section, we will continue setting out new and traditional awareness practices. We begin with multiple suggestions for a crucial moment: starting and orienting our day.

Daily Awareness Practices

A key component to living a life with awareness is setting a tone for the day. Traditional Jews pray the morning service (*Shaharit*), which can serve as a reminder to awaken to the possibilities of a new day. In fact, there are three services recited daily, preferably in a quorum of ten people (a minyan). If that is not possible, you can recite the prayers alone. While there are advantages to a group experience, the ease of an awareness practice at home that fits our morning schedules makes it more likely to happen. Moreover, a service that can take more than 30 minutes to complete can be challenging to people trying to get themselves or their children out the door in the morning.

Following are a variety of practices that you might consider adopting. Some of these practices are more traditional; others are a reformulation of traditional practices; and still others are new ideas. They can be done in a short period of time (between 5-15 minutes).

Like any practice, regularity makes it more likely to be effective. You need a place to do the practice where you can be undisturbed. Consider doing the practice either while lying in bed or after you get up and get dressed, but before you become actively engaged in your day. I would encourage you not to check your email first. A crisis at work or a negative email can too easily become your focus. The overall point of this practice is to give you a spiritual orientation to the day. It is to awaken to this day before all the tasks and responsibilities kick in. At this moment your responsibility is only to yourself, reminding you of the values you cherish. Another possibility is to do this practice as you commute to work or to take the first few moments as you arrive at your workplace. The following practices can serve as examples to create your own. You may want to have a different practice each morning as part of a weekly cycle. All such practices are forms of awareness that begin with a simple question: What do we want our focus to be for this new day? Broadly, these practices are meant to encourage us to be kinder, more thoughtful, and less afraid or anxious.

Modah/modeh ani—Gratitude

This awareness practice can be framed with the traditional phrase that is said upon awakening to the morning—**I give thanks before You, God of life and existence, that you have returned my spirit to me—Great is Your faith in me.** *Modeh/modah ani lefanekha melekh hai ve-kayam shehehezarta bi nishmati be-hemlah rabah emunatekha.*

Or: Thank you God for the renewed gift of life and consciousness, and for your compassionate spirit that is within me this day—great is your faith in my ability to bring goodness into the world.

Or: I give thanks for being part of all existence and that I have the blessing of another day of life. Let me strive to have faith in this day's potential for renewal.

This simple traditional prayer is a form of gratitude practice. It expresses thanks for beginning a new day of life. It suggests that we should never take that precious gift of life for granted. The last two words of this prayer—great is your faith in me—comes from a verse in the Book of Lamentations (3:23), a book which recalls in great detail the terrible destruction of the Temple in Jerusalem (586 B.C.E.). It seems a surprising choice for a prayer celebrating the new day. The full verse reads: "new things come with the dawn, great is Your faith." I understand this to mean that God has great faith in each of us to fully engage the changing world represented by the new day. This day has never happened before and will never come again. New things come with the dawn. Those new things include our ability to shape this world. The prayer expresses a profound belief in the possibility that we too can change. This prayer then is not just an expression of gratitude for another day of life; it is also a powerful affirmation of our potential to be who we deeply desire to be.

By implying that we should not take for granted that we are alive (since death can come at any moment), it also suggests we shouldn't take the blessings of this day for granted. We should strive for an awareness that everything passes and therefore we should not be caught up in minor annoyances. Instead, we should focus on what really matters: life and its blessings.

Awareness of goodness practice

There is a traditional phrase for acknowledging goodness: *hakarat ha-tov*. It is usually understood as recognizing the kind things that someone else has done for us. It emphasizes the importance of gratitude to others and by implication criticizes those who "forget" what others have done for them. The Hebrew *le-hakir* literally means to recognize, as in, "I recognize you even though we haven't seen each other in years." I suggest that *le-hakir* also means awareness as it is used in contemporary spirituality. Recognition is a process of seeing clearly and acknowledging what is. As we learned from the story of creation, God created a world of *tov*/good. We are meant to recognize that. Our acknowledgement of the goodness of our lives encourages us to spread goodness to others. Our purpose is not to ask God or the universe for more blessings, but to be like Abraham: a blessing to all we meet on our journey.

Here is an example of such a practice:

Let me remember to be grateful for this new day of life. It will not come again.

I am grateful for the people who are important in my life.

I am grateful for my ability to feel and to think.

I am grateful for my body.

May I be blessed with insights and wisdom on this day.

Repeat this three times to help bring your attention to what you are saying. Pause before the third repetition and see whether there are any specific actions you want to take this day to live these principles.

"Where are you?" practice

After eating of the Tree of Knowledge, Adam and Eve hear God coming and they hide. God asks: Where are you? (*Ayekha*). We all play this cosmic game of hide and seek even though we know we cannot really hide from God or the world; we can only successfully hide from ourselves. Each morning we can ask ourselves the question—*Where am I?* Can I see myself clearly in the light of the new day? Can I accept responsibility for my flaws even as I answer the real question—who do I want to be this day? Recite:

I want to remember to strive to see everyone as an image of God. Flawed and holy, just like me.

I want to be ready to help others with a kind word or gesture.

I want to strive to say *yes* instead of immediately going to a place of *no*.

I want to hold all three of the sage Hillel's teachings simultaneously: If I am not paying attention to my needs, who will do that for me? If I am only concerned about myself, then what kind of person am I? If not now, when? (*Ethics of our Ancestors* 1:14).

I want to live my life imbued with the wisdom of Judaism—*l'asok be-divrei torah*—to be engaged with words of Torah.

This practice could be combined with a *hineni*—**Here I am**—practice. Unlike Adam and Eve, who hide from God after eating from the Tree of Knowledge, a number of biblical characters, like Abraham and Moses, respond to God's calling by saying, *Here I am/hineni*, which can be understood as the definition of being present. To sit quietly with the intention of being spiritually present with a periodic chant of *hineni/here I am* could either be its own practice or a fitting response to the question, *Where are you/Ayekha*?

Practice of holding competing truths/eilu ve-eilu:

> It was the best of times, it was the worst of times, it was the age of wisdom, it was the age of foolishness, it was the epoch of belief, it was the epoch of incredulity, it was the season of Light, it was the season of Darkness, it was the spring of hope, it was the winter of despair, we had everything before us, we had nothing before us…
> —Charles Dickens, *A Tale of Two Cities*

The Jewish version of the Dickens quotation was suggested by Simcha Bunim, (a 19th-century Hasidic master): Each Jew should carry in one pocket the phrase "we are little lower than angels" and in the other pocket "we are dust and ashes." Judaism teaches that life is complicated. We live in grey areas where the correct choice is not always apparent. While many think religion is a place to find answers, liberal Judaism suggests that it is a form of hubris to think that is possible.

Bernie Glassman, a Zen teacher (1939-2018), wrote: "Yet, we still want to know. In some way we can't help it—we're human. As part of being human, we believe that the reason we're not happy or not successful is that somewhere in the world there is a piece of knowledge we haven't acquired yet. If we can find it with the help of the right book, the right religion, the right teacher, or the right job, we'll be happy and successful." Glassman suggested that at times we need to rest in unknowing. Whether this means accepting our limitations as human beings or understanding we need to hold competing truths, it can be a powerful practice to begin a day reminding ourselves of this challenging notion.

The Talmud (*Eruvin* 13b) says that despite the fact that the Schools of Shammai and Hillel strongly disagreed on many issues they still remained part of one community, marrying each other and eating in each other's homes. Why? Because of the principle *eilu ve'eilu divrei Elohim hayyim*—both these and those are the words of the living God. How can it be that the same act could be permitted and forbidden? I think the explanation lies in the notion that honestly held views can be contained in God. One of the points of Judaism is that there is an underlying unity in the world. Despite our experience of the world as a place of disconnection and separation, God is everywhere. Even for those who don't believe in God, a sense that the universe is tied together can be an important understanding to carry into the everyday world. The description of God as a living God or even the God of life also suggests that the world is constantly changing. Our understanding may change as well over the course of our lives.

In our divided world, where too often we think we are right and others are completely wrong, it is important to remember we are all human. The Talmud (Berakhot 58a) has a blessing that can be understood to celebrate the variety of human beings. This blessing could give expression to a practice acknowledging competing truths: Blessed is the wise one of secrets (God), for just as people's opinions vary one from the other, so are each of their faces unique—(*barukh hacham ha-razim she-ein da'atam domeh zeh la-zeh, ve-ain partzufeihem domim zeh la-zeh*). Perhaps God's unusual name here acknowledges that not only are people different but that we can't possibly fully know another person and their motivations.

Social justice practice

Recite the following:

I know
that poverty must cease.
I know this through the brokenness
and conflict in my heart.
I know
that protest is my most prophetic act
and that the world is longing
for a new soul, a new healing moment.
I know
that when we awaken to our origins
and become truly human
we bring hope to the children
and to the earth.
I feel called today
to bring the people together to break the bread
and tell the story.
I feel called today

to be a mystic in action,
aligned to the dynamics of the universe.
I feel called today
to give my gift,
to listen to the heartbeat of the broken world;
to heal the fragmentation of people and planet.
I feel called today
to celebrate the wonder of creation
and respond to sacredness and the
challenges of life.
I feel called today
to participate in the work of my time,
to fall in love,
to feel at home.
I feel called today
to be inflamed with enduring hope,
to be at one with the universe,
to be touched by God.
I feel called today
to compose a new paragraph for life.
—James Conlon

(For a different social justice practice, see Pesach section, p. 112).

Principles to live by practice

One purpose of the daily morning practice is to bring awareness to the important truths by which we want to live our lives. In the tradition, the most well-known prayer said in the morning is the *Shema*—**Hear O Israel, Adonai our God, Adonai is one.** In fact, this line and the paragraphs that follow it are not prayers. They are statements of faith. The *Shema* can serve as a model of a morning practice that reminds us of the principles and values we hold dear and we want to help guide us.

There is actually a traditional practice to help us remember important principles of Judaism that is found at the end of the weekday service in traditional prayer books. It is a private practice that is not part of the service; even many traditional Jews don't recite it. It consists of six remembrances to be recited daily. They quote biblical verses that tell us to:

1. Remember the Exodus from Egypt (Dt. 16:3).

2. Remember you stood at Sinai and received the Torah (Dt. 4:9-10).

3. Remember what Amalek did to you on the journey from Egypt (Dt. 25:17-19).

4. Remember how you provoked God during the 40 years in the desert (Dt. 9:7). (Traditionally this is understood as referring specifically to the worship of the Golden Calf.)

5. Remember how God punished Miriam in the desert with leprosy (Dt. 24:9). (The rabbis understood this incident as Miriam gossiping about her brother Moses).

6. Remember the Sabbath day to make it holy (Ex. 20:8).

Some of these are traditional commandments; others are not. We can understand why it is important to especially remember some of these moments from sacred history. It's not hard to understand, for example, why we should remember slavery and the Exodus all the time. Similarly, we are to remember that we, not just our ancestors, stood at Sinai. The covenant is with all Israel for eternity. The ongoing engagement with Torah is a ceaseless practice that should affect our daily lives. The midrash says that the Voice of Sinai calls to us every day, not just at the ancient moment of the revelation at Sinai. We are called to engage in Torah (both its study and practice) day and night.

The people of Amalek attack the Israelites as they travel in the desert after leaving Egypt, targeting the stragglers at the end of the Israelite line. In the tradition, Amalek has come to symbolize the evil forces in the world. We are commanded (Dt. 25:19) not to forget that our mission is to wipe out evil from this world—to literally wipe out the memory of Amalek. As much as we are to remember that we were once slaves and therefore should have compassion for those on the margins of our society, we must also commit ourselves to Judaism's ultimate vision of a world redeemed from evil and suffering. Both our past suffering and our commitment to a better future are meant to profoundly shape our role in the world.

The call to remember the Sabbath day reflects the importance of Shabbat in Jewish life. The concepts of resting on the seventh day and making time holy become part of the way the world is to be perceived. Traditionally, the weekdays are viewed as leading up to Shabbat and then flowing back into the work week. This weekly cycle becomes the dynamic of our existence, shaping both our work and our rest. Our responsibility is to continue the work of creation for six days and then we are to rest, reflect, and refresh. We are to remember each day that this cycle exists. It is an important example of how Judaism shapes time by giving the weekly cycle texture and meaning.

The last two items on the list seem much more minor then the first four. Yet, they too can be understood as reminding us of basic principles. Remembering the incident of the Golden Calf emphasizes that idolatry is an ever-present danger, especially to those who strive to live a religiously infused life, particularly as we understand idolatry as the worship of partial truth. Idolatry in its contemporary form would have us believe that God is knowable rather than unknowable. It is to proclaim this and only this is the God of Israel or the universe. (See Idolatry chapter, p. 164). Each day we need to engage in the challenging notion of reaffirming our principles even as we acknowledge the limits of our knowledge and understanding. We live in a world of many truths—some even in contradiction with other truths.

Finally, the last injunction on the list is to remember God's punishment of Miriam in the desert. Traditional commentators understand this to refer to the time that Miriam gossips to Aaron about their brother Moses and is punished with a form of leprosy. The story emphasizes the concept that God creates the world through speech, not action. We also create much of our world through speech. We need to be always aware of the power of our speech to hurt or to help.

Each call to awareness represents a specific way to frame our consciousness as we move through our daily tasks: remember our history of slavery and freedom; remember the revelation of Sinai; remember the Sabbath day, remember to strive to redeem the world; remember the falseness of idolatry; remember the power of speech.

A liturgy of awareness

1. **Remember the Exodus from Egypt (Dt. 16:3)**: Remember the potential that you have to free yourself from that which holds you back.

2. **Remember you stood at Sinai and received the Torah (Dt. 4:9-10)**: Remember that the tradition is a 3,000-year-long conversation about how to live life. You have a part in continuing to unroll the Torah scroll of the Jewish people.

3. **Remember what Amalek did to you on the journey from Egypt (Dt. 25:17-19)**: Remember the world is still unredeemed and you are tasked to help bring about its redemption.

4. **Remember how you provoked God during the 40 years wandering in the desert (Dt. 9:7)**: Remember not to be ensnared with the false idols of thinking there is an absolute truth just waiting over the next hill.

5. **Remember how God punished Miriam in the desert with leprosy (Dt. 24:9)**: Remember that we create our world through the power of words.

6. **Remember the Sabbath day to make it holy (Ex. 20:8)**: Remember that we need to reflect as much as we need to create. We need to rest and to let the planet rest as well.

These six remembrances can make us aware of the potential of this new day even as they suggest the challenges we will face. They are one example of an awareness practice you could adopt. You could frame the interpretation of each biblical verse using your own language. You could also decide to eliminate one or more of them. Finally, you could decide to pick your own points of awareness. These could be said instead of or in addition to the six listed above.

Daily creation practice

A more complex practice would change each day over the course of the week, paralleling the creation story beginning on Sunday. For this practice I use many of the traditional blessings recited at the beginning of the morning service every day. These blessings were originally said at home and were tied to a specific physical activity such as waking up and getting dressed. At some point the recital of the prayers was moved to the synagogue and the connection to the physical act was severed. Interestingly, the blessings were always metaphorical. "Praised are you God for clothing the naked" or "girding Israel with strength" were not meant to be taken literally, even though these lines were supposed to be said as you put on clothes or a belt. I have tried to reconnect the metaphorical aspect of these blessings to aspects of our lives and to the story of creation. (Note: I have included the concluding formula of each blessing. The opening formula is: *Barukh atah Adonai eloheinu melekh ha-olam*—**Blessed are You Adonai our God source of the universe**).

1. The first day focuses on light and darkness.

> Recite the blessing *asher natan la-sechvi vinah le-havhin bein yom u-vein laylah* **Who has given the mind the ability to distinguish day from night.**
> *Oteh or ka-salma*—**I wrap myself in the light** (of this new day) **as in a garment** (Ps. 104:2). Some have the practice of wrapping themselves in a tallit/ prayer shawl as a physical way of wrapping themselves in light, thereby seeing the world as filled with light and humans as a vessel for that light.

2. The second day focuses on the separation of sky from earth.

> We have the ability to distinguish between things. It is a critical aspect of being human and yet it too often can lead to becoming judgmental. The traditional commentators notice that this is the only day of creation that God doesn't say—*ki tov*—it is good. Why? Distinguishing has often led to division and argument.
> We recite the blessing *pokeah ivrim*—**who gives light to the blind**—hoping we can see clearly rather than be blinded to the truth that lies before us this day.

3. The third day focuses on earth and ocean and especially on growing plants.

> We recite the blessing *roka ha-aretz al ha-mayim* **grateful for a firm place to plant our feet**. We celebrate the possibility of our growth reflected in a world filled with an infinite variety of growing things that make this planet viable for all living beings.
> We recite the blessing *zokeif kefufim*—**who lifts up the bent-over**, enabling humans, not just plants, to grow upright.

4. The fourth day focuses on the sun and the moon and the stars as it says, "they shall serve as signs for the set times—the days and the years."

> Time is a key element of our lives. The challenge is not its management, but the understanding that we shape time by making certain days significant. Shabbat and festivals are ways we overlay structure and meaning on the astronomical course of the universe.
> We recite the blessing *mekadesh hazemanim*—**who makes holy certain times.**

5. The fifth day focuses on birds and fish.

While we are land creatures, our ability to fly in the air and travel both on and below the surface of water are powerful demonstrations of human capacity to overcome physical obstacles in the world.

We recite the blessing *ozeir bnai adam bi-gevurah*—**who strengthens humans with courage.**

(Or alternatively: *matir asurim*—**freed us from the bounds of nature**)

6. The sixth day focuses on the creation of animals and of humans.

We recite the blessing *malbish arumim*—**who clothes the naked**—thereby acknowledging the physicality of our bodies even as we distinguish ourselves from the animals with whom we share the need to eat and procreate.

We recite the blessing *she-asani be-tzelem Elohim*—**who made me in the image of God**—our most essential definition.

Some say:

She-asani yisrael—**made me a Jew.**

She-asani bat/ben horin—**made me free.** The ability to choose is a critical aspect of human beings.

She-asah li kol tzarki—**who has given me a heart and mind**—which is what I need to make choices.

Some will add anticipating a hard day.

Ozeir yisrael bi-gevurah—**who girds me with strength.**

Others conclude with *oseh ma'aseh bereishit*—**who continues the workings of creation.**

7. The seventh day is Shabbat and we rest and give thanks for the week that has passed.

We say *ha-ma'avir sheinah mei-anai utenumah mei-afapoi*—**who removes sleep from my eyes and slumber from my eyelids.**

You might have thought this should have been the blessing said upon awakening. I think it is last because the point of these blessings is to really awaken to the day, not just stumble out of bed and rush off to work. This blessing asks for help in coming to real awareness of the new day. While it could be said every day, it seems most appropriate to recite it on Shabbat, when we are not rushing off to work and therefore have a more spacious capacity to become fully aware.

Creating your own practice

There are, of course, many other principles or variations on these practices that you may want to use instead of my choices. You may want to combine some of these practices that are relatively short. You may want to alternate their use depending on which seems to best suit you that day. You also may want to quote more lines in Hebrew from the liturgy or Psalms to give this a more liturgical and traditional texture. In any case, I think the rabbis were correct to establish that prayers should be articulated quietly rather than just be thoughts in your head. There is a concreteness to the articulation, transforming thought into action.

During the day practices

The impact of your morning practice should carry into your day. The Hasidic notion that holiness can be found in the everyday means that striving to be aware or kind or grateful is how we want to be all the time, not just when we sit and reflect in the morning. You may want to consciously embrace that possibility. For example, you can continue to cultivate a feeling of gratitude by saying a "real" thank-you to people who have helped you. Since it is hard to do that all day long, my personal practice is always to say "have a nice day" to the cab driver as I am exiting. Paying attention to that one form of human interaction helps me to remember to do it. Figure out what is possible for you to do even as you try to push yourself to expand your practice. It is important to acknowledge nice things, especially since we may tend to get more caught up in unpleasant things that happen. Being kept on hold for a long time or getting delayed in commuting can darken our sense of the day. It seems easy for us to hold on to those negative moments, but harder to hold on to the good moments.

There is a traditional notion of reciting one hundred blessings a day, which is not so challenging to fulfill if you recite the traditional prayers of the three daily services that contain almost that number. I think the idea of reciting a hundred blessings was meant to encourage us to be aware of the blessings in our lives rather than a specific goal to say that number of blessings. In the liberal community, the recital of the *sheheheyanu* blessing has become widespread for a wide variety of special occasions such as a *bar/bat mitzvah* or special wedding anniversaries. (Note: in order to be as inclusive as possible, increasingly rabbis now refer to this life cycle moment as a b'mitzvah, which carries no gender and means *in the mitzvah*). The blessing praises God who gave us life, sustained us, and brought us to this moment (*sheheheyanu v' kiymanu ve-higiyanu lazman hazeh*). However, according to traditional *halakha,* the *sheheheyanu* blessing is said only when it is a moment of celebration for an individual (and also for each festival). There is a different blessing that is said when there is more than one person celebrating, such as two parents at a birth. *Ha-tov ve-ha-maytiv* is understood to mean God is good and beneficent. I would understand it as a blessing for the good thing that has happened (*ha-tov*) and a wish that goodness may increase (*ve-ha-maytiv*). It asks us to be grateful for the goodness of this moment, and also to strive to bring goodness into the world. It is not just an expression of a hope to celebrate many more joyous occasions in the life of an individual or family. Joy is to be shared and spread. Consider taking a moment to be grateful for something good that has happened, whether it is a little thing or something more significant. Saying one of the traditional blessings or just giving thanks to the universe is always a good practice that feeds the well-being of our soul.

In the last year of my father's life, my siblings and I decided he could no longer stay in his home even though he had a wonderful person taking care of him. He just needed too much care as his dementia got worse. I went down to Florida to escort him to the nursing home near where my sister lived in Washington, D.C. I brought his caretaker with me to help with the transition. Despite repeated explanations, my father was very confused about what was going on. After we settled him in his room, about a half dozen caretakers came in to introduce themselves to him. They were all African-American women. His caretaker explained who these women were and why they were there. My father was lying in his bed silently. Finally, he said to the women, "Sorry, I don't understand who you are." One replied, "We are here to take care of you." Again silence. Then my father said: "Well, that's certainly God's work." I was startled by the sudden moment of clarity by my father. I also imagined that the caretakers who also saw what they did as holy work felt connected to this old Jewish man born in Ukraine. They felt deeply appreciated by his understanding that this wasn't just a job for them. Despite coming from two very different backgrounds, this was a moment of real connection and mutual appreciation. We do create worlds with our words.

Kavanah before a meeting

Help me to come nearer to you and to all that you represent.
Remind me that perfection does not exist in an imperfect world.
Help me realize that I don't need approbation of others to feel worthy.
Let me remember that others' ways of doing things are not mine.
Lead me to patient understanding of those who seem annoyed

or angry.
Let me not dismiss people as being irrational when their response emerges out of fear and anxiety.
Most of all, let me remember people are neither better nor
worse than I am,
nor am I worse or better than they are.

Traditionally, there is an afternoon service called *minhah*, which means gift.
It refers to an offering that was brought to the Temple in Jerusalem in biblical
times. It is the shortest of the three services and can easily be recited in ten minutes. I want to suggest that it can be a "gift" to yourself to pause amidst your busy
day and take a breath, to disconnect electronically and just be with yourself.
Minhah is different from the other two daily services because it does not contain
the paragraphs of the *Shema*—Hear O Israel, Adonai our God, Adonai is one. I
wonder whether the oneness that is central to this prayer seemed too difficult to
achieve amidst the busyness of the workday. It could more easily be attained at
the beginning and ending of the day accompanied by the rising and the setting
of the sun. Find a place to sit quietly; if that is not possible at your desk, then go
outside for a short walk. There may be one of the morning practices or a piece
of them that you'd like to recite. Or listen to a favorite piece of music. Or use this
specific practice to reorient yourself in the middle of the day.

"Who am I?" practice

The phrase *Da lifnei mi atah omeid* is usually translated as "know before whom
you stand," which is intended to remind us that we are always in the presence
of God. It is often put on the walls of synagogues as a devotional text. I want to
suggest a different parsing of the words.
Da lifnei—**before** anything else, you need to strive to really **know**
Mi atah—**who are you** (in all your complexity) and then
Omeid—you can **stand up** before the world and do what needs to be done.
Sit with these notions in quiet. When you are ready to recite the above *kavanah*, stand.

Going to bed practice

The practice of examining your inner traits will be described more fully in
the chapter Walking in God's Ways. There is a particular practice called *heshbon
hanefesh*/the examination of yourself. Basically, it consists of focusing on an inner
quality, such as patience or generosity, for a week. Part of this practice is to keep
a diary in order to track how you did on maintaining that quality. You could also

keep a journal and write down moments of gratitude or wonder. It could be a delicious bread pudding that you ate at a restaurant or a performance that moved you or an especially meaningful interaction with someone. There is no need to feel a compulsion to make it complete. If you follow this practice, each night before you go to sleep you might want to find at least one thing to write down. I can imagine no better way to fall asleep than with a pleasant thought or a feeling of being blessed.

Lest we think that Judaism's practice is solely focused on our inner self, the next core principle explores Judaism's call for social justice.

Core Principle #4: Engaging in Social Justice

> Charity begins at home and justice begins next door.
> —Charles Dickens

Is there something unique about Judaism's approach to social justice? Some critics suggest that the essence of Judaism has been distorted by an overemphasis on social justice. This chapter will explore why social justice is one of Judaism's core values and not a distortion of it. There will be suggestions for ways to engage in a social justice practice imbued with particular Jewish values and based on Jewish texts.

Abraham: The first to speak truth to power

God said to Abram, "Go forth from your native land and from your father's house to the land that I will show you. I will make of you a great nation. And I will bless you; I will make your name great, and you shall be a blessing. . . . And all the families of the earth shall bless themselves by you" (Gen. 12:1-3). Abraham is the first Jew. God appears to Abraham and tells him to go forth on a journey to a promised land. If he takes that journey, he will be a blessing to those he will meet on the way. The biblical text doesn't tell us why God chose Abraham or what it means to be a Jew. A few chapters later there is an incident that makes this clearer.

Abraham is sitting by the entrance to his tent during the heat of the day when he sees three travelers who he runs to greet. He offers them the hospitality of his tent. The three strangers, actually angels, predict that his wife Sarah, already quite old, will give birth. They then leave to bring destruction upon neighboring Sodom because of its wickedness. After the angels leave, God asks: "Shall I hide from Abraham what I am about to do to Sodom?" (Gen. 18:17). God wants to make sure that Abraham understands what is expected of him. In verse 19, we are finally told explicitly what his journey (and all of our journeys) are about. Abraham must understand and teach his children to observe the way of God (*derekh Adonai*). What does that mean? To do righteousness and justice—*tzedakah u-mishpat*.

Up until now we have no idea how Abraham is to live as a Jew. Now we know that the journey is not through space but through deed. He is supposed to live a life of righteousness and justice. We see from Abraham's response why he is chosen to be the founder of the Jewish people. When Abraham is told of Sodom's imminent destruction by God, he takes up the mantle of responsibility.

This emphasis on responsibility is highlighted in Abraham's story but the motif runs through the beginning chapters of Genesis. When Adam and Eve are "caught" eating of the Tree of Knowledge of Good and Evil, they don't take responsibility; rather, they blame someone else. When Cain kills his brother Abel, he proclaims, "Am I my brother's keeper?" It is the ultimate statement of non-responsibility. In the face of the imminent cataclysmic flood, Noah doesn't seem to feel responsible to save the lives of anybody but his family.

God challenges Abraham to become a blessing in the world by feeling responsible not just for his family or even just his neighbors, but for all the families of the world. Abraham understands that responsibility. In the face of injustice Abraham does not ask: *Am I my brother's keeper?* He takes up his responsibility by challenging God. In the face of the imminent destruction by God of the people of Sodom, Abraham asks, "Will the judge of the whole world not do justice?" (Gen.18:25). Will innocent people die with the guilty? You too, God, are bound by the laws of justice. Abraham speaks truth to power.

That has always been our task as Jews. Abraham and Sarah are the first immigrants in the world. We are their children. We carry the baggage of difference wherever we travel. Abraham and Sarah were strangers in a strange land. Yet, they welcomed other strangers to their tent. We strive to travel the world via the way of righteousness and justice. There is no righteousness without justice. There is no justice without the righteous teaching that all people are created in the image of God. We still strive as individuals and as a people to be a blessing to all the families of the earth—all of them with the same dream—looking finally to be welcomed home to a promised land filled with righteousness and justice. Later, the Torah makes explicit this call to act justly.

> **Justice, justice** (*tzedek, tzedek*) **you shall pursue in order to be truly alive. (Dt. 16:20)**

The best translation of *tzedek* is social justice. Strangely, the importance of social justice in Judaism has become a matter of controversy in the last decade. There are those who think that social justice is just code for liberal politics. They criticize Jews who make social justice central to their Judaism and who downplay other aspects of Judaism, such as ritual or study. This critique ignores numerous biblical verses and rabbinic teachings about social justice. We know from the story of Abraham that "God's way" is to do *tzedakah u-mishpat*—righteousness and justice. "Justice, justice you shall pursue" is one of the core principles of Judaism.

Judaism's teachings about social justice do not translate simply to public policies that are consistently liberal or conservative. The claims that Judaism's solutions to social issues can only be in consonance with contemporary liberal ideas or in consonance with contemporary conservative ideas are equally mistaken. Part of the greatness of the Jewish tradition is that it contains many opinions and teachings that are often contradictory. Yet, the Torah is clear that we must care for the stranger and feed the poor. Our ongoing challenge is to try to apply that tradition to the contemporary issues we face as individuals and as a society. This chapter will not be a presentation of solutions to homelessness or poverty or any other contemporary issues. Instead, it will present some of the basic concepts embodied in Judaism as ways for each of us to think about how to engage in social justice.

On an action level, the contemporary response to social justice can be broadly categorized as volunteering, donating money, and working for political change. These three categories have Jewish equivalents. The first—volunteering—is called *gemilut hasadim*, acts of lovingkindness or, more simply, *hesed*—kindness, such as working in a soup kitchen or in a literacy program. Yet, acts of lovingkindness also can include interpersonal interactions with family, friends or strangers. Helping my neighbor with a task is not an act of social justice, but it is an act of kindness. As we shall see, kindness is an attribute to be cultivated.

Donating money (*tzedakah*) and working toward systemic change (*tzedek*) share the same Hebrew root. The word *tzedakah* is usually, and misleadingly, translated as charity. The English word (derived from the Latin *caritas*) connotes giving out of compassion to those who are in need. However, the Hebrew suggests that we help those in need not just out of the goodness of our hearts, but because justice requires it. In Judaism, helping others is something we are required to do. It is not voluntary. This is why the term social justice as a translation of *tzedek* may better capture Judaism's attitude than compassion or concern. It is a matter of justice rather than just being nice. Whether or not we are moved by a person's plight, we are called to help them. Underlying this notion of social justice is that everyone deserves access to food, shelter, healthcare and other basic necessities to be able to live a fulfilling existence. Therefore, both these rubrics—giving money and systemic change—are seen as traditional commandments. Or in a more contemporary understanding, we are to bring godliness/goodness to the world by being caring people.

The truth is that these three categories of acts of kindness, donating money and working for social justice overlap. They are all related to being a mensch—a caring human being. The impact of these actions is first and foremost on those in need. Being a mensch means cultivating generosity and caring as ways of being in the world. Ultimately, *tzedek* has an impact on what kind of human being we are.

Who is the focus of the concern for social justice?

In the Torah, we are told that after leaving Egypt, at the first stages of that journey, the Israelites were attacked by Amalek. In Jewish tradition Amalek has come to symbolize all that stands in opposition to the Divine, the holy, and basic goodness. The text tells us that Amalek specifically attacked those stragglers who were too tired to keep up with the Israelite line of march. What makes Amalek particularly reprehensible is its attack on the most vulnerable Israelites. Rabbi Warren Goldstein sets forth a vulnerability principle in his book, *Defending the Human Spirit*. He contrasts the Torah's protection of those who are vulnerable with Western society's attitude toward the poor, which until recent times, often saw the poor as vagrants and beggars who should be imprisoned. He suggests that Judaism stresses a collective responsibility to act on behalf of the most vulnerable members of society. In the Torah, the most frequently mentioned vulnerable class of people is the stranger (*ger*). "You shall not wrong a stranger or oppress him, for you were strangers in the land of Egypt" (Ex. 22:20). There are a number of interpretations regarding who the stranger is in the Bible. A common one is the resident alien, someone who is not a "citizen" but who resides in the land of Israel. The next verse lists two other categories of the vulnerable: "You shall not ill-treat any widow or orphan" (Ex. 22:21). What links these three categories is that none has a traditional family structure that can protect them. While some commentators understand the Torah as being specifically concerned with widows and orphans, other sources see them more as examples of those who are vulnerable (see Mekhilta on Ex. 22:21).

Our ancient experience of being outsiders in Egypt and therefore vulnerable to Pharaoh's oppression reminds us to care for the stranger. No matter how far we have come from the slavery in Egypt, it remains the foundational story of the Jewish people. More than remembering our triumphant Exodus from Egypt, we are to remember how easy it is to oppress those who are seen as strange. The call to take care of the stranger is repeated many times in the Torah text. In one count, the Talmud says it appears thirty-six times in the Torah (Bava Metzia 59b).

Oppression

Throughout human history, it has been common for some people to take advantage of the vulnerable. At its worst, this has led to a dehumanizing of the other. Discrimination and persecution have followed. Too often it has ended in genocide. Yet, oppression does not only occur in its most blatant forms. The rabbinic tradition is concerned with the concept of oppression through words (*o'naat devarim*) as well. This oppression occurs when we stereotype people or make belittling comments about them, such as reminding them of past failures.

This too is prohibited. This concept is expanded to include deception through speech. One interesting example is that we should not pretend to be interested in something for sale that we really have no interest in buying. It is seen as unfairly raising the hopes of a storekeeper and wasting his time. For example, this principle could be applied to the frequent practice of being helped by a salesperson in a store, getting the model number and then going home to order it online at a cheaper price. While capitalism might suggest this is okay, the concept of oppression through words would say otherwise. The Torah acknowledges that oppression can have subtler effects. The Netziv, a 19th-century rabbinic scholar, comments on Dt. 10:19, "You too must befriend the stranger, for you were strangers in the land of Egypt...You were slaves and now live lives of worth. Who knows what potential lies hidden within this stranger!" I think the Netziv recognized the lost achievements of those who are oppressed and thus not given a chance to fully contribute to society.

Areivut: Responsibility

There is a core expression in Jewish tradition that all Jews are responsible for each other (*kol yisrael areivim zeh ba-zeh*). Being part of the Jewish people, we need to take care of each other. We should feel some responsibility even when we know we did not contribute directly to the difficult life that someone is leading. This is even more true if we live in proximity to the person in need.

This principle of responsibility is demonstrated by a strange ritual found in the book of Deuteronomy (chapter 21). The corpse of someone who has been murdered has been found in an uninhabited area and the murderer is unknown. The Torah instructs us to measure the distance from the body to the nearest town. The elders of the town must then perform a ritual that involves breaking the neck of a heifer by a wadi, followed by the following declaration: "Our hands did not shed this blood, nor did our eyes see it done." While the purpose of the specific details of the ritual is not clear, the ritual is meant to remove blood guilt for this murder.

The Talmud wonders: "Why did the elders make that declaration? Did anyone suspect that the elders were actually the murderers? Rather the elders are stating the victim did not come to us in the city and we sent him off without food. Also, we did not see him and let him go on his way unescorted" (*Sotah* 46b).

It is clear that no one is suggesting that the elders are the murderers. It is also clear that the murder occurred in a no-man's land. It appears that the ritual exists because there needs to be some sense of responsibility for the murder. Something has gone wrong in a society when a murder takes place. This may be especially true because there is a sense the murderer is unlikely to be caught. Is it possible the elders bear some responsibility? Perhaps the victim came to the elders in the town and was looking for assistance on his journey. Had the elders refused the assistance (whether for food or an escort), they may have increased the danger of the next stage of his travel. In biblical times travel was dangerous because of robbers and there were plenty of uninhabited areas. The elders therefore must declare that they didn't fail in their duty to take care of the traveler passing through the town.

What, then, is our responsibility to the world around us? What is my responsibility to my neighbors and the people who live in adjacent neighborhoods and in other parts of my city? Can I really be expected to feed everyone who is traveling through my city? Am I responsible to feed everyone who lives in my city? What about all the other problems in my city, such as homelessness or unemployment? *Areivut*/mutual responsibility is a nice principle, but aren't there realistic limits as to what I as an individual can do? Aren't solutions to such problems as crime or homelessness beyond even the capability of society to find?

We can certainly agree that while only some people are guilty of injustices in our society, we all bear some responsibility for participating in a society that allows, ignores, and at times abets the societal problems we have. Rashi, the 11th-century Bible commentator, suggests that in our story, the traveler was not given food. He then resorted to being a highwayman and was killed in an attempted robbery (*Sotah* 45b). This interpretation suggests that society bears some responsibility for poverty, which can lead to the poor resorting to criminal behavior. While this doesn't absolve the criminal of his misdeed, this notion of responsibility is a challenge to our society.

The text teaches we should feel some responsibility and strive to make our society better. Even when we can't fix it all, we would do well to focus on the last word of our text—*le'va-yah*—escort. The Talmud continues: Rabbi Meir would say we compel someone to accompany a traveler—*kofin le'va-yah* from the city, for the reward for accompanying a person is without limit. This is a powerful statement. Accompanying someone on the road isn't just a nice thing to do or something highly recommended. You can be compelled by the authorities to do it. That it is not a choice but an obligation emphasizes the importance the Talmud puts on accompanying a person.

While our society's problems are no longer about the dangers of traveling from one city to another, I want to suggest that this concept of accompanying remains important. We cannot fix all our problems, but we can strive to make people feel accompanied rather than ignored. Those most in need in our society often feel invisible. There is much talk of economic success; yet not everyone partakes of that success. Many people feel their lives don't matter. They feel left behind. What if we could instill in those around us a sense that we all are accompanied?

We all share a neighborhood, a city, and a country.

Interestingly, *le'va-yah*—accompaniment—is the term used for escorting a dead body for burial. Traditionally the dead are seen as the "neediest" because they can't do anything on their own behalf. It is considered an especially great *mitzvah*/good deed to ensure the burial of a corpse, in part because there is no ulterior motive. You can't curry favor with the dead. Lest you think that a body without life is no longer an image of God, the tradition stresses the honor that is due to the body. The Talmud states we blaspheme God when we fail to accompany the body. How could *le'va-yah*—accompaniment—be better actualized in our society? I think the question and concept is a good one to add to our national conversation. Certainly, one place to start is to listen.

There is another Jewish text that makes an important point about the inequities in society. The Talmud (*Bava Batra* 7b) states: "We compel the residents of a courtyard to help build a gatehouse and a door for the gatehouse." In rabbinic times people lived in houses leading off a shared courtyard. The text says that even if a resident was uninterested in having a gatehouse for the courtyard, they can be compelled to contribute to the cost of building a gatehouse. The subsequent discussion makes clear that the gatehouse provided both security and privacy for those living off the courtyard. Both are legitimate concerns of residents and so all the residents can be compelled to contribute.

The Talmud continues by suggesting that a gatehouse is a good thing (which is why someone who is unwilling can be compelled to contribute). Yet, the following story suggests otherwise: There was a pious person with whom Elijah the prophet would regularly visit. Then the pious person built a gatehouse and Elijah stopped visiting him. (Note: In the Bible, the Prophet Elijah goes up to heaven in a fiery chariot. He never died. In Jewish folklore, Elijah reappears in moments of crisis and celebration. For instance, he visits every Seder at Passover. He also visits pious people). If Elijah stopped his visits, this would imply building a gatehouse is a bad thing. The Talmud answers its own question. There is a right way to build a gatehouse and a wrong way. The wrong way prevents the poor from being able to communicate with the people in the courtyard. The pious person had built the gatehouse in such a fashion. This is why Elijah stopped visiting him. The correct way to build the gatehouse provides security and privacy but still allows for the voice of those in need to be heard.

This remarkable text states that the people living in the courtyard have legitimate needs, such as security and privacy. However, there is another factor that must be included in the equation—the rights of the needy. The point here is that we cannot ignore those who need our help. They will become invisible or, in the metaphor used here, the walls between us will prevent us from hearing their cry for help. We can't construct our lives in such a way as to wall ourselves off from the needs of the poor. We don't have to give up our comforts, but we also must make it possible to hear what is going on all around us. All communities need ways for those outside to have access to those inside. This text resonates with the ideas of Bryan Stevenson, the activist attorney, who suggests that we need to be proximate to those struggling in our society in order to be responsive to their needs.

Sodom

Besides Amalek, another example of injustice in the Bible occurs in the city of Sodom. In the midrash, the people of Sodom are described as ingenious in the ways they are cruel and inhospitable to strangers. One midrash tells how they each gave a poor traveler a coin with their name on it, thereby appearing to be generous to the traveler. However, they then refused to sell the traveler any food. When the traveler died from starvation, each "generous" citizen took their coin back (*Sanhedrin* 109b).

What made the people of Sodom exemplars of evil was their underlying attitude, as described in another midrash. The inhabitants of Sodom said, "We live in peace and plenty—food can be got from our land, gold and silver can be mined from our land. What need have we to look after wayfarers, who come to us only to deprive us? Come, let us see to it that the duty of entertaining travelers be forgotten in our land" (Numbers Rabbah 9:24). It was not scarcity of resources that pushed the inhabitants to discourage travelers. It was greed.

The real evil of Sodom was that this uncaring attitude toward the needy traveler was ensconced in law. It wasn't just that a lack of generosity was encouraged in Sodom. Their persecution of travelers wasn't a momentary passion. In Sodom, it was against the law to help the stranger; anyone caught helping them was put to death (See Malbim, 19th-century commentator, on Gen 19:2). Society itself had been corrupted, not just some individuals. This is why God condemned the city to destruction.

The rabbis had a term for acting like the inhabitants of Sodom—*midat s'dom*. A classic source about acting in the manner of Sodom can be found in *Ethics of our Ancestors* (*Pirkei Avot* 5:12):

> There are four character traits among people.
> Some say:
> Mine is mine and yours is yours—this is the trait of the average.
> Others say: This trait is characteristic of Sodom.
> Mine is yours and yours is mine—this is the trait of an ignoramus.

Mine is yours and yours is yours—this is the trait of the saintly.
Yours is mine and mine is mine—this is the trait of the wicked.

The commentators discuss why the first category might be seen as similar to the attitude of the people of Sodom. It does seem like average people are neither generous nor miserly. Is it really wrong to think that what is yours is yours?

The Talmud discusses a number of cases that define what it means to act like the people of Sodom. In one case, there is a family with two brothers, one of whom had bought a parcel of land adjacent to his father's property (*Bava Batra* 12b). When their father died, that brother said to his sibling: When our father's estate is divided in equal parts, please assign me the land adjacent to my property. The other brother refused to do so. This refusal was considered acting like the people of Sodom. Why? Because all the parcels of land of their father's estate were of equal value. For obvious reasons, one brother wanted the land to abut his existing property. It was a convenience to him with no loss to his brother. *Midat s'dom* is being ungenerous for no justifiable reason. It is just being spiteful and mean. Remarkably, the Talmud states that we compel (*kofin*) the brother to give him the parcel that abuts his land to prevent people from acting like the people of Sodom. Once again, we see an attitude or action that is simply not the ideal way to behave. The tradition states we sometimes need to compel people to act in generous ways.

This may help us understand our original text. While it is legally correct that the things I own are mine and your things are yours, when that attitude limits my concern only to my property and well-being, we have a problem. This is particularly true when being generous or helpful comes at no cost to yourself.

Being a mensch

More broadly, I think this suggests that being legally right isn't the goal. Being right isn't enough if it forgoes generosity or compassion. In today's society there is a great deal of emphasis on people's rights, but we need to pay attention to obligations as well. What must we do for individuals in need and for the society as a whole? The people of Sodom wanted to keep the wealth they had legitimately earned. Yet, they also wanted to prevent anyone from having any access to those resources. We can imagine them saying, *Why can't these people work their way up as we did?* Yet they had restructured their society in a way that prevented anyone new from having the opportunities and access they had. Making that discrimination legal ensured that the barrier was insurmountable. At times, enforcing the strict letter of the law without concern for its impact on the lives of others is not justice but injustice. The Talmud says that the reason the Second Temple in Jerusalem was destroyed by God was as a punishment for the focus solely on that which was legal (*Bava Metzia* 30b):

> Rabbi Yohanan says: Jerusalem was destroyed only for the fact that they adjudicated cases on the basis of Torah law in the city. The Talmud asks: Rather, what else should they have done? Should they rather have adjudicated cases on the basis of arbitrary decisions? Rather, say: That they established their rulings on the basis of Torah law and did not go beyond the letter of the law.

This striking text suggests that following the law is not enough. It could be that the law had been twisted to benefit one group of people at the expense of another, as in the case of the people of Sodom. Perhaps the courts in Jerusalem ignored extenuating circumstances and other principles, which suggests that real justice is not served by slavishly following the law.

Legal scholars wrestle with the tension between law and equity or, more simply, between law and justice. They recognize the challenge of laws that need to apply generally to everyone and every situation. They also know that this can lead to an outcome that, in specific circumstances, is unjust. This tension is reflected in a Talmudic debate on the meaning of the verse: "you will be doing what is good and right in the sight of the Lord your God" (Dt. 12:28). The opinion of Rabbi Akiva is that "good" is the law but "right" is justice, which is an even higher standard than "good" (Tosefta Shekalim 2:2). This suggests that we must strive for justice by taking into account the circumstances of each person. While most rabbinic sources present the principle of going beyond the letter of the law as motivated by generosity and piety, over time it became a legal principle that can be applied in Jewish law. This challenges us to appreciate that following the law doesn't always result in justice. Nor does it mean that having a legal right allows us to ignore the inequalities that are the legacy of our society's past.

The tradition also tries to shape our underlying attitudes by encouraging generosity, especially when it doesn't come at our expense. Sodom is an example of a society corrupted by its attitude. The tradition strongly discourages limiting your concern for others. Similarly, when it comes to accompanying a traveler or discouraging meanness, the tradition doesn't just suggest "best practices." Instead, it uses the language of *kofin*—coercion to demand behavior or attitudes that can serve as the foundation for a just society.

We saw that Ramban, a 13th-century Bible commentator, regarded the commandment "Do what is right and good" as an overarching commandment about how to act in the world. In that commentary, he suggests that the commandment also teaches us to go beyond the letter of the law (*lifnim me-shurat ha-din*). Judaism was never intended to be only a system of commandments and laws. The purpose of Judaism is to encourage us to act with justice and compassion. The law isn't the ultimate goal—being a mensch is. The law is the minimum standard—going beyond the letter of the law is meant to be the practice.

Expanding the circle of concern beyond Jews

I have been presenting texts and values from the Jewish tradition that can help shape our response to the social inequities of our time. There is, however, an important historical value in the Jewish tradition that needs to be rejected. Often such concepts as *areivut*—responsibility—were understood to apply only to other Jews. However, there are statements found in rabbinic literature advocating our responsibility to take care of needy people who weren't Jewish. The reason given was *darkhei shalom*—the ways of peace, or *tikkun olam*—repair of the world (*Gittin* 61a). While interpreted in different ways, the most common understanding is that we should take care of neighbors who are not Jewish because it makes for good relations with them. It is done for the sake of expediency rather than on moral grounds. Basically, the biblical verses of Lev. 19 that talk of loving or taking care of your neighbor were understood by the majority of traditional commentators to refer to your kin—that is, fellow Jews. We can seek to justify such interpretations in pre-modern times when universalism was a non-existent value and when the Jewish people too often suffered from antisemitism. However, it is past time to discard such limiting notions. These notions are contradicted by the book of Genesis, where in chapter one we are told that humans are created by God in God's image—all humans, not just Jews.

Similarly, the basic thrust of Jewish mystical and Hasidic teachings is about the divine sparks that are found in everything that exists in the world. If our task is to redeem those sparks and restore the Godhead (Lurianic kabbalah) or find the divine light in everything (Hasidism), who is going to redeem those sparks in all the many places in the world where there are no Jews? We remain a tiny minority in a vast world. The traditional mystical understanding that only Jews can redeem the sparks is counterintuitive to the underlying Kabbalistic myth that is universal in the scope of its vision of redemption.

Finally, Judaism is about a particularistic experience within a universal context. Over and over again, the Torah tells us we should take care of the stranger because we were strangers in the land of Egypt. Do we really think the text is telling us to be friendly to Jewish "strangers"? The opposite is true—specifically, we are to help those who are not "us." The whole point of these commandments is to be concerned for those who are marginalized because it is so easy to distort our tradition (or any tradition) to mean that we only take care of our own. Nowhere is the tradition clearer in its understanding of the balance between the particular and the universal than in the area of social justice. Our concern is for all of those who are in need, personified by the stranger.

Tikkun olam

The Hebrew phrase for repairing the world is *tikkun olam*. It has had a number of meanings in the Jewish tradition over the centuries, but in the modern period, it has come to mean engaging in social justice in order to fix the wrongs of the world. In fact, the term ought to be used specifically for political action to fix the wrongs of our society or in the world. It is important to distinguish between political action, giving money (*tzedakah*) and acts of kindness (*hesed*). While we need to engage in all three aspects of social justice, systemic change/political action challenges us the most. Why? Because it is not always clear what the solution is. Reasonable people can disagree. People with very different notions of the role of government will certainly disagree about what needs to be done. Solutions to societal problems will be found at the expense of one group of people in favor of another (e.g., landlords and tenants). Political action is often controversial. It also requires a lot of work to bring about change to the status quo. Donating money or time is simpler and often rests on an individual decision.

Tzedakah: Charity

As we have seen, honoring all human beings (*kavod ha-beriyot*) is a major principle underlying the pursuit of social justice—*tzedek*. It applies to the act of *tzedakah* as well. *Tzedakah* refers to giving money to help those in need, either directly to the poor or through an organization that helps the poor. This concern for people in need includes paying attention to their dignity in addition to offering financial support. Maimonides, the 12th-century philosopher and rabbinic scholar, created a hierarchy for giving support to those in need. Giving generously with a gracious manner while trying not to humiliate the recipient is near the top of the list. He recognized that it is not only how much you give, but how you give that is important. He understood that the process of giving affects the self-worth of a person in need. Giving reluctantly is demeaning to the recipient. Even when giving graciously and generously, recipients are still reminded that they are needy while the giver has money to give. Therefore, Maimonides said that the best way to give charity is a generous gift that is given anonymously, where neither the recipient nor the giver knows who the other is. He realized that even if the giver doesn't know who the needy person is, if the recipient knows who the benefactor is, it still can be awkward for the recipient. Thus, respect for the person in need is a crucial aspect of providing assistance.

Maimonides believed that the best way to respond to those in need is to help them become financially self-sufficient so that they no longer need charity. To help a person get a job is the highest form of *tzedakah*. Much has been written about Maimonides and Jewish approaches to *tzedakah*/charity, including the chapter on *gemilut hesed*/lovingkindness in my book: *A Book of Life: Embracing Judaism as a Spiritual Practice*. I talk there about the challenges that those of us who live in cities face when confronted with people who ask for money on the street. Living in cities has seemingly exacerbated the problem of poverty. Walking down a street and being stopped by a number of people asking for money can feel overwhelming. Complex problems like homelessness can leave us with a sense that there is nothing we as individuals can do. These are challenging issues made more difficult by the size of the population of modern cities. Yet, the problem of people in need has been part of human history from its beginnings. The rabbis talk about the problem of how to tell whether a beggar is genuine or a fake.

> Two scholars on their way to the bath house pass a person who asks them for money. They reply we will give you money on the way out. When they exit the bathhouse, they find the person has died. The scholars say since we failed to take care of him while he was alive, we will take care of him in death by preparing his body for burial. They discover the corpse had a bag with lots of money in it. They express relief that there are fake beggars because otherwise there would be no excuse for refusing to give to every person who asks for money. (Leviticus Rabbah 34:10)

There are no simple solutions to these challenges. My Manhattan friends have different ways of dealing with people who ask for money on the street. Some will give only to the same people regularly. Some will give to everybody on Fridays before Shabbat. Some will set aside a certain amount of money and give it until the money runs out. Making eye contact goes to the heart of how you are giving. All these variations are ways to deal with the overwhelming needs in many cities.

Hesed: Acts of kindness

> Our masters taught: Lovingkindness is greater than charity in three ways. Charity is done with one's money, while lovingkindness may be done with one's money or with one's person.

Charity is given only to the poor, while lovingkindness may be
given both to the poor and to the rich. Charity is given only
to the living, while lovingkindness may be shown to both the
living and the dead. (Sukkot 49b)

This final category, kindness, does not contain the word *tzedek*—justice. If
giving money to the poor is seen as required, kindness is seen as voluntary. Yet,
the text above suggests that kindness is greater than *tzedakah*. Why? Because ultimately it is even holier to act out of lovingkindness, to go beyond what is required
by justice. To act out of lovingkindness is to empathize with other people and to
want to help them or ease their burdens, even if simple justice would not require
it. To act out of lovingkindness is to understand we are all lost in a broken world,
yet together we can improve the journey of life. *Gemilut hesed* means to care even
when it is "not deserved." It also means to understand that we all need acts of
lovingkindness to be done for us, regardless of our economic status.

The Hafetz Hayyim (1839-1933) was a rabbinic scholar who wrote a small
book entitled *Ahavat Chesed*—love of kindness. This title is from a verse in Micah
(6:8): "God has told you what is good [*tov*] and what God asks of you: to act justly
and to love kindness and to walk humbly with your God" (Micah 6:8).

The Hafetz Hayyim wonders why the verse doesn't say either "act justly and
kindly" or "love justice and kindness." Why vary the verb? He notes that while
the prophet says we are obligated to act justly, we must cultivate kindness so that
that it becomes second nature. The Hafetz Hayyim suggests that too often we feel
coerced and respond reluctantly to a request, whether it is from a person who asks
for money on the street or a friend who needs help. Instead, you should strive to
act kindly with a willing heart. There is a big difference between something you
do reluctantly and that which you do with a full heart. The Hafetz Hayyim uses
the analogy of a parent with a child. It is not duty but love that motivates a parent's
giving to a child. A parent happily gives even when the child hasn't asked. The
Hafetz Hayyim is suggesting that we anticipate the needs of others, particularly
of people we know.

These acts of kindness can include simply being present with the person.
Maimonides suggests that acting in Godly ways means that we should celebrate
with people at moments of joy and comfort them at times of sorrow. The opportunities for acts of kindness are numerous each day. We just need to be thoughtful
about who is before us and what they need.

Creating a money practice/tzedek practice

The Hafetz Hayyim said that the amount of wealth you possess beyond what you need to live is a trust deposited with you by God to administer on behalf of the needy. This notion is both challenging and inspiring. He is not preaching a life of asceticism. We are supposed to enjoy the benefits of our labor just as we should appreciate the beauty of this world. Yet we are never to forget our responsibility to continue God's creation by improving the world in which we live.

A social justice practice starts with the broad principles laid out in this chapter and then concretizes them in each area: 1) political action/systemic change (*tikkun olam*); 2) poverty relief (*tzedakah*); 3) acts of kindness (*hesed*). We have seen that broadly the Torah calls upon us to pursue social justice, to care for those on the margins of society, especially the stranger, and to provide relief to the poor. How we should actually do this is, for the most part, not spelled out.

"If your kinsman, being in straits...do not exact from him...interest" (Lev. 25:35-36). The rabbis interpret these verses to mean that you need to help out those who are in dire straits. One way to do this is to lend a person money without charging interest. The notion that in many circumstances it was forbidden to make money by lending money was challenged in the modern period with the rise of a money economy. Laws have been created in effect to indirectly charge interest. However, the notion of lending money to those in need without interest is still around, particularly in traditional communities. These interest-free loan funds are often known as *gemilut hesed* funds (deeds of lovingkindness funds or more simply by the acronym GMaH). In the recent Israeli TV series *Shtisl*, the main character started his own GMaH to lend out electric heaters to people. Often these funds will focus on lending objects instead of money, like extra dishes for a celebration. In his book, the Hafetz Hayyim encourages the establishment of such funds. In fact, he says that everyone should create their own interest-free loan fund in addition to giving money to the needy. According to tradition, each person is supposed to give 10% of their income away to those in need. The Hafetz Hayyim says that a third of that money should be set aside to create an interest-free free loan fund. He extolls the importance of such funds. He suggests that some needy people might be embarrassed to take "charity" dollars but would feel differently about a loan. Most importantly, the loan fund has the potential to create systemic change. Whether as a bridge loan over troubled financial waters or money to start a business, the loan could enable a person to escape the cycle of financial insecurity.

I was struck by the Hafetz Hayyim's notion that we should each have an interest-free loan fund. I had only known of communal examples of such funds. As a congregational rabbi I had a discretionary account that I occasionally used for congregants in need—sometimes as a loan, more often as an outright gift. Frankly, that experience convinced me that the Hafetz Hayyim's idea of a personal loan fund was too difficult for most people. It requires administration, finding a person or persons who could benefit from such a loan, and making judgements about the appropriate amount to loan. On the other hand, these interest-free loan funds evoke the idea of microcredit. In the last decades, there has been a tremendous growth in small lending in developing countries. Many people don't have access to a regular bank loan, but small loans could enable someone to start a business and begin to escape poverty. Jonathan Morduch and Rachel Schneider write about the kinds of people who can benefit from small loans in their book *Financial Diaries*. There are millions of people in the U.S. who work in jobs that should enable them and their families to live modest lives but there is no backup for a sudden expense like a car repair or a medical emergency. For some, the dilemma is that their income comes in unevenly. While their annual income is sufficient, there are months when their income is significantly lower and yet fixed costs like rent stay the same and are due each month. For such families this means not only going without meals in the lean months, but worrying all the time about whether they will make it to the end of the month. There are also other unseen costs. There is the amount of time they have to spend juggling their cash to make it last rather than spending time with their children or even being able to pick up an odd job to supplement their income. For people like this, an interest-free loan is a lifesaver. It is also an alternative to what should be a solution of last resort—payday loans at very high interest rates which are difficult to ever repay.

Was there a different way to make the Hafetz Hayyim's vision a reality? The Hebrew Free Loan Society of New York City makes exactly the kinds of loans that the Hafetz Hayyim had in mind—bridge loans and starting-new-business loans. Their model is to lend the money interest-free, but they do require each borrower to ask two people they know to guarantee the loan. They have an extraordinarily high rate of loan repayment. They also have the experience and the staff to help choose loan recipients and to oversee them, including their monthly repayment.

The truth is, it is very hard to effect systemic social justice change; but these free loan funds can have a substantial impact on a family's financial situation. It is, after all, a way to achieve Maimonides' highest form of tzedakah—help someone to earn a living. An average loan from New York's Hebrew Free Loan Fund is $7,500. Some people donate that amount all at once. This is a charity contribution—you don't get the money back. It also means that your one-time gift will be loaned over and over again as each borrower pays back the loan. In the course of 40 years (a generation in the Torah), your gift of $7,500 will be, in effect, a gift of $150,000 and make a difference in the lives of 20 families. You will have created a free loan that is administered by a Hebrew Free Loan society. Before I retired, our synagogue created the SAJ Hebrew Free Loan Fund. We were able to raise $130,000 in small and large gifts for the fund, which we hope will be a model to other Jewish institutions.

While you will not know the recipient of your donation—and in fact your money is mixed in with all the other donations to Hebrew Free Loan—your contribution is helping people in significant ways. If you can't give the average loan in a one-time gift, you could donate each year until you have given that amount. The Hafetz Hayyim says you give until you create the fund and then you can stop and redirect your annual giving to tzedakah/charity. Obviously, any money given to Hebrew Free Loan will be used toward their loans. There are over 40 Hebrew Free Loan funds in North America. You can find the one nearest to you by searching online for *International Association of Hebrew Free Loans*.

Giving circles enable people to pool their money and decide as a group which organizations to support. This is both an opportunity to do research and reflect on your *tzedakah* priorities, as well as a way to increase the potential impact of your giving by pooling the financial resources of a number of people. One such organization in the Jewish community is Amplifier (amplifiergiving.org).

A social justice practice can also be shaped around time. Many Americans will sit down in December before the end of the tax year and decide which charitable organizations they want to support. You could decide that you want to do this quarterly rather than waiting for the end of the year. The Hafetz Hayyim says it is better to give 100 one-dollar donations than a single donation of 100 dollars because you then become accustomed to giving as a practice. Some people put all their change in a *pushka*—*tzedakah* box—Friday afternoon before Shabbat. This becomes part of the preparation for Shabbat.

The holiday cycle is another way Judaism seeks to shape our lives and offers us new ways to think about social justice. The three pilgrimage festivals could be used as an organized way to focus on the three types of social justice. With its themes of liberation, Passover can be a time to focus on systemic change. The story of the Exodus demonstrates that society can change and that even the most oppressed can go free. As a week-long holiday, there is more time to take on one issue of change. The holiday of Shavuot can be connected with poverty relief. The book of Ruth, read on Shavuot in the synagogue, describes an episode where Ruth, out of desperate need, goes to a field to gather some leftover wheat after the harvest. We celebrate Sukkot by inviting guests into the sukkah, a temporary structure that enables us to focus on ways to be more hospitable in the new year. As a week-long holiday, Sukkot also provides more time to engage in acts of kindness related to homelessness or to the environment. (See Sukkot chapter for specific suggestions).

Torah of kosher money

The Jewish tradition asks us to consider what our relationship should be to the things of this world—to our bodies, to food, and to relationships. Our enjoyment of life is linked to a commitment to help those in need. In ancient agricultural societies, most people had little money. The Torah addresses such poverty by instructing farmers to leave behind some of their harvest for the poor to gather. Dropped or forgotten sheaves were left for the poor. The corners of the fields were not harvested, but rather considered a portion for the poor. Are there any equivalents in the money economy in which we live? The biblical tithe has become the model for giving 10% to *tzedakah*. Is there a broader thinking about money that is now required? We have very detailed laws about which foods we can eat and which foods should not be eaten together. Has there been less thought about money because, until relatively recently, it was not something that many people had in any great quantity? On the surface, a dollar is like any other dollar. Are there different types of money that we should treat differently?

For instance, I wondered whether "found" money is analogous to the forgotten wheat of biblical times. The found money is not only the $20 bill you see lying on the street or money you discover in a drawer. It could be money that you weren't counting on, like an unexpected refund from the IRS or money from a class action suit against a company. A different category of money is passively earned money. Such money could include the interest you earn on a bank account or in the stock market. After all, unless you are actively buying and selling stocks yourself, you are not working to make the money that your investments are earning. While this is certainly not found money, should you give more of that away than the money you earn from your job by dint of your hard work? If you are like me, you ignore that money when you calculate what you earn a year. You become conscious of it when you are preparing your taxes. I am not suggesting that you should give it all away. I am suggesting that in thinking about what our responsibility is to others less fortunate, we could be giving away passively earned money at a higher rate than money we earn from our work. Obviously, this will differ depending on your own economic circumstances. Now that I have retired, passively earned income has become more necessary to pay my bills. A related but a somewhat different category is if you are lucky enough to invest in a stock that does unbelievably well. Wouldn't it be "kosher" to see a self-imposed "windfall tax" as an appropriate way to share your good fortune?

Having money is a responsibility. The Hafetz Hayyim suggests figuring out how much money you need to live on and then giving the rest away. I think that most people would find that notion too extreme, but we ought to think about our attitudes toward money and its use when we are constructing our Jewish lives.

Your perspective will vary greatly whether you are struggling financially or have significant discretionary financial resources. Each of us feels differently regarding how much money we need. Beyond need, the next category is what we like to have. We could agree that food and shelter are necessary, while nicer furniture or an extra room are things we might want, beyond what we need. In general, Judaism encourages us to partake of the bounties of life rather than renounce all worldly things. Since the world is the creation of God, it is appropriate to express gratitude to God by enjoying the things in it, whether made by nature (God) or by humans. That enjoyment should be balanced with an ongoing commitment to help those in need.

What about a second home, a piece of art, or a collection of objects? None of these are necessary, but Judaism sees them as part of the blessings of this world to be enjoyed. *Is this object worth it?* is a question we ask ourselves all the time. Each of us must answer that question for ourselves. Yet, we should answer with an awareness that we share this planet with all humans and it is our responsibility to help improve their lives. Perhaps when you feel that you are really splurging to buy a particular item, you may consider donating an extra amount to charity. Consider it a luxury tax. While I know I don't need this item, I believe I will get a great deal of pleasure from having it. At the same time, I can also make a contribution in addition to my regular *tzedakah*/charity donations so that others may have an easier life.

In the past, ethical issues related to money had to do with being honest in business. Now that we live in a money economy, many of us need to think about what we do with the money we have earned. Money can be used in a mostly neutral way, by depositing it in a bank account where it can earn interest. We can deposit our money in a bank that has a policy of investing a specific percentage of its money in local non-profits. Recently, the practice of socially responsible investing has raised important questions. Do you want to buy stocks in companies that sell products that from your point of view are ethically problematic? For instance, some people don't want to own stocks in companies that sell tobacco. What about the company that has a reputation of not treating its employees well, or uses child labor in a foreign country to make its clothing? This can be complicated; a conglomerate may make many fine things but also have one subsidiary that does something you find morally objectionable. Socially responsible investment funds have recently been established to help screen out certain categories of companies. There is a form of investment known as an ETF (exchange-traded fund) that is like an index fund, but also screens for a variety of social issues.

There is also impact investing, which enables you to invest in companies that have a positive impact on societal issues. This goes beyond avoiding investing in morally problematic companies; impact investing allows you to use your money to do good in the world even as you expect a return on your investment.

Certified B corporations balance purpose and profit. While most public-ly-held corporations are legally required to focus on profits and dividends to shareholders, B corporations are legally required to consider the impact of their decisions on their workers, community, and environment. There can be a trade-off between the social impact and the return on your investment, but all of these companies are in the business of making money.

In our world, how we use our money makes a difference. Each of us will decide how our practice with money will reflect that understanding, but an aware-ness of its value is an important part of religious life.

The Maharal, a 16th-century rabbinic scholar, taught in his book *The Path of Lovingkindness* (*Netiv Gemilut Hasadim*) that you should not act out of a sense of being commanded, but because you want to be compassionate. It is in your very essence (*oseh hesed mei-atzmo*) to act in that way. There is an interesting progression in the tradition about social justice. First, we should understand that *tzedakah* is not charity. It is an obligation. Our actions should not be limited to giving money to those in need. We must also work for a just society, which means working for systemic change. But even those acts of justice on behalf of the vulnerable in society are not enough. We must also act with kindness—not only to those in need, but to everyone—since all humans need a helping hand. We must go beyond the letter of the law, especially when it is at no cost to our-selves. It ultimately is about cultivating a generosity of spirit, in order to be the opposite of the people of Sodom. It is to love kindness. We begin with a sense of justice, but our goal is to move beyond justice to act out of kindness. It is to imitate God by "building a world through lovingkindness" as in the verse Ps. 89:3. For the Maharal, this is the essence of Torah; to be a student of Torah is to make kindness second nature.

Justice of peace

We began this chapter with the verse: Justice, justice (*tzedek, tzedek*) you shall pursue in order to be truly alive. The Talmud posits: "It is written in one verse: In justice you shall judge your neighbor (Lev. 19:15). It is written in another verse: Justice, justice you shall pursue (Dt. 16:20)" (*Sanhedrin* 32b). The Talmud won-ders why the word *justice* is repeated in the second verse. It implies that judging your neighbor with justice is inadequate.

The Talmud replies that the first time the word justice is used it means judge-ment and law, but the second time it means compromise. The Talmud then gives examples of a conflict where neither party has more of a claim than the other (such as a question of the right of way at a crossroads). The resolution is to arrive at a compromise. We live in a society that is very divided and where many see compromise as a dirty word. I suggest we apply this text to social justice issues. Such issues often have competing claims (consider the debate over immigration, for instance). This text suggests that compromise does not betray our principles, but potentially creates a way to move forward that both sides can feel is progress. This is known as the justice of peace (*mishpat shalom*) rather than justice imposed by one side on another. Certainly, there are issues that do not lend themselves to compromise, but there are many times where compromise might be a process that benefits everyone. After all, peace—real peace—is the ultimate goal of justice.

Passover:
Reexperiencing slavery and freedom

The Passover Seder is not just a time to remember our past, but to experience the story as though it happened to us. By eating bitter herbs and dipping vegetables into salt water (thereby tasting our tears), we experience the slavery with our mouths. We also drink wine to taste the sweetness and joy of freedom. Yet, the story of freedom is not simple. The primary symbolic food of the Seder is matzah, unleavened bread. It is both the bread of affliction that the Israelites ate as slaves in Egypt and the bread they took with them as they hurriedly left Egypt. Leaving in the middle of the night, they had no time to let their dough rise, and so matzah also became the bread of liberation. Matzah represents the tension underlying the Seder. We are free, and yet we begin the Seder by reciting the words, "This year we are slaves; next year we will be free." Since the Exodus, we know that freedom is a possibility. Our fates are not inexorable. It is also true that slavery isn't only physical; we can also be enslaved to the pharaohs of our minds that tell us that change is a delusion. Of course, there are still many people whose freedom is restricted by oppressive governments, by prejudice, or by their economic circumstances.

Seder practice

While still one of the most widely observed Jewish traditions, the Seder's effectiveness in focusing us on the issues of freedom is hampered by a lengthy traditional text in the *Haggadah*, which does not tell the story of the Exodus in a straightforward manner. Where once the Four Questions were mere examples of what we might ask, they have become a required performance by the youngest child reciting the same questions each year.

The Seder can be an opportunity to reflect upon how we are free, how we are held back, or how we hold ourselves back. One major challenge is that many Seders have competing constituencies present, such as small children and adults, or people who see the Seder as a time for family or friends to gather—a Jewish Thanksgiving—and people who want to discuss freedom and contemporary political issues.

One common challenge is easy to address: When do we eat? At our Seder, we treat the dipping of the vegetables (*karpas*) as crudité. We put out enough vegetables and dips to assuage people's hunger. Scholars suggest that the Seder is modeled after the Greek symposia where discussions of issues took place over food.

With some planning, you can meet the needs of everyone at your table. It may require focusing on young children early on in the evening and only later having a more serious discussion with adults. At the same time, the authors of the *Haggadah* clearly understood that it is essential for the next generation to feel they are a part of the Jewish story. Children became engaged when asking the Four Questions and hiding the afikomen. The 20th-century German Jewish philosopher Franz Rosenzweig saw the children's role as providing an insight into the nature of freedom.

> The freedom of this meal at which all are equally free is expressed in a number of rites, which distinguish this night from all other nights. This particular freedom expresses itself in the fact that the youngest child is the one to speak, and that what the father says at the table is adapted to the child's personality and degree of maturity. In contrast to all instruction which is necessarily autocratic and never on the basis of equality, the sign of true and free social intercourse is this, that the one who stands—relatively speaking—nearest the periphery of the circle give the cue for the level on which the conversation is to be conducted. For this conversation must include everyone. ... The freedom of a society is always the freedom of everyone who belongs to it.

Here are some issues you might want to raise with guests at the Seder:

1) Is matzah the symbol of slavery or freedom? Why do we say we are slaves, when we clearly are not? Does that undercut the meaning of the Exodus? What could slavery mean today?

2) The story of the Israelites on their way to the Promised Land is not a triumphant march to freedom. Instead, the Israelites not only complain constantly along the way; they repeatedly express a wish to return to Egypt. Why is it so hard to feel grateful for the freedom we have?

3) "In every generation a person should see themselves as if they left Egypt." What does that line from the *Haggadah* mean?

3) The four children: Do we want to call any child wicked? What do they say that is so bad? Who is the simple child and who is the one who doesn't know how to ask?

4) Would it really have been *dayyenu* (enough) if we left Egypt and didn't receive the Torah?

5) Does one people's liberation always have to come at the expense of another people (the Egyptians)?

All of these questions raise issues about the nature of freedom. There may be other texts, such as Roosevelt's Four Freedoms, that can serve as a rich resource for a discussion on the nature of freedom. The Seder can be both a gathering of family and friends and also a time to focus on the themes of oppression and freedom in the biblical story and in today's world.

Social justice practice for the week of Passover

Since Pesach is a week-long holiday, it is a good time to review your social justice practice over the past year. What causes have you supported politically and/or financially? Are there new causes to take up or old ones to put aside? There is a traditional concept of devotion called *mesirat nefesh*. At its extreme, it means giving up your life, but more commonly it means devoting yourself to something that you feel is very important. While you may feel committed to a number of social justice causes, is there one that you want to make a priority for the coming year in an attempt to make an impact? With its themes of freedom and concern for the stranger, Pesach is an appropriate time to set such a goal.

We should use both the Seder and the week of Passover to engage in the essential theme of freedom—both for ourselves and our world. The following is a social justice kavanah/intention to be recited each day of Passover to aid us in that process. It is composed of biblical verses and quotations from the Haggadah with new liturgy in italics.

> I behold you in acts of justice when done with awareness I am filled with Your vision. (Ps.17:15)

> Open to me the gates of justice, I will enter them expressing God's name. This is the gateway to God; the righteous will engage through it. (Ps. 118:19-20)

Thus, God says: Let not the wise glory in their wisdom; let not the powerful glory in their strength; let not the wealthy glory in their financial success. But only in this should they glory: In their knowledge and understanding of Me. For I, God, act with lovingkindness and justice and equity in this world; For these I desire. (Jer. 9:22-23)

Don't place your trust in illusions saying, "The Temple of God, the Temple of God, the Temple of God are these." No, only by mending your ways and deeds wholeheartedly, only if you bring justice between one person and another. Only if you do not oppress the stranger, the orphan and the widow... (Jer. 7:4-6).

Through justice will you be established, and kept far from oppression; you shall have no fear... (Is. 54:14)

For the work of justice shall be peace, and the effect of justice, calm and confidence forever. (Is. 32:17).

Ani ve-lo malakh

I, not a perfect being

Ani ve-lo saraf

I, not one consumed with fury at the oppressors

Ani ve-lo shaliah

I myself, not someone acting on my behalf

Ani hu/hi ve-lo aheir

For I am the one to fight for redemption, there is no other

She-ani aheir

For I am other!

For I was a stranger in the land of Egypt and went out with the determination and strength to fight for freedom and with an outstretched arm to help lift up those that are oppressed.

Therefore, we should work, speak out, strive, and fight for the redemption of all the peoples of the world, as it is written: "You shall not oppress the stranger, for you know the feelings of the stranger, having yourself been strangers in the land of Egypt" (Ex. 23:9). *Then the power of Your rule will repair the world, and all the creatures of flesh will call on Your name, as it is written:* "A time is coming—declares my Eternal God—when I will send a famine upon the land: not a hunger for bread or a thirst for water, but for hearing the words of the Eternal One. ... So, let justice well up like water, righteousness like an unfailing stream." (Amos 8:11, 5:24)

For I am my fellow's keeper who awakens myself with them to oppression, who imagines with them dreams of a different world, who gives voice with them against the silence suppressing unpleasant truths, who frees myself with them from a society that has unequal opportunities, who joins hands with them to ensure no one falls behind, who encourages all of us weary of the struggle.

Happy are those who act justly, who do what is right in every hour. (Ps. 106:3)

Justice, justice you shall pursue in order to be truly alive. (Deut. 16:20)

Seeking personal freedom

Freedom is not just about social justice. It is also about living our individual lives as free as possible. It is not a one-time achievement. As we see from the story of the Exodus, as soon as the Israelites leave Egypt, they yearn to return. How can we make ourselves freer?

A place to start is understanding the difference between the process of *teshuvah*/repentance and the process of seeking freedom. *Teshuvah* involves a recognition that you have done something wrong. It requires a healing or mending of the past as a way to move on to a better tomorrow. Freedom involves breaking out of long-established patterns of our lives. You may not have done anything wrong. You might simply be afraid of taking on something you have never done before, or of being seen as foolish. You may be haunted by a difficult moment in your past.

An event in the life of Moses illustrates this point. The first time Moses draws water from a rock in the desert, he strikes the rock with his staff. The second time, God instructs Moses to speak to the rock to draw the water; Moses strikes the rock instead. What was once the correct response is now wrong, but Moses is locked into an automatic response. Moses resorts to the past, not understanding that this is a different situation.

How often do past challenging experiences trigger a response that is more about the past than the present? How often do we hear in the voice of a person we are talking with, the long-ago voice of a parent, lover, or family member? As long as we are not responding to the actual moment, we are not free from past patterns. We are chained to an automatic and often unwise response.

Why are we not supposed to eat bread on Passover? Fifty-one weeks a year it is perfectly okay to eat bread, but for one week it is strictly forbidden. Is there something wrong about bread? Is it, as some commentators suggest, that leavened bread is a metaphor for being puffed up about ourselves? I think there is nothing wrong with bread, but the prohibition on Passover invites us to rethink our relationship to food, a major aspect of our patterned life. What are the patterns of our eating that have become routine, and with which patterns do we struggle?

What are the other patterns in our behavior that keep us from responding freely to what is happening? On Passover, we remember that once upon a time we were strangers feeling vulnerable and insecure in Egypt and that truth still lingers with us. Passover offers the opportunity to leave the constrictions of Egypt behind, carrying with us the matzah of freedom.

More about food

Pesach asks us to focus on what we eat. During the week, we may rush through a meal because we are busy. We might eat at our desk while we check emails. Even if we go out for lunch, how often is it a business lunch? We don't often pay attention to the act of eating. While there may be some occasions for a leisurely meal during the week or on Shabbat, Pesach can be a time to pay attention to our eating. This would not just involve observing the restrictions on bread during the holiday. It could mean setting aside time for an "eating meditation," which involves slowly chewing on our food. Try eating a raisin with intention. You feel the texture of the raisin, put it in your mouth, and take a first bite. (I am not suggesting that you try this during the Seder because your other guests will start pelting you with matzah balls for eating so slowly.) The intermediate days of Pesach offer an opportunity for an eating meditation experience. It needn't be a slow eating of a raisin. You could eat a regular meal, but take the time to slowly eat your food. It doesn't have to be at an exaggeratedly slow pace. It should just be slower and more focused than our normal eating. You could do this for one meal a day. Besides a method for focusing our attention, it could serve as a means to reflect on both how we eat and what we eat. Pesach is the holiday to give thought to this basic life activity.

Simplicity practice

Both Pesach and Sukkot encourage a focus on simplicity. Sukkot's theme of shelter and home in the context of eating in the simple structure of the sukkah/booth can help us to reflect on the nature of home itself. Pesach can do the same for food. What happens to all the food in our pantry? Do we use Pesach as an opportunity to give away unopened boxes to a food pantry? Do we clear our cabinets of opened boxes and bags of food that have been sitting there for many months? Do we try to use up that food rather than just throwing it out, knowing that the average American family discards twenty-five percent of the food they buy each year?

Beyond food, do we see the prohibition of bread and the requirement to clean our home as an opportunity to declutter? Besides the old food in your pantry, isn't there a lot of stuff lying around your home that you really have no need for? Do you have a good feeling when you clear out accumulated things that no longer have a purpose? You can feel really free from the burden of those piles. This process can encourage us to question whether we need or really want that new gadget or that article of clothing. Perhaps our journey is weighed down by all that stuff and we'd rather be more like the Israelites who, in one biblical image, left Egypt only with the matzah on their shoulders, the clothes on their backs and with a faith (sometimes challenged) that the journey to freedom would work out. The pandemic accelerated this process for many of us. Month after month staring at clothes we weren't wearing and objects in our apartment that did not, as Marie Kondo would say, spark joy, forced us to rethink what we carry with us, what we need, and what we actually find helpful on the journey. We can create a new practice by seeing Pesach as an opportunity to continue our life's travels with somewhat less weight slowing us down.

Core Principle #5:
Finding Holiness Everywhere

Our first four principles recognize the equality of all human beings and our responsibility to treat everyone with goodness. Awareness helps us remember our values and enables us to be more attentive to our surroundings. Core Principle Four upholds the importance of striving for justice for all, while recognizing that all of us need help, not just those who are struggling to get by. These principles are consistent with the traditional category of mitzvot/practices that focus on relationships between people (*mitzvot bein adam le-havero*). The fifth principle shifts our focus to the relationship of people to God (*mitzvot bein adam le-makom*). We begin that exploration with the idea of holiness.

Holiness is a word unique to religion and describes the essence of God. It can also describe objects like the Torah or a holy space—a sanctuary. It can be used to describe a person such as the Pope or the Dalai Lama. In the Torah, only God is described as intrinsically holy. Places like the Temple in Jerusalem and time, like the holidays, are holy because God ascribes them as such.

What quality makes something holy?

Leviticus 19:1 declares: "You shall be holy, for I, the Lord your God, am holy." Chapters 17-26 of the book of Leviticus are known by Bible scholars as the holiness code, wherein we are called to strive to be holy.

We might find it hard to define exactly what it means to be good or even ethical, but we have a broad understanding of what those words mean. But what does it mean to be holy?

Two of the classic Bible commentators represent different schools of thought on this question.

Rashi, the 11th-century commentator, understands holiness as calling us to separate from that which is unholy, meaning the materiality of this world. A life of the spirit consists of resisting worldly temptations. In this view, the material and the spiritual or the holy and the ordinary are in perpetual conflict. The less material you are, the more spiritual you can be.

In contrast, Ramban, a 13th-century Bible commentator, believes that holiness is not separate from, but rather connected to, the oneness of the world. This definition resonates more with me. Holiness is a basic way of seeing and experiencing life, as we strive to be present in each moment (even as we know that often we will be distracted). It reminds us to celebrate the gift of our lives. It is more than being kind and compassionate, though of course that is essential. To be holy is to be in touch with the oneness that underlies all creation. It acknowledges the preciousness of existence. Even as we experience existential aloneness, holiness fosters a sense of connectedness to the universe. When we experience that connectedness, we are able to respond to others as our best selves, meeting them with openness and compassion.

This concept of the holy distinguishes Judaism as a spiritual practice rather than just an ethical system. The components of holiness include an underlying unity with the universe (whether called God or not); that each person is an image of God; and that life has meaning, all of which serve as motivations to strive to increase good/*tov* in our world. Holiness is what Judaism is about and what life is about. It is about taking care of those on the margin of our society. It is also about the daily interactions with the people with whom we live and work. Holiness is the potential in every interaction to really hear what is being said, and to choose the generous response.

As we have seen in Leviticus Chapter 19, holiness is lived not through withdrawing from the world but through engaging in it. It is in the world of everyday relations that holiness is fostered.

The Holiness Code commands: Don't bear a grudge, don't gossip, don't put a stumbling block before the blind, and don't stand idly by injustice. This weave of commandments urges us to create a holy community and society by treating everyone with respect, and by confronting wrongs, either personal or societal, in order to try to fix things. This is at the core of Judaism.

Finally, holiness is an assertion that our world contains more than what we can see and touch. The Sefat Emet, a 19th-century Hasidic master, comments frequently that Torah enables us to achieve a way of being that is not limited by the laws of nature (*le-ma'alah mi-derekh ha-teva*). He does not mean that we can do miracles or escape death. He means that there is an added dimension to life—a dimension that rests on faith, not proof.

Shabbat: Holiness in time

In the Torah, we first encounter the term *holiness* in Gen. 2:3 when God completes the week of creation and rests on the Sabbath day. This verse states that God blessed the seventh day and declared it holy. Centuries before there were Jews, God established the Sabbath. Here is the second example of the Torah's attempt to superimpose a structure over the natural world. The first was when God described each day of creation as *tov*—good. God brings a moral value into the world of nature which otherwise could be viewed as neutral. Now we are told that the seventh day is different from the other six days. While the other days are known only by numbers, the seventh day is known as Shabbat—the day of rest. It is blessed by God and declared holy. Shabbat is holy—*kodesh*—and the other six days are ordinary—*hol*. The six days are for creation and work; Shabbat is for rest. Shabbat gives us time to reflect in order to regain a sense of perspective and purpose so easily forgotten in the busyness of the work week. Shabbat is an opportunity to reacquaint ourselves with the holy.

Stepping away from work

In our ever faster moving world, a Shabbat practice is even more crucial. We live in a time of instant messaging. In many jobs, checking your email regularly, even when you are not at work, is seen as part of an employee's responsibilities. Cell phones allow us to be in touch all the time. There is no downtime while you travel to work. Even in the theater, your phone is on vibrate "just in case." When do you have the time to reflect or just *be*?

Shabbat is a practice of stepping away from the work week. It is a time to slow down from the hectic pace of our lives. It is a time for reflection. It is at its heart an awareness practice, asking us to pause to consider where we are, where we are going, and how well that path fits with our vision of our lives. It gives us an opportunity to spend more time with loved ones or friends or even just ourselves. It is a gift to ourselves that only we can give. It is a gift of the most precious element in the world—time. The Torah tells us to cease work on Shabbat. The rabbis developed in great detail the definition of work as "creative enterprise"—*melakhah mahshevet*.

> The melakhah which is forbidden on the Sabbath is conceived as the execution of an intelligent purpose by the practical skill of man. Or, more generally, production, creation, transforming an object for human purposes; but not physical exertion. Even if you tired yourself out the whole day, as long as you have produced nothing within the meaning of melakhah; as long as your activity has not been a constructive exercise of your intelligence, you have performed no melakhah. On the other hand, if you have engendered, without the slightest exertion, even the smallest change in an object for human purposes, then you have profaned the Sabbath, flouted God, and undermined your calling as a Jew. Your physical power belongs to your animal nature; it is with your technical skill which serves your spirit that you master the world—and it is with this that, as a human being, you

should subject yourself to God on the Sabbath.
—Samson Raphael Hirsch, 19th-century rabbinic scholar

In this traditional definition, it is not physical exertion but rather the engagement in creative processes linked with physical efforts that define work. The work of creation is the human task, but on Shabbat we must cease from that goal and rest and reflect. While this cessation from work can be seen as good ecological practice and beneficial to the health of human beings, ultimately, we are to cease work in order to create the experience of Shabbat. The Torah tells us to both stop work on Shabbat as well as celebrate it. The cessation of work creates space for us to rest and reflect. Without pausing from the everyday, rest and reflection might rarely happen, if ever.

A sanctuary in time
Yet, ceasing from work doesn't mean creating a 24-hour period of doing nothing. Abraham Joshua Heschel, a 20th-century theologian, described Shabbat as an opportunity to build a sanctuary in time. Most of the week, we are building various sanctuaries and structures in space. On Shabbat, we are meant to build a sanctuary in time. This too is a creative enterprise, but with a different purpose than our activities during the week. We are not occupied or even preoccupied with earning a living. We are focused on living our lives. It may be a sanctuary from the pressures and pace of the work week, but its purpose is to take a breath before moving on. It seems like an essential practice for life. Perhaps that is why it exists from the first week of creation. Some form of awareness is required to live life fully.

A contemporary Shabbat practice
Our world is very different from the pre-modern world. Today many people think of what they do as a career, not just a job. They work not only to earn enough to survive but also to have a sense of personal fulfillment. They feel defined by their work. They may feel a sense of success from it. What could be some of the elements of a revised Shabbat practice based on this contemporary understanding? Traditional Jewish law forbade a whole variety of activities such as cooking, lighting a fire, and writing. This resulted from the rabbis' attempt to define what the Torah meant by work. In a pre-modern world, most people were not specialists. The majority of people were farmers. People weren't going to stores to buy clothes or other goods; they made almost everything themselves. Sewing, dyeing, and building were activities of every household in addition to farming work such as planting and harvesting. Rather than using these traditional categories, which may be unrelated to how we spend our work days today, we could focus a Shabbat

practice on simply not doing what we do to earn a living. Some people might want to add to that household work: cooking, cleaning, or doing laundry. Some might want to include running errands (dropping clothes at the dry cleaner or going to the bank)—refraining from activities that you may need to do but not necessarily want to do.

All this is to create the time for reflection and relaxation. This "free" time can be used to have a more leisurely meal with family or friends. Families often don't eat dinner together during the week because of different schedules or work or homework pressures. Meals are usually rushed or eaten while doing something else, like checking your cell phone. I know one family whose rule is that on Friday night everyone has to be home for dinner. While that is the extent of their Shabbat practice, it resets their family dynamic in a meaningful way.

Oneg: Shabbat as celebration

A new form of Shabbat practice can also involve spending time doing things that you enjoy. The concept of *oneg Shabbat*—the pleasures of Shabbat—is just as important as the work prohibitions. In the past, this has meant reserving special food for Shabbat and wearing your best clothes. The term *oneg* is now used for the reception after Shabbat services. Shabbat is meant to be celebratory, enabling us to do things we enjoy but often can't do during the week. These could include reading for pleasure, being in touch with friends, or going for a leisurely walk. A slower pace is part of the tradition of Shabbat. *Oneg* might mean exploring hobbies such as art or writing—even though they are traditionally forbidden activities. In this reframed Shabbat, we focus our energies away from our workweek rather than simply avoiding the traditional categories of work. The distinction is not the act itself (e.g., painting) but whether that act is how you earn your living or is a hobby that you enjoy. Oneg can also mean doing something special on Shabbat. Echoing the tradition of special food on Shabbat, some parents allow their children a Shabbat treat each week. Part of this Shabbat practice could include studying Torah or attending services.

In the spirit of Shabbat

According to traditional Jewish law, you are not allowed to carry anything outside your home on Shabbat, which would include something as light as a handkerchief. On the other hand, you could move 50 boxes of books up two flights of stairs if it was within your home. The issue isn't how strenuous the activity is, but whether it falls under the general categories of work. Any attempt to cover every possible situation will lead to applications that don't seem to make sense or that adhere to the law but seem to contradict its spirit. For some people, the most important value is staying out of the consumer culture, so they won't go shopping. As a retired person, I have found it a challenge to think of what replaces work. I refrain from doing errands, especially ones that provoke tension or anxiety in anticipation of doing them. The overall point of the Shabbat experience is to get a different perspective on our lives by refraining from doing much of what we do during the week.

There is a traditional concept that describes activities that are technically permitted (like moving 50 boxes of books at home) but violate the spirit of Shabbat. The term for this in Yiddish is *shabbosdik*, or *ruach shabbat* (the spirit of Shabbat) in Hebrew. You can and should decide for yourself where to draw the line to enhance your Shabbat experience. I like to use the example of a friend who is a doctor. He says he gets a lot of pleasure reading medical journals and therefore he doesn't consider that work on Shabbat. However, he won't read medical journals in his specialty because that could be work-related.

Besides being a time to connect with others, Shabbat could be devoted to reflecting on good moments from the past week. It could also include thinking about a spiritual to-do list for the coming week—saying something nice to a friend, or trying to be more patient with clients.

In America, because we have something called a weekend, it is important to figure out how to make Shabbat a special day. One obvious difference is you don't have to refrain from any activity on Sunday. Sunday could be a good day to do errands that you are too busy to get done during the week. Sunday can also be a time to do work because of an upcoming important deadline.

Shabbat unplugged

Some people have decided to go unplugged as part of their Shabbat practice. Social media has become something of an addiction in our society, so unplugging our devices helps us focus on creating an environment and a pace that is different from our everyday activities.

In traditional Jewish law, there are a variety of things that are forbidden because they are viewed as a "fence" around the Torah. One example is carrying money. Since commercial transactions are forbidden on Shabbat, you shouldn't carry money or credit cards lest you forget it's Shabbat and accidently use them. Can this idea of a "fence" be helpful? Some people might prefer to remain plugged in so they can stay in touch with friends or read personal emails that they didn't get a chance to read during the week. What happens when you see a work-related email or a personal email from someone with whom you have an uneasy relationship? Can you just ignore it? Or will you spend all Shabbat wondering what the email says? If you think you can't ignore it, then a "fence" around all social media might be useful.

Shabbat as an environmental practice

Increasingly, I believe we should see Shabbat as an environmental practice. When we stop our work, we renounce our mastery of the world. Instead of being in control, we are to just *be*. The traditional Shabbat prohibition of the use of fire means that using a car is forbidden. However, other traditional Shabbat work-arounds, such as leaving your stove burner on for all 24 hours of Shabbat, clearly wastes energy. As a result, some people have decided to turn lights and the stove on and off as needed rather than leave them on for all of Shabbat. The goal is to think of Shabbat as a time to leave the world as untouched as possible. Therefore, some people try to walk, ride a bicycle, or take public transportation instead of using private cars or taxis (despite the traditional prohibition of using motor vehicles or even bicycles). In general, we can try to use less energy. The rationale for prohibiting certain activities such as the ones mentioned here seems focused on human activity. Shabbat then becomes a time when we move away from an anthropocentric orientation and can feel more connected to the universe.

One interesting side note in this regard is the category of *muktzah*. In Jewish law, these are objects that we are forbidden to move on Shabbat. Mostly these are things such as pens or tools, the use of which are forbidden on Shabbat. This principle forbids the moving of anything that is not needed on Shabbat. Thus, twigs lying in your yard should not be moved since there is no particular purpose to moving them. Basically, it encourages us to leave the world at rest. On Shabbat, we can try to do as little as possible not because we think this radically changes our carbon footprint but because we think it is important to be conscious of our imprint on the environment.

Shabbat as an experience of a more perfect world

Shabbat is described in the tradition as a taste of the world to come—meaning it should have a bit of the flavor of a perfect world. This notion takes on additional meaning when Shabbat is an environmental experience. We live our lives in an imperfect world. Judaism doesn't ask us to make it perfect, but we are supposed to make it better. There are moments like Shabbat when we are encouraged to get closer to that perfection. If we don't cook on Shabbat, we use our car less, are more conscious of conserving energy, Shabbat becomes a taste of the world to come. Yet, the tradition acknowledges that we need to use our refrigerators, heat or cool our homes and use electricity if Shabbat is also to be a day to relax and to enjoy. We do the best we can and hold both the reality of our existence and our hopes and vision of a world to come. After all, the greeting for the day is Shabbat

Shalom—wishing each other a day of peace, pointing to the vision of the prophets of when the lion and lamb shall lie down together. The Yiddish greeting is *Gut Shabbos*—wishing a good Shabbat, hearkening back to the first week of creation where each day ended with—it is good/*ki tov*.

The oneness of Shabbat

As a spiritual practice, Shabbat can take this one step further. We live in a world of *us* and *them*, even of *you* and *me*. Shabbat can be a day when we strive toward a sense of oneness. You can see this in the opening and closing rituals of Shabbat. We light two candles Friday night to announce the beginning of Shabbat. We conclude Shabbat with the ritual of *Havdalah*, during which we use one candle that is actually a number of candles braided together. Duality has become one. At its best, Shabbat can bring us to a sense of oneness. It could be a sense of oneness with nature as we have time to take a walk or notice the sunset. It could be a sense of oneness with God who is One or a sense of being connected to the universe rather than alienated from it. Finally, it could be a sense of oneness with ourselves, giving ourselves the time just to reflect on our life or being more aware of the thoughts and feelings that arise when we create space and give them the time to appear.

The Sefat Emet, a 19th-century Hasidic master, teaches that when everyone participated in the building of the *mishkan*/sanctuary in the desert, the whole Jewish people came together in unity. That unity was destroyed when the people built the Golden Calf. The Sefat Emet suggests that we can still find that unity on Shabbat. For him, Shabbat is one of the ways we can experience not being limited by nature. Shabbat brings holiness into our lives. We carry that aspect of Shabbat into our work week. Our intention should be to foster oneness and peace through our work and interactions. The pattern of our lives should be a weekly return to the *shalom*/peace of Shabbat (from his commentary on *Parashat Ha-Hodesh* in the years 5631 and 5634).

Elsewhere, the Sefat Emet points out that the letters of the word Shabbat can be scrambled to spell the word *BoSheT*, meaning embarrassment or distress. Shabbat is a time to rebalance our inner lives. It is not just stopping from working; it is also putting down the weight of our worries. It suggests that another form of Shabbat practice would be striving to live as though you were living in the world to come. In such a Shabbat practice, being nasty to someone is as much a violation of the spirit of Shabbat as driving heavy machinery. Going to synagogue to hear or share the latest gossip would be detrimental to the goal of experiencing the sense of oneness of Shabbat. We will never be perfect human beings; but fostering our connection to all of life should be the essence of Shabbat.

Every seven days Judaism asks us to take a spiritual retreat. It is not a call to reject materiality and embrace asceticism. On the contrary, traditional Shabbat practice involves drinking wine and eating the best foods. It is a retreat from the busyness of our work week so we can immerse ourselves in our inner life, in creation, and with our family and friends. We step back in order to better step forward, requiring the quiet of Shabbat rest in order to hear our inner selves over the din of the week. It is an opportunity to reset our bearings before we set off on next week's journey.

Shabbat is a unique gift. Perhaps that is why it appears in the Torah before there are any Jews and its only practitioner is God, who rests after a week of creation. "More than the Jews have kept the Sabbath, the Sabbath has kept the Jews," proclaimed Ahad Ha'am, a 20th-century Zionist thinker. Today, more than ever, the world needs to have a practice of Shabbat for the sake of all who inhabit this planet.

The spirituality of the everyday

Can we experience the holy only on Shabbat? What is its place during the everydayness of the week? Hasidism suggested that holiness can be experienced at any moment, not only on Shabbat or moments when doing religious activities such as praying or studying Torah. This notion is called by scholars *avodah she-be-gashmiyut*—service through the material. The tradition often viewed spiritual and the material or the holy and the ordinary in perpetual conflict. The material was a temptation leading us away from the true service of God. Hasidism's emphasis on joy was rooted in a much broader world view, rejecting the asceticism of earlier Jewish mystics. It fully embraced the notion that the divine is embedded in everything. Therefore, the holy was not just accessible when fulfilling one of the 613 commandments. Holiness was not found just in extraordinary moments but in ordinary moments as well. A conversation with a friend, an unexpected smile, a beautiful flower or a moment of insight all had the potential to connect us to the wholeness underlying the universe. Touching holiness came not by rejecting the material but by embracing it. In this way, Hasidism is very modern in its orientation to the world by broadening the definition of the sacred.

It's not about doing the Jewishly Jewish things

People often think that Judaism is about observing a certain set of laws and customs that are particularistic in nature—practices like keeping kosher, observing Shabbat, or celebrating holidays—the "Jewishly Jewish" things, those rituals that only Jews observe. From a traditional viewpoint, if you do a lot of these rituals, you are considered "a good Jew." In fact, Judaism is not about making you a good Jew but rather helping you to become a good person and to live a life of meaning. The giving of *tzedakah* or helping the stranger are central to leading a Jewish life, but we do them in order to make our world a better place. Observing Shabbat, having a practice that helps us pay attention to what we eat (tradition-ally, keeping kosher), or taking time to be grateful are all practices that help bring awareness to our lives and remind us that we are connected to something larger than ourselves. The concept of holiness encourages us, through deeds of caring and practices of awareness, to strive for such a life.

Mitzvah as connection

Hasidism teaches that the word *mitzvah*/commandment is related to the Aramaic word *tzavta*, which means connection. The *mitzvot* are not items to check off a list, but rather opportunities for connection. For me, *mitzvot* provide opportunities for connection to other people, to our vision of life, to this planet, to the unity underlying the universe and, finally, to ourselves. They provide a way of being in the world that helps us pay attention to the blessings and challenges that each of us face on our journey.

Every moment has the potential for connection in the Hasidic understanding of holiness. Opportunities exist even in such mundane places as the workplace. It isn't simply that you shouldn't cheat your customers; in a positive sense, every interaction has the potential to be holy or at least helpful. It's all about connection in a world of aloneness. Our story begins with the exile from the Garden of Eden; this is the human condition. Many mystical traditions suggest that connection to the Divine Presence can only happen by withdrawing from the distractions of the world and engaging in a lengthy practice to bring about an elevated state of consciousness. Hasidism does talk about that elevated state of consciousness but it encourages everyone, not just a few spiritual masters, to strive for a sense of connection to the Holy One, or to the holy, or simply to their fellow Jew. It is true that Hasidism suggests that its followers could attain that connection by being connected to their *rebbe*/spiritual teacher, but its adherents also suggest that the spirituality of the everyday is possible for anyone. Hasidism holds that there is a spark of the holy in everything in the world, including a spark within each one of us. It is always right there waiting to be uncovered—both in the world and within us. We need only to pay attention to connect to it.

This is how I have come to understand Judaism. Although these teachings date from the 18th and 19th centuries, they give Jewish expression to contempo-rary notions of spirituality and still feel very fresh.

Rav Kook (20th-century theologian) declared:

Ha-yashan yithadesh Ve-he-hadash yitkadesh

Take that which is old/tired/routine and make it new
And take the new and make it holy.

Shaping time with holiness: The Jewish holidays

While holiness can be found in the everyday, we experience it especially when we shape the most basic element in our lives: time.

This is true not just on Shabbat. Time reminds us that we are mortal. Our time will come to an end. No matter how much we exercise or eat healthy food, we cannot escape death. Judaism uses time not to focus on our mortality but on life itself.

Sanctifying time offers a critical awareness practice because it is easy for one day to follow another until too much of our life has passed.

Judaism attempts to disrupt time through an annual festival cycle that urges us to pay attention to important themes of life.

The High Holidays are a good example. We should always pay attention to the people we have hurt. We should always strive to improve our inner qualities. But it is next to impossible to consistently pay attention to others and to ourselves. We can easily end up never paying attention and putting off that focus to the proverbial tomorrow, when we have time. The High Holidays encourage us to take time to examine our lives and to seek to change. Hopefully, that will lead to an awareness and a change in behavior that will carry through the rest of the year.

The Torah refers to the holidays as *mikra'ei kodesh*/holy convocations. While we know that holiness can be found at any moment, the holidays are times especially devoted to holiness. We bring our attention to the themes of each holiday by pausing from our regular routine. On Pesach, we focus our attention on the holiness of freedom. On the High Holidays, we focus on change. We turn our thoughts to nature on Sukkot.

The Torah says: "Three times a year ... [they] shall appear before God...They shall not appear before God empty-handed, but each with his own gift, according to the blessing that God has bestowed upon you" (Dt 16:16-17).

This verse tells us that Jews who were making a pilgrimage to Jerusalem were supposed to bring gifts from their crops or their herds. This verse can serve as a *kavanah*/intention as we celebrate the festivals of Pesach, Shavuot and Sukkot. Each festival is an opportunity to reflect on the blessings of our life and to think about our own "gift." The verse implies that each of us has a unique gift. No one is "empty-handed." What combination of qualities defines who we are? What would it mean to bring them to this holiday? Does a commitment to help others echo the Passover theme of freedom? Does patience reverberate with the story of the Exodus, which unfolds in stages rather than all at once? Is a willingness to try new things the embodiment of the spirit of the Israelites at the crossing of the sea?

We prepare spiritually for each of these holidays by discovering the gifts that are particularly relevant to the themes of that holiday. In that way these festivals will be moments of reflection and inspiration on our journey through the year and through our lives.

Core Principle #6:
Caring For the Planet

The Torah talks about settling the earth (*yishuv ha-aretz*). To the inhabitants of the ancient world, the earth must have seemed to be a vast universe of unexplored mystery. For centuries, societies have faced the challenge of clearing land for human habitation and crops. Our challenge is that we have over-settled the world. We are polluting the environment, exterminating species, and causing global warming. This requires new thinking and practices related to the environment. We need a new way to frame this issue.

The traditional *halakha* is woefully inadequate here, because the circumstances of our relationship to the planet have radically changed since ancient times. In other areas, the *halakha* has strived to apply ancient principles and understandings to new circumstances. This was not difficult when it came to new technology. Is electricity similar to fire or dissimilar? Depending on the answer, its use on Shabbat would be forbidden or not (since lighting a fire is traditionally prohibited). When it comes to the environment, it is not a question whether fracking is kosher or not, but a more fundamental issue—what is the role of humans in the ecology of the world?

Bal tashchit: Don't wantonly destroy

The defining traditional source for relating to the environment is found in Deuteronomy 20:19-20 and is known as *bal tashchit*—do not destroy:

> When you besiege a city for a long time, in making war against it to capture it, you shall not destroy its trees by wielding an ax against them. You may eat of them but you shall not cut them down…Only the trees that are not trees for food, you may destroy and cut down to construct siege · works against the city that is waging war against you…

It is striking that even in war there is a limit to permissible destruction. The rabbis apply this law not just to the specific situation described in the verse. They prohibit any wanton destruction, whether of food or objects. The problem for us is found in the second verse, which allows non-fruit trees to be chopped down in order to create siege works. This is understood in the tradition to mean that wanton destruction is prohibited but destruction for a purpose is permitted. What is a purpose? In general, anything that is of benefit to human beings.

Environmental ethics

In current discussions of environmental ethics, there are debates about the limits of human activities. Can a valley be flooded to create a dam for hydroelectric power in a new city? What if doing so would destroy a plant species that grows only in that valley? Do the benefits to humans outweigh the loss of that species? Some would argue that saving a species should take priority because it is possible some vital use for this plant could be discovered in the future, such as a cure for a disease. Deep ecologists reject this anthropomorphic view in which anything that humans benefit from is permitted. They believe we are in the midst of the current climate change crisis in part because we prioritize human need when we set policies about the environment. Instead, they maintain that all living beings and even inanimate things have a value in the world and should be considered when setting environmental policies.

Bal tashchit suffers from an anthropocentric view. It prohibits wanton destruction but not destruction for a purpose. There is nothing in *Bal tashchit* which would prohibit clearing all of the Amazon rainforest to make homes for people or farms for raising crops. For centuries, the emphasis has been on settling the land (*yishuv ha-aretz*) in a world where human habitation seemed tiny compared to the vastness of the earth. The story of America and the ongoing settlement of its frontier is a specific example of this process. Our situation is now very different. There are no vast unexplored or unsettled areas. It took over two million years of human history for the world's population to reach one billion people, and only two hundred years more to reach seven billion. The world no longer needs to be settled—it needs to be protected. How can Judaism frame a response to the environmental crisis?

Can we use the word sin when we pollute this world? When we destroy the ozone layer, we haven't actually hurt another person, but we have hurt the world. I want to suggest that we reinterpret a biblical category that has basically fallen into disuse: *tum'ah*/impurity. In the Torah, especially in the Book of Leviticus, the category of *tum'ah* is not the same thing as sinning. It defines something that is impure, either because you did something wrong or through no fault of your own. Death is the most powerful form of impurity; touching a dead body makes you impure. In the Torah, people could become impure. Certain creepy-crawly creatures were always considered impure. Menstrual blood was impure. There is even a puzzling passage about houses that became impure through some form of biblical leprosy that grows on the walls (even the rabbis of the Talmud did not know what the Bible meant by that). There were rituals supervised by the priests that involved immersions of the impure person and/or sacrifices that could be offered in order to be returned to a state of *taharah*/purity. With the destruction of the Temple, this category became irrelevant, since purification rituals couldn't be performed without the Temple.

Only remnants of this idea have survived among traditional Jews. People who trace their lineage to the priestly caste (*kohanim*) in general don't attend funerals. Menstrual blood still makes women impure until they immerse in a ritual bath (*mikvah*). Some argue that *tum'ah* as a category should be discarded. The fact that it now applies only to women is troubling, to say the least. It is part and parcel of rabbinic Judaism's emphasis on dividing the world into the good and the bad. It is not surprising that the laws about menstruation continue to exist, but the parallel impurity laws about men are no longer observed.

I still wonder whether *tum'ah* as impurity is redeemable as a term to describe the pollution of the earth. Pollution seems to me not just a modern term for destroying the environment, but echoes the biblical sense that *tum'ah* can affect the world in ways that might not be visible but still have a negative impact. In Leviticus, there is an understanding that impurity is an inevitable byproduct of existence. The task of the priests and Levites was to try to protect the sanctuary from impurity in part by purifying people who had become impure. The fear was that over time too much impurity would build up and drive God from the sanctuary.

We can reconstruct the notion of impurity, not by understanding it as an invisible force infecting society, but as a consequence of human activity that is detrimental to the environment. To put it in contemporary terms, *tum'ah* would make the world uninhabitable to human beings. *Tum'ah* is toxic to life. Such a state hearkens back to the story of Noah and the flood.

> The earth became corrupt before God; the earth was filled with lawlessness. When God saw how corrupt the earth was, for all flesh had corrupted its ways on earth, God said to Noah, "I have decided to put an end to all flesh, for the earth is filled with lawlessness because of them: I am about to destroy them with the earth." (Gen. 6:11-13)

Finding that the deeds of humans have corrupted the earth itself, God decides to destroy everything and to cleanse the earth in the waters of the flood—the birth waters for a new world. What happens after the flood? Noah and his family and the animals of the ark reestablish the world. However, some things have changed. God has established a covenant that ensures there will never be another flood to destroy the whole world.

> I now establish My covenant with you and your offspring to come, and with every living thing that is with you—birds, cattle, and every wild beast as well—all that have come out of the ark, every living thing on earth. (Gen. 9:9-10)

The covenant not to destroy the world is made with all living things, not just humans. This covenant argues against an anthropocentric notion of the world. It is now up to us, whom God has given power over the world, to make sure that we do not pollute the world and thereby bring a flood or any other disaster that could bring an end to all living things. The rainbow, then, may be a sign that God will no longer destroy the world, but it is also a warning that we humans have now been given that power to either give respect (*kavod*) to the earth or to pollute it (make it *tameh*) and cause its destruction. For me, reclaiming the category of *tum'ah* as pollution is a useful way to frame the challenge of living a life with an awareness of the need to protect the environment. Just as the Torah states that you cannot live without causing impurity, however unintentional, so too we cannot live without leaving a carbon footprint on this planet. How can we offset or minimize our negative impact on the earth's environment?

Environmental principles drawn from the tradition

1) It is not ours—it belongs to God.

> Our rabbis have taught: It is forbidden for a person to enjoy anything of this world without a *berakhah*/blessing… R. Levi contrasted two texts. It is written: "The earth is the Lord's and the fullness thereof" (Ps. 24:1); and it is also written: "The heavens are the heavens of the Lord, but the earth God has given to human beings" (Ps.115: 16). There is no contradiction: in the one case, it is before a blessing has been said; in the other case, after. (*Berakhot* 35a)

Blessings are said before we eat in part to acknowledge that this is God's world, not ours. Thus, all anthropocentrism is tempered in Judaism by acknowledgment of the Creator. We may have a lot of power in this world but, at best, this world is on loan to us. We are only the managers, not the owners.

2) We are to protect the earth

And God took the human, and put the human into the garden of Eden to till it and to tend it" (Gen. 2:15). Here, humans are tasked with the work of tilling and tending this world. The responsibility that humans have to protect or watch over the garden/the world is explicit. Later midrash interprets this biblical text:

> In the hour when the Holy One created the first human, God took the human and let the human pass before all the trees in the Garden of Eden. God said: "See My works, how fine and excellent they are! Now all that I have created for you have I created. Think upon this, and do not corrupt and desolate My world; for if you corrupt it, there is no one to set it right after you." (Ecclesiastes Rabbah 7:28)

Here the midrash understands that Genesis is assigning ultimate responsibility for the world to humans. As ongoing creators of the world, we must preserve it. Humans are not masters but responsible actors.

3) To everything, there is a purpose

> Our rabbis said: "Even those things that you may regard as completely superfluous to creation, such as fleas, gnats, and flies, even they too were included in creation; and God's purpose is carried out through everything—even through a snake, a scorpion, a gnat, or a frog."(Genesis Rabbah 10:7)

There is a reason why God made the covenant after the flood not only with all humankind but also with the animals of the world. We learn an important lesson about the place of human beings in the world. It is too easy for us to think we are the pinnacle of creation and the world is here for our benefit. Perhaps that is why humans felt it was okay to corrupt the world before the flood. The covenant after the flood is with all living creatures to remind us that life—all life—is the pinnacle of creation, as we see in the following midrash.

> Why did God create loathsome reptiles and creeping things?... God created Adam and brought him into the world. And God created Adam for no other purpose than to serve God with a whole heart and God would thus find contentment in him and in his descendants after him until the end of all generations.

But then after Adam complied with the command to be fruitful and multiply, one [descendant] worshiped the sun and the
moon, another worshiped wood and stone, and thus every day
Adam's descendants came to be deemed by God as deserving
annihilation. Nevertheless, upon considering all the work of
God's hands in the world of creation, God said: "These [human
beings] have life, and those [other creatures] have life. These
have breath and those have breath; these have desire for food
and drink, and those have desire for food and drink. Human
beings ought to be deemed as important as cattle, as beasts,
at least as important as the variety of loathsome reptiles and
creeping things which I created upon the earth." At once God
felt some measure of contentment and resolved not to anni-
hilate humankind. And so, you see that reptiles and creeping
things were created in the world as a means of humankind's
preservation. (Eliyahu Rabbah, Ch. 1)

Here, the creepy-crawly things remind God that all life is sacred, even the life
of human beings who have lost their way. Maybe God made a covenant after the
flood with all living creatures in order to try to prevent the future destruction of
the planet. Humans need to take responsibility for all living creatures, even those
we think the world could do without.

4) Recycle: Expanding the notion of sheymot

According to tradition, books and paper with God's name cannot be discarded in the usual way, but must be buried in the earth. This practice came from
a sense of respect and honor. I want to expand this practice. If we understand
that everything in this world has God's name on it (*sheymot*), then everything
should be recycled appropriately. I make sure to recycle 100% of the paper I use,
as a personal *humra*/stringency. I have come to believe that recycling paper with
God's name on it is even more respectful than burying it.

5) Conserve: Simple living

Our environmental crisis has come about in part because of the conspicuous
consumption in our society. Our numerous appliances consume enormous energy
resources. The manufacturing, packaging, and selling of consumer products use
up other resources. The garbage we produce literally overwhelms our means of

disposal. Some medieval Jewish communities issued sumptuary laws that regulated the amount of money that could be spent on clothes or on parties or feasts. These existed for a number of reasons, but one was to discourage conspicuous consumption. Some Hasidic communities have continued this tradition to prevent a keeping-up-with-the-Joneses, (or rather the Goldsteins), that drives up the cost of weddings. Such laws could serve as a model to help us to police ourselves with regard to our consumer purchasing. There is nothing we buy that does not also come at a cost to the environment. We should constantly ask ourselves: *Do we need this item?* Although need can be broadly defined to include things that give us pleasure, the question still remains.

6) *Humrot/*stringencies

There is a strand in the tradition that asks us to be extra careful (*humrot*) when it comes to observing Jewish law. The most well-known example is Glatt kosher (extra restrictions on what makes meat kosher). Mostly, these extra stringencies were the individual practices of people who wanted to be extra pious. In modern times, some of these stringencies are widely observed. Today, much of the Orthodox world consumes only Glatt kosher meat. I want to suggest that people use this notion of stringencies/*humrot* with the environment. In my effort to recycle 100% of paper, I'll go across the apartment to where we have a bin for paper recycling rather than just throw a receipt in the nearest wastebasket. There are many things we can do as individuals. While trying to do them all can be overwhelming, try to pick one area in which to be super-strict, even as you remain aware of an individual's limited environmental impact.

Everything in this world is a creation of God. Nothing should be taken for granted. Life is an amazing interconnectedness of all beings. We need to be careful making changes because we have seen over and over again that the impact of what we do can have far-ranging and unexpected consequences. Whether it's acid rain or plastic bags, the consequences of what we do can affect people living far away from us.

Sinning against God

What happens to the idea of *mitzvot*/commandments when we attempt to reimagine how to apply traditional categories to contemporary issues such as climate change? While commandments between people fit very well in *Minhag America*, those between us and God are more challenging. Many of the ritual commandments from that category have been reinterpreted as part of the practice of awareness. The purpose of these rituals is to make us more aware in our lives. They are no longer about sinning against God as parallel to sinning against our fellow human beings. Does the concept of sinning against God still have meaning?

Sinning against God could mean failing to live up to the values represented by God. If we fail to live up to being an image of God, haven't we besmirched God's name or God's honor? There is a traditional notion of *hillul hashem*, desecrating God's name. It is not only other human beings we can hurt with our actions, but also God's name—or at least the values of Judaism.

A place to begin our rethinking is the traditional name for this category—*mitzvot bein adam la-makom*—commandments between a person and God. The name used for God in describing this category is *makom*/place. It is a rabbinic name for God, not a biblical one. Midrash Rabbah (68:9) states: "God is the place (*makom*) of the world, and the world is not God's place." The midrashic comment is usually understood to mean that God is everywhere in the universe, which is also the creation of God. Yet, God is not limited by the universe.

It is not an accident that *mitzvot bein adam la-makom*—commandments between people and God—use the name of God that means place. As the midrash says, God is the place of the world. Being careless about how we treat this planet is being disrespectful to God. In fact, I would suggest that today this is a primary way that humans are desecrating the name of God. Instead of being co-creators of the world, we are destroying *makom*/God as manifest in the diverse world of creation. Each time a species disappears from this world, haven't we in effect diminished God's name? As we reconstruct *halakha*, we need to think of how this category of *mitzvot*/commandments related to the *makom*/world needs to be expanded in order to preserve God's name, which is the same as our planet. One way to focus our attention on the environment is through the celebration of Sukkot.

Sukkot: A week living with nature

Sukkot is the third and final pilgrimage festival on the Hebrew calendar. Its origin is as a harvest festival. While Pesach and Shavuot are connected to two events that are at the center of the Jewish story (the Exodus from Egypt and the revelation of the Torah at Sinai), the historical connection of Sukkot is to a time period—the 40 years of wandering in the desert on the way to the Promised Land.

It seems an odd choice because the 40 years is usually understood as a story of failure. Originally, the Israelites were supposed to journey from their experience at Mount Sinai directly to the Promised Land. When spies were sent to check out the land flowing with milk and honey, they returned with a report of the land's fruitfulness but also reported that the inhabitants of the land were giants that could not be overcome. The people rebelled once more and God condemned that generation of Israelites to wander in the desert for 40 years, where they would die before seeing the Promised Land.

There are two main observances of the Sukkot festival: eating in a *sukkah,* or booth (the plural gives the holiday its name, Sukkot); and the waving of the four species (*lulav* and *etrog*) during services.

The booths remind us of the dwellings in which the Israelites supposedly lived while wandering in the desert. They also evoke an image of the temporary shelters erected by workers who needed to live out in the fields during harvest time in the land of Israel.

The *lulav* and *etrog* comprise four species: the *lulav* is a palm branch tied together with myrtle and willow branches; the *etrog* is a citron fruit similar to a lemon. The reason these four plants were chosen is not clear from the Torah text. Perhaps we gather them in and wave them in the direction of the four compass points to imitate the harvesting process. It could be both a way to express gratitude for the harvest as well as to express hopes for next year's crops. Success for a crop in the land of Israel depends on the amount of rain that falls during the winter. If there is not sufficient rain, next year's crop is in trouble. Therefore, there are a number of rituals associated with Sukkot that give expression to the concern about and hopes for the rainfall. This may be a reason for waving the four species, one of which (willow) is associated with water.

In the ancient world, the harvest was both a time of celebration and anxiety, depending on the success of the past year's crops and the uncertainty about the coming year. The sukkah became a symbol of both these elements. When we sit under a roof that offers no real protection from the elements, we give concrete expression to the notion that life is uncertain. We also express a sense of accomplishment with the harvest and, because of its proximity to Yom Kippur, with the process of *teshuvah*/change of the High Holidays. Our complex relationship to nature and the world is at the heart of this holiday, which makes it an appropriate time to focus on the environment.

Environmental Sukkot

The connection between Sukkot and the environment is so pervasive that it calls for creating new practices. We might undertake a review of what we are doing in our personal life to lessen our carbon footprint and explore what policy issues we could work to support. This annual assessment of the ecological state of our lives can go beyond such things as replacing our regular bulbs with LED bulbs or recommitting to recycling. We can give new meaning to the intermediate days of Sukkot by actively focusing on how we can help to heal the world.

An environmental practice

We can try to live with as little carbon impact on the world as possible during Sukkot. We do this knowing that for the other 51 weeks a year, we can't or won't live that way, but we want to acknowledge that this issue may be the most important challenge to the future of life on this planet. We are not claiming that by living for a week with reduced impact that we have slowed global warming in even an infinitesimal way. Rather we believe that living closer to the ideal, even for just a week, is an expression of our commitment to work for improvement. There are a variety of actions we could take in order to reduce the resources we are using for the week. We could stop eating meat for the week, reducing the environmental impact of raising animals for human consumption. We could commit to eating only locally grown produce. We could cut down on the use of fossil fuel by walking to more places than we normally do. We could also bike or take public transportation rather than drive to work.

There is a traditional principle that if necessity requires you to bend or break a Shabbat law, that you do it in a way that acknowledges that you know you are bending it. For instance, if you forgot your key to get into your apartment building, you can ring the doorbell to get someone's attention. However, you ring the doorbell with your elbow rather than by using your finger. The point is to minimize the seriousness of the violation. A personal example: Many years ago, I decided I was going to carry my house keys in my pocket on Shabbat despite the prohibition against carrying items. In recognition of Shabbat, however, I carried my keys in my left pants pocket instead of my right pants pocket, where I usually carry them. Part of my Shabbat ritual is to switch the pocket for my keys as Shabbat starts. While this may sound silly, such acts are a form of awareness practice. It is useful to be aware that what you are doing is less than perfect even if the impact is only on your awareness.

Therefore, even if you are driving on Sukkot, what if you parked a walkable distance from your destination in order to acknowledge that it would have been better had you avoided using the car altogether? You could also eat less cooked food and more fresh, raw fruits and vegetables. Any of these things might be too difficult or too costly to do all year round, but you could manage them for a week. There may be some of these practices that you decide to continue to do on a more modest basis—for example, taking public transportation to work once a week.

Carbon footprint offset annual calculation

The Torah lists a series of tithes the Israelites were expected to give from their crops to the priests and Levites. When the Israelites came to the land of Israel, everyone inherited a piece of land, except for the priests and Levites. In contemporary *halakha*, these practices, while still on the books, are only symbolic. The underlying notion of tithing is that the land and its harvest belong to God. At best, we are long-term leaseholders on the land.

I want to suggest adapting the tithe as a way to acknowledge that, as leaseholders on this planet, along with the right to benefit from its produce, we must also be stewards of that land. The challenge is that the earth pays a price for our being here. We cause inevitable wear and tear on this planet. By using fossil fuels to heat our homes and power our cars, we are contributing to global warming. A number of websites have calculators so you can see how much impact you are having. One such website, the Carbon Fund, estimates that the average American contributes 50,000 tons of carbon emissions each year. They suggest an amount of money to contribute to offset the 50,000 tons. The money can go to support alternative energy sources such as wind and solar power. If more of our electricity came from fossil fuel-free sources, we could reduce carbon emissions. Another project is planting trees, because they absorb carbon dioxide. Some environmentalists argue that projects that reduce carbon emissions are better than ones that absorb existing carbon emissions. Therefore, they argue that planting trees, while a good thing, is not the best choice. Also consider the fact that it takes many years for trees to grow. When choosing to contribute to a carbon offset, check that the projects you are supporting meet the CDM Gold standard to ensure that they have an actual impact on the carbon emission problem. Rather than using the average number suggested by the Carbon Fund, Sukkot could be an appropriate time to calculate your own specific carbon footprint and take steps to offset it through a combination of changing habits and contributing money to environmentally appropriate projects.

Preparing for the journey into the New Year

As the final annual holiday in the festival cycle, Sukkot commemorates the journey. This is an important teaching of the Torah. We end the book of Deuteronomy on the wrong side of the Jordan. The generation of the desert will not make it to the Promised Land—even Moses. We complete the Torah reading cycle with the death of Moses. Instead of continuing with the Book of Joshua, which describes the entrance into the land, we begin again with the creation of the world. Ultimately, the story of the Jewish people in the Torah is a real story. There is no heroic ending with the triumph of good over evil. In fact, the hero, Moses, dies. His death is not in a climactic final battle—it is the death of old age. The story needs to move on with the next generation. It is a real story because it parallels every person's story. We can never reach the Promised Land. What we can do is live a life of goodness and meaning.

Sukkot is the harvest festival where we metaphorically gather the harvest of our past year's planting and the fruits of our efforts at self-examination. There is an element of review as well as preparation for the new year that has only just begun. The holiday is an opportunity to think about how we want to shape our lives in this new year. With its theme of harvesting, Sukkot shifts our focus from the ways we have failed, which seem so prominent during the High Holidays, and allows us to focus on what we have accomplished during the past year that we can carry with us. A harvesting practice could involve the listing of such accomplishments. They might range from mundane successes, such as finally cleaning out the basement, to more consequential accomplishments. The criteria for making the list are things that give you a real sense of satisfaction and accomplishment. It is more than something you do all the time, like paying bills or doing the laundry. As much as we need to be self-critical, it is also important to appreciate what we have accomplished. Knowing yourself is not just about understanding your limitations; it's also about valuing your strengths.

The harvesting practice

Review the lists out loud and end each one with the phrase—*tov le-hodot*—it is good to acknowledge what I have accomplished. *Yishar orhoteikha*—and may your path ahead be straight and clear (Prv. 3:6).

Sukkot and sheltering

The pilgrimage festivals focus on major pieces of human identity: freedom and food on Passover; commitment and values on Shavuot; and shelter and security on Sukkot. The central ritual of Sukkot is the commandment to build and eat in a booth (*sukkah*). We are supposed to live in the sukkah during the festival, both eating and sleeping there unless the weather is inclement. However, it is too cold for most North American Jews to sleep in the sukkah. Its standard use then is the other main activity we do at home—eat our meals. Just as Passover asks us to pay attention to what we eat 51 weeks a year by forbidding it for one week, Sukkot asks us to examine what it means to live in a home by symbolically moving out one week a year.

The rules about what constitutes a sukkah point us to the issues about home and shelter. The most important feature of a sukkah is its roof. It is made of leafy branches cut from trees. It lacks the most essential feature of roofs—it offers no protection from the elements. It is forbidden to have a roof for your sukkah that prevents rain falling into the sukkah. The rules about its walls are more flexible, but most commonly they are not permanent. The sukkah has a feel of impermanence. Originally, the sukkah reflected a nomadic lifestyle. Today, the impermanence of the sukkah structure conveys a challenge to most North Americans who live in permanent structures.

We look to home as a place where we are safe and warm, and where we can relax. For many it is a place of intimacy with our partners and/or family. It can be a refuge from the fast-paced world of work. Perhaps, like those who built the Tower of Babel, we imagine nothing can overcome us in our castle. Yet, we would be wrong. Misconceptions and miscommunication can cause the strongest castle walls to topple. While the point of Sukkot isn't to be worried about your safety, it teaches us that nothing is permanent and that vulnerability and shelter coexist. Security comes from building relationships of trust and caring that serve, like the sukkah, as partial shelters from the daily winds of life. Walls do offer protection, but we must be careful not to turn our homes into a Fortress of Solitude, like Superman's retreat from the world—aptly named because Superman was a unique being in the world, and his superpowers set him apart from everyone else. Sukkot reminds us that strength and security come from an awareness of vulnerability, not from imagined invulnerability. Like the sukkah, our walls need to be porous enough to let the outside world in. We need to create a sense of security that we can carry with us when we travel the streets of our life's journey. Security comes from trust, not from isolation. Living with the tension between walls and openness helps prepare us for those moments when the carefully constructed walls of our lives collapse. Then we will need to find the inner strength to rebuild rather than just sit among the ruins of our sense of invulnerability. With its themes of harvest and its anxiety about the future, Sukkot is a model for the tension with which we live.

The book of *Kohelet*/Ecclesiastes is the appropriate biblical book to be associated with Sukkot; it recognizes that our lives are like a passing wind or a vanity of vanities. It is true that fundamentally there is nothing new under heaven. The voice of Ecclesiastes is not that of the pessimist or the skeptic. It is the realistic voice of someone who has lived life. Yet, despite that underlying truth, or perhaps because of it, we are free to accomplish what we can. Our lives are not graded pass/fail. They are "graded" by the efforts we make to live up to our vision of ourselves. Yet knowing we are imperfect; we can let go of the vanity of perfection and be free to be the best we can be.

At this moment of harvest, we have come to the end of the year. The earth lies slumbering under its coat (*kittel*) of white for the winter. We don't know what the new year will bring to our story, but we do know that spring will come and new plants will grow and new experiences will occur shaped in part by our efforts.

Bitahon/faith:
A Sukkot spiritual quality (*midah*) practice

Another aspect of Sukkot is the spiritual quality of trust or faith. In Jewish tradition, trust (*bitahon*) means having trust in God. In the face of anxiety about the future, the world is not a world of chance. God makes everything happen and therefore what happens to people happens for a reason. Faith was understood to mean that even when people couldn't fathom a tragedy, they believed that there was some unknown reason for it.

This traditional notion that God intervened in the world didn't mean that you should be passive in the face of life's challenges. If you are sick, you should go to the doctor, not just leave it in God's hands. Neither should you not bother making a living and just trust in God to provide. There is a traditional principle that it is wrong to depend upon miracles as a way out of difficult situations. Trust in God was more often applied to accepting things as they happened.

A contemporary understanding of the quality of trust focuses on the negative aspect of anxiety. We can get caught up in being worried about what will happen. We are very good at imagining all the things that could go wrong or that explain how other people think of us—stories that are based on little or no information. At the extreme, these stories can be paralyzing, causing us to avoid new experiences just because they are new or passing on opportunities to avoid imagined rejections. Even if they don't paralyze us, we can spend enormous amounts of time playing out the *what-ifs* of these stories. Ultimately, they can affect what we think of ourselves and our capabilities.

Rebbe Nahman of Bratslav said: "If you have faith in your ability to mess things up, then you should certainly also have faith in your ability to repair what is broken." As humans, we are not immortal, all-powerful, or all-knowing. It is inevitable that we will make mistakes, but we need to have faith that we also have the ability to do the right thing or to fix what is wrong. The same ability to choose the mistaken path can lead us to choose the wise path. We need to have faith in ourselves, even as we acknowledge that we will continue to be imperfect. Mostly, we try to do the best we can. In any case, worrying about it doesn't actually change anything and can distract us from getting the clarity to make the right choice. There are a lot of factors that come into play when we need to make complicated decisions. Sometimes the decisions we really thought were the correct ones turn out to be mistakes. Other times desire or habit influence us to choose unwisely. Yet, we are always choosing.

Buddhism teaches that we live in a world of suffering. Yet spending energy worrying about suffering doesn't lessen the suffering; often, it increases it. Acknowledging suffering can allow us to see it clearly. The loss of a job or the end of a relationship is a painful experience, but it is part of life; adding anxiety to the loss only makes it worse. Understanding that you can't change the outcome, but that you can figure out how best to move forward, reflects a realistic faith in our ability to live with adversity. Fear and worry lead to an attitude of clutching. Trust can lead to an openness to what comes next, without denying the real sadness or loss we feel.

In this contemporary sense of trust, we no longer believe everything happens for a reason. Instead, we believe that life happens—both the good and the bad. We believe that we are part of a universe that is larger than our individual story. We reject the notion that there is no purpose to existence, that our time here on earth has no meaning. Yet that belief doesn't prevent us from suffering or death.

Sukkot follows the High Holiday period, during which we focus a lot on how we failed during the past year. Yet we also are committed to changing for the better, given the promise of a chance to start over in the new year. We echo Rebbe Nahman's teaching: we can and will do both—mess up and improve. The verse (Ps. 32:10): "One who has faith in God, will feel surrounded by love [*haboteah b'adonai hesed yisoveveinu*]" suggests that a belief in God, Torah, or a belief that there is a purpose to existence enables us to embrace lovingkindness. Lovingkindness reminds us that overall, life is a gift. If we can minimize anxiety then we will be more in touch with the love of friends and family, and our own deepest desire to love and care for others. If a sukkah is not a secure shelter from the world with its challenges, it is a partial shelter that we symbolically carry with us along whatever roads we travel. As an open shelter, it urges us to embrace our many encounters on the road.

Core Principle #7: Wrestling With God

For many people, God is the most challenging aspect of religion. Perhaps more than any other people, Jews have embraced modernity, which offered a way out of the ghettos of Europe and an end to the restrictions on professions open to Jews. Jews also embraced modern culture, with its emphasis on rational thinking and science. Like others, Jews focused on the world of the here and now, downplaying the importance of the doctrines of life after death or the resurrection of the dead. What you did in this world defined your life. If the Middle Ages were characterized by being otherworldly-focused, the modern world is very focused on this world. While in the past, God was the center of the universe, in the modern world humans have taken center stage.

Traditional notion of God

What do I believe about God? The more I think about it, the more the traditional idea of God doesn't make sense to me. In today's world, having doubts about the existence of God is not a unique perspective, but one still not typically expressed by a rabbi. Is there really a being out there that is all-knowing and all-powerful? Did this being create the world, and if so, why? I am not troubled by questions that seem rather silly—if God can create anything, can God create a rock too heavy for God to lift? Such abstract questions seem irrelevant. God should be relevant to how I live my life. Religion is about life truths, not philosophical truths.

Do I really think God freed the Israelites from Egypt by bringing ten plagues? Did God speak at Sinai? Or more broadly, is there a God in which I can believe? If so, what does "God" mean? What is God's nature? Have I experienced God's presence? Let me begin my answers by returning to the Torah text.

A changing God

Some scholars have argued that the God of the Bible develops over time. I would agree and suggest that the balance between God and humans shifts over the course of the Torah. God is the powerful actor in Genesis and yet still seems to be trying to understand humans. Already by the Exodus, while God brings the plagues, Moses and Aaron have an important role to play both as the spokespeople to Pharaoh and the leaders who take the Israelites toward freedom. As I have suggested, God is a God of change. When God calls upon Moses at the burning bush, Moses asks God what he should say when the Israelites ask what is God's name. God responds, *"Ehyeh asher ehyeh"*—I will be what I will be (Ex. 3:14). It is not the God of Abraham, Isaac and Jacob, the God of the past. It is the God of change who will lead the people from slavery to freedom, as if to say the nature of God is ever-changing. It is a mistake to proclaim that God is fixed in one name or conception. God redeems Israel from Egypt so we will know that redemption from slavery is possible. Now it is up to us humans to continue the work of redemption by bringing freedom to the world. Increasingly, humans become the main actors in the Bible. In a later book of the Bible, the author portrays God as favoring King David at various moments in his life, though God performs no miracles for David. David defeats Goliath by using shrewd military strategy. Our understanding of God has changed over time, helping us expand our idea of God. But the question remains: What does God mean in our lives?

When bad things happen to good people

The tradition holds that God rewards the righteous and punishes the wicked. This leads to the dilemma made famous by Harold Kushner in his bestselling book *When Bad Things Happen to Good People*. Ever since Judaism promoted the notion of one God (monotheism), this question has been a challenge. If there is only one God, tragedies can't be blamed on other gods. What makes this even harder is that we believe that God is concerned about morality. If God is neither evil nor capricious, why do innocent children suffer? Monotheistic religions have always struggled with this question.

The bottom line for me is that I can no longer believe in a traditional notion of an omnipotent God. As Kushner wrote, we can choose to believe in an all-powerful God who is not good or a good God who is not all-powerful. If you believe in a God who acts in the world by rewarding and punishing people, how do you explain bad things happening to good people? Why should any innocent baby die? Why should six million Jews be murdered in the Holocaust? If God is ethical and not capricious, how could these things happen? The tradition suggests two responses to these challenging questions. First, we will be rewarded in the world to come, to balance the suffering in this world. Second, these tragedies are part of God's plan, which human beings cannot know (or perhaps comprehend).

The God of Mordecai Kaplan

Neither formulation is acceptable to me. Even if I was certain that there is a world to come, I don't think being rewarded there justifies the suffering people experience in this world. Like Harold Kushner, I would rather believe in an ethical God who is not all-powerful. This means I reject the idea that God acts in the world, either rewarding the righteous or punishing the wicked. This is the notion of God propounded by Kushner's teacher, Rabbi Mordecai Kaplan, the 20th-century founder of Reconstructionism. Kaplan suggested that God is not some entity running the universe. He described God as the "power that makes for salvation." Kaplan maintained that we experience God by experiencing human beings acting in caring ways to each other. At the death of a loved one, God is not to be experienced as the Lord High Executioner. Death occurs not because God decided this person's life should end today but because death is the fate of all human beings. Everyone, even the saintly, will die. Where can God be found at a time of grief? For Kaplan, God is found in the gathering of friends to embrace us in our loss. The best we can do as the living is to hold hands in the face of the encroaching darkness and do our best to remember all the deceased meant to us.

Mordecai Kaplan didn't see God as a noun but rather as an adjective. Rather than claim that God is merciful, Kaplan and his disciples describe mercy as Godly. A more contemporary language describes God as the impulse to be compassionate to others. In Hasidism, the impulse to love or to feel connected to the Holy One is understood as the basic motivating force in the universe. A less deistic version would be to say that the motivating force is to feel connected to the underlying unity in the universe.

God is unknowable

What can we say about God? Very little. God is unknowable. Metaphors that describe God as lord or king, which may have been helpful to our ancestors, are inadequate for us. They no more describe God than those that describe God as an old man with a white beard. The mystics described God as the infinite (*ein sof*) or as Nothingness (*ayin*), acknowledging the inadequacy of words to describe God. Maimonides, the 12th-century philosopher and rabbinic scholar, came to a similar understanding. Though a philosopher and a rationalist, he also maintained that God is indescribable and railed against anthropomorphic descriptions of God in the Bible. Maimonides believed that describing God's outstretched arm or God's anger were at most metaphors for demonstrating God's actions in the world, but ultimately did not describe in any way the character or form of God.

Have I resolved my rational doubts? In part. I have come to a place where I don't have to answer all the contradictions about God. On the one hand, it still doesn't make sense to me that there is some being that runs the universe, but I also don't believe we live in a random universe. I believe life has a purpose. Whenever I think about it rationally, I can't believe in a God. Whenever I sit with my heart, I have faith that we live in a universe of meaning.

What I do know about God (maybe)

I find God a useful way to express other important beliefs. The first is that there is something larger than myself, and it is important to live my life with that consciousness. I believe religion reminds us of a truth that contradicts our experience—the world is larger than me despite the many ways my experience suggests otherwise. This is an essential teaching of Judaism. Traditionally, Jews call this understanding God. I also believe there is an underlying unity to the universe. We need to seek that existential oneness rather than just settle for existential aloneness. These are my beliefs about God. I have no need to prove them to myself or to anyone else. By definition, beliefs are unprovable. Belief requires a leap of faith across the void of doubt. Whether you understand God as some kind of entity or as an expression of an ideal, I hope you can find some belief to carry with you on your life's journey.

The question remains: Why did God create the universe? When I ask myself that question, I again come to a place of disbelief. Why would God create the world? Was God bored? Is the universe some form of a cosmic game? Did God want to be worshipped? Any answer to that question seems ridiculous. In the end I come back to the notion that we live in a universe of meaning.

God's gift of consciousness

That last statement was good enough to start writing this book. While I live my life as though God (of some kind) exists and life has meaning and purpose, I have been forced to reexamine these views in the process of writing this book. Why did God create the world? Maybe God created the world as an act of generosity. This world has enabled billions of people to experience consciousness, which is a gift to each one of us. The world doesn't exist because we deserve it or as a test to see how well we could live. It was an act of generosity when God created the world. One way to interpret the verse in Psalm 89:3 is that the world was built through lovingkindness. When all is said and done, while I remain uncertain about so much, of this I am sure: consciousness is an amazing gift to human beings.

What about the nature of God?

I think Maimonides is correct—there is very little we can say about the nature of God. The midrash says that the Torah begins with the letter *bet*, beginning the word *bereishit* (in the beginning) because its shape is closed on three sides and open only on the left side. This is to teach us that we cannot know what is above or below or what came before the moment of creation. We can only understand what follows creation (Midrash Rabbah 1:10). What were things like before creation? What did God "do" before the universe existed? Did the universe always exist? This question was essential for philosophers like Maimonides but ultimately unknowable.

Sometimes resting in "unknowing" can be a valuable spiritual practice. We learn to accept that being human may mean that there are limits on what our minds can comprehend. Instead, we try to focus on what is accessible to human beings—our past and present—even as we ponder the future. Ultimately, God's importance is in how our faith helps shape our life here and now.

For me, God is the expression of goodness. God is a vision of a world of peace, of connection and of meaning. Life isn't just about my achievements and my acquisitions. It isn't even about my family and my relationships. It is about the universe. Judaism is a call to act in Godly ways. It is a call to awareness.

An awareness of the universe

The *Shulhan Arukh*, the 16th-century classic code of Jewish law, opens by stating:

> One should strengthen oneself like a lion to get up in the morning for the service of the Creator… "*Shiviti YHVH le-negdi tamid*/I have placed God before me always" (Ps. 16:8). This verse states an important principle in Torah and among the righteous who walk before God. For the way in which such a person sits and behaves, and does his business when he is alone in his home is not the same as if he conceives of himself before a great king… All the more so if a person understands in her heart that it is the Great King, the Holy One whose glory fills the whole earth that stands before her and sees what she does…. Even when lying in bed, know before whom you lie, and when you get up, get up with diligence to worship your Creator.

The goal of life is not just to observe every Jewish ritual and law. It is to *place God before me always*. The challenge here lies in the underlying attitude of Joseph Karo, the author of the *Shulhan Arukh*, who suggests the reason to be conscious of God is so we will be on our best behavior in front of an all-powerful king. I don't think placing God before us always is about fear and awe but about being aware of what life is about. We are called to walk through life with a persistent consciousness of the presence of the Holy One. We should have this consciousness as we walk, do business, and interact with people—in other words, when we are engaged in all of the mundane activities of daily life. For the *Shulhan Arukh*, awareness is the goal of life. The whole rest of that code is commentary on how to achieve that awareness. Too often, this underlying purpose is lost, while attention is paid to making sure the commandment is fulfilled properly. Hasidism refers to this as rote ritual done for the sake of its performance, not its meaning. The religious life is about our being aware of the gift and purpose of our lives.

Jews don't bow to idols. Nor do Jews bow to God.

Up until modern times the most common image of God was as king. Earthly kings wielding power and judgment were familiar images that seem to best represent God. Approaching the king/God with awe and some trepidation seemed appropriate for One who held the power of life and death. This idea is reflected in the Amidah, the central prayer of every Jewish prayer service. We bow at the beginning and end of the first blessing as follows: On the first word *barukh/* Praised—we bend our knees. On the second word *atah/*You—we bend forward at our waist. On the third word *Adonai/*God—we stand up straight.

Why do we stand up straight rather than bow when we say God's name? Overall, this bowing practice is to teach us to recognize our limitations. We are human and therefore mortal. We are bound to make mistakes. We express this recognition as we bend and bow to a reality that we too often forget in our hubris. Yet, God does not seek cringing servants. When we actually say God's name, we stand erect. God wants us to stand up straight before God. Actually, it would be more accurate to say God wants us to stand with God. We are to remember that each of us is an image of God. Standing with God reminds us that, despite our limitations, we are also powerful. We are the ongoing creators of this world and must strive to bring about its redemption. This small ritual also reminds us that we are to be upstanders, even to God. As we have seen, Abraham speaks truth to power when he challenges God's justice over the plan to destroy Sodom.

As we move away from the notion of God as king and humans as God's lowly subjects, we take upon ourselves the responsibility for being God's partners. First, we do bend our knees and bow to acknowledge that we are human beings and therefore flawed and mortal. Yet we are ready to stand shoulder to shoulder with the Divine rather than keeping our head lower than "His majesty."

A teaching by Levi Isaac of Berditchev (19th-century Hasidic master) suggests that humans have power in the Divine/human relationship (*Kedushat Levi*, Be-shallah *oh yevuar az yashir*). Based on the verse Psalm 121:5, instead of reading it as "God is your protection," (*adonai tzilkha*) Levi Isaac teaches the words should be read as "God is your shadow." In life, our shadows imitate the movement of our bodies. For Levi Isaac, this verse means that when we act in caring and compassionate ways, God "must" follow suit. In Mordecai Kaplan's theology, we can see God acting in the world not through miracles but by seeing humans act in Godly ways. Levi Isaac and Kaplan are suggesting similar ways to understand the Divine/human dynamic. Humans are important actors in the world. Redemption can come about through human activity. While Levi Isaac has a more traditional view of God, at least in this teaching, he emphasizes the power of human activity.

God and humans: A religious view

The Declaration of Independence states: *We hold these truths to be self-evident: that all men are created equal.* Let's read the Declaration as if it said all *people* or humans rather than all *men*. The Torah says that all human beings are created in the image of God. Is there any significant difference between these two powerful statements of the equality of all human beings?

The answer to that question is the whole point of this book. Religion says that life isn't only a result of evolution or of human creation. There is something larger at stake when we understand that we are all created in the image of God. The Declaration of Independence is an extraordinary document, but it is also a document written by human beings. Judaism claims that there is something in the universe greater than human beings. God is not limited by the current state of human wisdom and understanding. Being created in God's image means that paradoxically, while humans are limited, we also can strive to reach what is beyond us—God. Revelation means the universe continues to unfold and we strive to discover that unfolding. We are stretching to reach higher, deeper, and wiser. Being created in the image of God means that we have the potential to be better and create a world of *tov*/good. It also means that we are empowered with the ability to destroy the world. What makes us uniquely human is our capacity to reach beyond ourselves even as we remain rooted in our fallible selves.

> Issachar Baer of Zlochzow, an 18th-century Hasidic master, taught that we first reflect and realize: "Who am I, a mere man and contemptible as I am…to pray… before the great…King." When he thinks further and realizes he is himself naught but a portion of the Godhead then to the contrary he will pray with great ardor. (*Hasidism as Mysticism*, Rivka Schatz Uffenheimer)

At first, when a person wishes to pray, they think of God's greatness and say to themselves: *Who am I, a mere flawed mortal, to pray before the great and exalted God?* But upon further reflection, they realize that there is no place absent of God, and therefore they, too, are part of the Divine. In this teaching we can see the shift in perception. First the person realizes that they are just a tiny speck in the universe but then realize that speck is of infinite significance because it is part of the Holy One. Judaism is about holding both truths simultaneously. God is the reminder of that human potential. Whether God is a being or an expression of that potential, God calls us to live our lives beyond the mundane. This powerful teaching about the Godlike quality of human beings is a profound statement about a religious view of the relationship between God and humans. We are not God, neither all-powerful nor able to escape death; but we are not just to live life—we are to feel empowered to create and innovate in this world. While we share the basic characteristics of all humans, we are also unique. God's greatest gift is not just consciousness but also the ability to play our part in the unfolding of the world.

We are Godwrestlers

We are the children of Israel, the patriarch, who had a mysterious encounter in the night as he returned back to the land of Canaan after many years of exile.

"And a man wrestled with him until the break of dawn." While the "man" does not prevail, he wrenches Jacob's hip. Jacob will limp the rest of his life. The "man" wishes to leave before sunrise. Jacob won't let him leave without a blessing. The "man" responds: "Your name shall no longer be Jacob, but Israel for you have striven (*sarita*—a play on *yisrael*/Israel) with beings divine and human and have prevailed" (Gen. 32:25, 29).

Who is this "man" with whom Jacob wrestles throughout the night? Is it a being divine, human, or both? In the felicitous phrase of the social justice advocate Arthur Waskow, Jacob/Israel has become a Godwrestler. The people of Israel are wrestlers with beings divine and human. The point isn't to win. The point is to confront what needs to be confronted, whether that is our inner demons, external evil, or even God. It will be painful. We may come away limping, but questioning is an essential part of "the journey into the heart of darkness," as Joseph Conrad so powerfully described it.

Seeing God

I have re-read this chapter many times wondering whether I have been helpful to you, the reader. It is clear that many people these days don't believe in God and therefore don't believe they are religious. I have tried to answer why or what I believe in a variety of ways, even as I acknowledge that ultimately it is a matter of faith. There is no proof.

If you have never experienced God, it is very hard to believe in God. This is an old anxiety. The Israelites, even after experiencing God at Mt. Sinai, will be uncertain only 40 days later. They will ask for something tangible that they could proclaim as their God; the Golden Calf is the response. Despite that disaster and despite the fact that Moses spent those 40 days receiving the written Torah directly from God, even Moses wants more proof of God. In the aftermath of the Golden Calf incident, the relationship between God and the Jewish people seems shattered. God tells Moses and the people that they should go on with the journey to the promised land but God won't accompany them. The people are in despair. Moses pleads for God to accompany them on their journey in the desert. God agrees and Moses responds "Oh, let me behold Your Presence—*kavod!*" (Ex. 33:18).

After the Golden Calf episode, it seems odd that Moses asks to be reassured by seeing God! Wasn't the whole mistake of that episode that the people sought reassurance of God's existence by making a way to "see" God? Aaron and the people made the Golden Calf, a finite physical representation of an infinite and changing God. Apparently, we all want reassurance. We all want to feel protected or cared for by a benevolent God—even Moses. In response to this request, God explains to Moses that a human being cannot see God and live. Therefore, God says, "I will place you, Moses, in the cleft of a rock and shield you with My hand until I pass by and then when I remove My hand you will see My back but not My face" (Ex. 33:22-23).

What did Moses actually see? God says, "I will pass (*tuvi*)—My goodness before you…and the grace and compassion that I show" (Ex. 33:19). Moses doesn't see a being but rather how God acts in the world with grace and compassion. The essence of God is described by the word *tov*—goodness. At the end of each day of creation, God says "it is good." Ours is a moral universe. God is about goodness, yet much of the universe is amoral. A plant doesn't choose to act in good or bad ways; humans do. It is our responsibility to bring more goodness into the world. In the language of the mystics, it is up to humans to redeem the sparks of holiness that are scattered throughout the world. We are the force that makes for redemption. Moses can't see God literally, but he can experience God's compassion toward the world and thereby "see" God.

Some commentators suggest that Moses doesn't see God's "back" but God's *ahorei*—the aftermath of God's passing by. Or more radically, Moses sees the world through God's "back," meaning Moses sees the world from God's perspective. It is as though Moses sees the world through God's eyes. In that moment, Moses sees the world in its vastness and its suffering, in its struggles and its strivings, and in its love. It is that vision of God's goodness that gives Moses the strength to continue on the journey ahead. Perhaps that moment of vision is the "God" that will accompany Moses and the Israelites on the long journey ahead.

In all my years of being involved in Jewish life, have I ever experienced God?

Did I ever feel I was in the presence? There are moments when I am singing Hasidic *niggunim*/melodies and I am present to the music and entirely unselfconscious. I am not wondering or concerned about what people are thinking of me. I am just singing. There is a feeling of openness. There is only music. This doesn't happen all the time. Most often it is when I am leading services and repeating a melody again and again. It happens more when it is a wordless melody than one with words. When I lead services and when I sing, I don't look at people (I look down) because I don't want to be distracted by someone looking uninterested. Yet, I am very aware of the other people present and their participation in the singing. I lead them in the singing and they inspire me by their joining in the singing. We inspire each other. Perhaps those moments are times when I touch the oneness that underlies the world. Perhaps in those moments I experience a different consciousness. Music is special. Opening our mouths in song is for many people one of the easiest ways to open ourselves up. The dropping of barriers allows us to connect to the oneness of the world. Ultimately, religion, God and Judaism are about that openness. They are about touching that truth.

In that cleft of rock, Moses sees the universe as ever-expanding and understands that the world is infinite. Maybe that explains both what it means to be in the image of God, who has no image, and simultaneously hints to the nature of God, described as *ein sof*—infinite—by the mystics. We are human and mortal, but we have the capacity to be Godlike. There is no limit to our capacity to love. We don't say to our third child, "Sorry, we used up all our love with your older siblings." There is no limit to our capacity to work for redemption or to create art or literature. There is no limit to discovering insights or to be in wonder of nature.

Whether we understand God as a being, as the universe, or as a vision of our limitless potential, ultimately, Judaism is about understanding the infinite possibilities.

The end of traditional prayer

Despite a lifetime of praying and leading services, I have come to believe that traditional prayer no longer works for most Jews and requires radical reconstruction. Prayer and its music have been central to my Jewish life. I led services at both Maimonides Day School and at Hillel at Brandeis, but my real introduction to leading services was at Havurat Shalom. While traditional in style, the services emphasized *kavanah*—praying with intention. The mood of the services ranged from contemplative to joyous. This was especially apparent in the use of *niggunim*/ wordless Hasidic melodies that were sung in a repetitive style that could last for many minutes.

This model of services continued to work for me over the next few decades even as I realized some of its problems. It was a model that depended heavily on the person who was leading services. Needless to say, there were some very skilled leaders and some much less so. Some of this had to do with creativity and musical ability. Mostly it had to do with how well the leader could engage and inspire those attending the services. Unlike traditional service-leading, these services required constant creativity in order to keep things fresh week after week. This is especially a challenge when the services are led by volunteers. Nobody was paid to plan these services. Over time, these services had little variation from one week to the next except the selection of music that was drawn from a large repertoire.

In the *New York Times Magazine*, there was an article more than a decade ago provocatively entitled "Is there a right way to pray?" by Zev Chafets. It includes a description of prayer by a Baptist minister: "Let God begin the conversation. Keep your prayers brief and clear. Repeat simple, Scripture-based phrases. Pray standing up to fight torpor. And pray directly facing others, eye to eye, in a loud clear voice." Were someone to describe Jewish prayer, *brief, clear* and *simple* do not immediately spring to mind. Instead, the description might read: Make sure your Shabbat morning services are at least two to three hours long, thereby ensuring people will vote with their feet by showing up an hour late. Most importantly, make sure those prayers are in a language the vast majority of attendees don't understand. Even if someone does understand Hebrew or is following the prayers in English, they will find the language old fashioned. They may wonder why God is praised over and over again. Some find the God language troubling because it is always referring to God as masculine or uses outdated metaphors such as king or lord. Liberal modern prayer books have tried to address these issues with commentary, new translations and English readings. Some have tried to address the issue of God language. No matter how much editing we do, *brief, simple*, and *clear* remain elusive.

Disconnected prayer

The more fundamental challenge is the act of praying itself. If you ask people to define prayer, most would answer that prayer is asking God for things like a new job or the healing of a loved one. Yet an increasing number of Jews don't believe in a God who makes such things happen. Like the notion of God rewarding and punishing individuals, the notion that God says *yes* even occasionally to someone who prays for a loved one who is dying contradicts most Jews' understanding of how the world works.

For liberal Jews, prayer takes place almost exclusively in synagogue and only on Shabbat and High Holidays. In our increasingly fast-paced world, services are one of the few things that last for several hours. While Broadway plays and musical concerts can last that long, compare the amount of planning, creativity, resources and staffing that go in to creating and staging a performance to that of a Shabbat service. Some of the most successful synagogues today have added musicians to services to help fill the room with sound, and most liberal synagogues have shifted from a performative style with musical solos to congregational singing of Jewish folk music. Adding energy and music has helped, but still has not solved the problem.

Prayer was never an easy enterprise but is now far less likely to succeed because of the erosion in the belief in the enterprise itself. It is not just that we wonder about the value of praising God. I think we wonder what anything we are saying has to do with our lives. I attended a conference on religion and healing many years ago where a nun shared with the audience a sample of the prayers she composes for her hospital patients. They were individualized and reflected the various experiences of those patients. When the rabbi's turn to speak came, he talked about the *mi-sheberakh* prayer. The *mi-sheberakh* is the traditional prayer that asks God to heal a person who is sick. It is individualized only to the extent that people can add the person's name to the general prayer. Whether the patient was dying, had just gotten a good prognosis, was on the way to surgery, or was suffering from a chronic disease, there is only one formulaic prayer to recite. Unlike the nun, the rabbi had never composed an individualized prayer for a patient. There simply hasn't been a culture of improvisation within Jewish tradition.

Prayer that connects to people's lives

Prayer needs to connect people to the most important issues of their lives. The beginning of that process is to reframe prayer. The next challenge is how to use the traditional liturgy or parts of it to make those connections to the spiritual life of individuals. The Friday night after September 11th, I reflected in my Manhattan synagogue on the image in the hymn *Lekhah Dodi* of a city in ruins. Suddenly, a prayer people sang without much thought resonated with what was foremost on every one's mind. Certainly, in many synagogues rabbis reflected on 9/11 and perhaps inserted a traditional prayer for those suffering. Yet, in most synagogue services, the liturgy the week before 9/11 and the week of 9/11 was the same. A while ago I was at a synagogue community that had gathered to pray for an adult member who was about to undergo major surgery. The gathering consisted of the evening service. Yet, the imagery of the evening prayers was absent. The imagery of rolling darkness into light, God's love for us, crossing the sea of difficulty to the other shore, going and coming in peace, and lying under God's sheltering presence as connected to this moment went unmentioned. There was a complete disconnect between the liturgy and what was on the mind of every single person who was in that room, despite the fact that the themes in the liturgy might very well have been helpful if the leader stopped for a moment and brought our attention to the way they connected to our concern for our friend. Whatever was said about the situation, it was said as an add-on to the service. It was a telling example of how the traditional liturgy is made irrelevant to people's lives.

The model of healing services

A person responsible for helping me rethink prayer was Debbie Friedman, singer and musician (1951-2011), who tragically died too young. Suffering from illness herself, Debbie was one of the leaders in the Jewish healing movement, which sought to create space for people who looked to the Jewish tradition for support. Debbie and I decided to lead a once-a-month healing service together. When we met to begin planning the service, we realized that we were beginning with a tabula rasa—a blank page. Not having a real model liberated and challenged us to create something new. We decided that the service would consist of readings, songs, and reflective teachings on a theme. The theme would not be illness, but would focus on related topics such as brokenness and wholeness, or light and darkness. Most months we tied the theme to the Jewish holiday of the month. The music was a mixture of Debbie's songs and Hasidic music. We would end each service by singing Debbie's *mi-sheberakh* (written by Debbie and Drorah Setel) during which people could say the name of anyone they wanted included in the prayer, including themselves.

We led services together for nine years. They became a model to me of what services could be. The people who came were either sick or had relatives or friends who were sick. There were also people who were in neither of those categories who came regularly. They came because these were spiritual themes in their lives. They struggled with darkness and disappointment. They sought hope and celebration.

Everyone at the service knew why they were there and what they hoped to get out of the experience. They saw the connection between their lives and the readings and the teachings and the songs. They never asked themselves why we were saying a particular prayer. The gap between what is in the prayer book and what is in peoples' hearts and their guts didn't exist in these services. The healing services were not just accessible; they were immediately meaningful. Nothing in this hour-long service seemed irrelevant. Neither did it need a five-minute explanation by the rabbi of how you could interpret this prayer so it made sense.

Despite the success of these services, and my attempt to improve on Shabbat services in the various experiences and communities of which I had been a part, I still struggled to understand what wasn't working and what might be a solution.

The basic elements of rabbinic prayer

Before suggesting ways to reconstruct prayer, it might be helpful to set out the basic structure of rabbinic prayer. There are three basic elements of prayer—praise of God, requests of God, and gratitude to God. While prayers of request are basically absent from our Shabbat and holiday liturgy, they are central to the daily liturgy and I would suggest are at the heart of how most Jews think of prayer. Is there a way to re-envision these three elements of rabbinic prayer—praise, request, and gratitude? What if instead of praising God, we take a moment to acknowledge that the universe is much larger than ourselves. We strive to regain a perspective that we are not the center of the universe. For some, that would be acknowledging a God who created the universe. For others, it would be recognizing that they are only one person in a world of eight billion people and an uncountable number of living creatures. The point isn't to feel worthless; it is to regain perspective. While I can only see the world from my perspective, it is good to remember that everyone else sees from their own perspective as well.

Instead of thanking God, we might simply express gratitude for the blessings that we enjoy in our life. Feeling grateful is a central spiritual practice. It is not only that we too often take things for granted. By being grateful, we bring to our consciousness that we have many blessings—health, relationships, and life itself. It is also a better spiritual place to live—a sense of having rather than a sense of lacking.

This leaves only one traditional rubric—that of requests. This requires a sharper reimagining. Rather than requests of God, we might consider these as requests we make of ourselves. In what ways have we not lived up to our own values? The service becomes a time for inner work on our spiritual and ethical qualities. We sit in reflection. Where are we spiritually? What can we leave behind from the last week? What should we make a point of carrying forward into the new week? What can we celebrate and what can we acknowledge can be done better going forward?

Prayer in my retirement

When I retired, I had to find a synagogue. I had decided not to attend the synagogue where I had served as rabbi for 14 years so that the new rabbi would have plenty of room without my presence. At first, I was fine about not going to synagogue on Shabbat. It felt good to have a break. After leading the service for so many years (even before I became a rabbi), the transition to being a congregant was not so simple and my frustrations about services were only exacerbated when I was sitting in the pews. Manhattan is blessed with many synagogues and my wife and I tried out a good many of them. I found that the more traditional the service, the more restless I felt with the length of the liturgy. In the end, we joined a synagogue where we liked the music and respected and admired the clergy.

I was surprised to discover that my dissatisfaction with services was shared by many of our friends, most of whom are Jewish professionals. They all regularly attended Shabbat services but were also unhappy with the experience. From these conversations I created the non-minyan with several of our friends and colleagues. It is called the non-minyan not because it lacked a traditionally required quorum of 10 adults, but because I wanted to be clear up front that what was going to happen would not resemble a traditional minyan service. I told the group I wanted to experiment with a format that began with the assumption that there would be no recitation of traditional liturgy. We would meet once a month for an hour-and-a-half on Shabbat morning. We would spend half the time in a spiritual practice (formerly called prayer) and half the time studying/discussing a topic in the current Torah portion or a theme of an upcoming Jewish holiday. Each month I put together a handout with lines from the liturgy or other Jewish sacred texts, together with readings. Each month we would focus on one such theme, like holiness, open-heartedness, or the power of words. We would move back and forth, singing a line of Hebrew, reading a poem or a *kavanah*/intention, and then singing again. The idea was to reflect on a spiritual theme aided by teaching, singing, and the readings. Sometimes we would begin with study and discussion, which helped support the theme during the prayer part of the morning. Other times we would spend the first half of our time in "prayer" and then study—a pattern that follows the traditional structure of Shabbat morning services. We rarely did a whole paragraph of liturgy. We never recited the *Shema* or the *Amidah*. We never ended with *Adon Olam*. The only prayer we recited consistently was the mourner's Kaddish. We didn't chant the weekly portion from a Torah scroll. In other words, no one would confuse this with a traditional prayer service.

Overall, I found this new model was successful and have even expanded it to the High Holidays, which are open to a wider public. Whether this is a sustainable model over time is unclear. It requires real work on my part to put it together each month. Does it feel like a spiritual practice? Yes. Does it feel similar as an experience to what happens in services in synagogue? Yes. Could this model work in a synagogue setting? Certainly. There are of course many issues to consider. What happens to the existing service? To the Torah reading? To life cycle celebrations? Do the current clergy have the skill set to pull this off successfully? These are difficult and challenging questions without simple answers. What I do believe is that the current model of synagogue service is failing for a large number of Jews. We need to explore new models that combine spirituality, learning and community if synagogues are not just to survive but to thrive by the end of the 21st century.

The effect of the Covid pandemic on services

Most synagogues closed during the pandemic and live services were suspended. For liberal synagogues the answer was to use Zoom or livestreaming to allow people to participate from their homes. The biggest drawback of the experience was that there could not be communal singing because the time lag on Zoom turned singing into cacophony. The second drawback was screen fatigue, which is particularly problematic during the High Holidays, which are quite lengthy. Many synagogues tried to shorten the service. The biggest advantage of Zoom was that it allowed people easy access to services. They didn't need to leave their homes. It was possible to sign on to services all across the country. Some of the large synagogues that invested resources in creating a produced experience saw their attendance numbers skyrocket. Even smaller synagogues with less technological capability increased their numbers, perhaps because people found it easier to attend services and perhaps because they were craving community at a time of isolation. For halakhic reasons, Orthodox synagogues considered Zoom or streaming forbidden on Shabbat and festivals, which has had a significant impact on a community that is strongly committed to weekly synagogue attendance.

By the spring of 2021, synagogues started to reopen, at least on a limited basis. Anecdotally, I've heard a number of Orthodox people expressing reluctance about going back to synagogue because they discovered they didn't miss it during Covid. There is also talk among liberal Jews that services are too long, especially on High Holidays, and they are reluctant to return to the way it was pre-Covid. Whether these are fleeting feelings or will lead to real change, time will tell. However, I believe that Covid made the problems of synagogue services all the more apparent.

The end of prayer?

I believe that we have come to the end of traditional prayer as a central aspect of Judaism. This isn't the first time in Jewish history where such a radical break has occurred. Just as Judaism moved from a sacrificial cult with priests in a Temple to communal prayer in synagogues, we must now reconstruct how Jews come together to focus on the spiritual aspects of our lives. In reconstructing prayer, we no longer direct our words to an unanswering God, but rather see prayer as a time to focus on our inner lives. One of the ways the rabbis referred to prayer is *avodah she-belev*— the service of the heart. In our busy lives, services must become an opportunity for self-reflection that brings us back in touch with some of our deeper values. Services need to help us acknowledge that we are part of a universe larger than ourselves; that we are neither all-powerful nor powerless; that we are unique and yet not alone in the universe. Services become a time to articulate a set of values:

To celebrate community.

To be grateful for the wonders of creation.

To be grateful for the gift of life.

To strive toward compassion and understanding toward everyone.

To seek to work on such qualities as patience, equanimity, and generosity.

These values can be in relationship to God: *I am grateful to You for creating nature.* Or *I feel connected to the Oneness that underlies all creation.* Or it can be "godless." *I feel grateful for the community, for my life, for the wonders of creation.* For some, services will still be a time to strive to experience being in the presence of God (as it was for the Hasidim). There is a place for a more mystical understanding of *avodah she-belev*/service of the heart. Some will want to experience feeling connected to that which is beyond themselves by temporarily erasing the sharp boundaries between ourselves and God, either by losing oneself in song or meditating on a word that embodies service of the heart. We are seeking an experience of connection, not an answer to a request.

Services in this post-rabbinic Judaism would provide time to reflect on our *kavanah*/intention of the past week and prepare for the coming week. The liturgy would give structure and focus to the time. I am not suggesting *avodah she-belev* just be an hour of silent meditation. What of the traditional liturgy? While it remains a rich source of material that might give expression to our deepest spiritual questions, its length, archaic language, difficult theology, and the way it is organized in the traditional prayer service simply fails to bring us in touch with those spiritual truths. I disagree with those who think its length is intended to lead to one moment of meaningful prayer. I no longer believe in the value of reciting the service from beginning to end, even in an abbreviated manner.

What about petitionary prayer? Many of us will resort to it at the moments we feel the need. We do not need a fixed liturgy to pray for someone whom we love deeply who is sick. At those moments we all know what to say because we speak from our hearts—that too is literally *avodah she-belev.*

Is this notion of *avodah she-belev*—this turning inward—just another manifestation of the narcissistic qualities of our society or another form of pop psychology self-treatment? It could be; everything has within it the possibility of becoming trivial. A key element is that *avodah she-belev* will often take place in community. After all, the Jewish tradition emphasizes that while solitary prayer is clearly possible, it is optimal when prayer takes place in a minyan—a community of 10 or more people. Why? Because it is important for us to remember our common humanity. The inner life is not lived alone in a cave but rather in the complexity of daily interactions with all those around us. Most of all we pray together—and mostly in the plural—to remind us that the purpose of *avodah she-belev* is not for you or me to achieve *nirvana*/perfection. Rather, the goal of *avodah she-belev* is to enrich our lives so we can be better positioned to touch the lives of everyone around us, so we all live in a more compassionate and caring world. Where is prayer in this description? If you think prayer means asking God for things, then nowhere. If you think prayer provides a way to reflect on our spiritual lives, to give expression to our goals and hopes, to help make the coming week better, then it is all over the place. What is Jewish about this? It is Jewish because Jews are doing it together using verses from Psalms and the prayer book accompanied by Jewish teachings. But mostly I believe it is Jewish because it offers the potential of connection to our deepest, best selves, because it offers the potential of holiness in our lives and in our world.

A vision of what could be

Is this a radical suggestion? Perhaps. But perhaps it is just acknowledging the truth of many of our experiences of prayer. As difficult and challenging as it is to imagine *avodah she-belev* replacing prayer as we know it, it also offers an opportunity to answer an essential question. Imagine for a moment:

Your friend asks you: *Why do you belong to a synagogue?* and, even more puzzling, *Why would you attend on a regular basis?* You answer: Because it is one of the most important things in my life. I join with a community of others to explore critical issues of my life: Who am I? Who do I want to be? Where do I find or create meaning in my life? What is it all about? In the synagogue, one of the few refuges from cell phones, I have the ability to disconnect from the distractions of the world in order to renew the connections to the deepest places within myself that some call the soul. While I acknowledge that my time here on earth is the equivalent of a blink of the eye in the timeline of the universe, I connect to a tradition that precedes me and will continue long after I'm gone, and thereby touch eternity. I engage with the texts of that tradition and am inspired by its ancient insights and the contemporary insights of my fellow congregants. I sit here with no other agenda than to be present in the moment, to explore and reflect on the spiritual qualities that I strive for, to remind myself of the challenges of this broken world and commit myself to engage in acts of *tikkun*, of repair.

Wouldn't you want to be part of that experience?

Idolatry: How religion fails God

I have tried to explain the positive nature of religion and of God. Whether you believe in God and especially if you don't, you most likely see the Torah's focus on idolatry as irrelevant to modern life. I want to suggest that idolatry remains important in understanding Judaism.

In the Bible, the great sin is idolatry. The kings of Israel and Judah are judged on whether they allowed the worship of other gods. According to the rabbis, the first Temple in Jerusalem was destroyed because the people worshipped other gods. How is idolatry a relevant category today? Some suggest that idolatry is still a challenge because we have new false gods that we worship. The gods of money and fame have replaced Baal and Astarte. There are new false gods in whom we put our trust and think will save us from the challenges of life.

There is a different way that idolatry is still very much alive in our world. It is a danger that is inherent in religion; its dark side. Even as the biblical text describes what could be the highpoint of the Jewish story—the encounter with God at Sinai—we are warned about this danger that lies within religion. The Torah text quickly moves from the supreme religious moment of the revelation at Sinai to the depths of the story of the Golden Calf.

Frustration and impatience at Sinai

After the revelation of the Ten Commandments, God tells Moses to come up on Mount Sinai to receive the tablets with the Ten Commandments and the accompanying teachings. Moses is to be with God for 40 days and nights receiving the Torah. In traditional Judaism, Moses is given the books of the Torah—Genesis, Exodus, Leviticus, Numbers, and Deuteronomy during this period, as well as the Oral Torah that helps to explicate the written text. Meanwhile, the people become increasingly concerned because of Moses' prolonged absence, detailed in Exodus 32. "They gathered against Aaron (Moses' brother) and said to him: 'Come, make for us a god who shall go before us, for that man Moses, who brought us from the land of Egypt, we do not know what has happened to him.'" Aaron tells them to take the gold earrings from their wives. Then Aaron casts the gold in a mold and makes a golden calf. "And they exclaimed *eleh elohekha yisrael* (This is your god O Israel)... Early the next day the people celebrated a festival to the god and they brought offerings and ate and drank and danced."

Meanwhile, up on the mountain, God informs Moses that the people have turned away from the right path and are worshipping a golden calf. Moses comes down from Mt. Sinai, smashes the tablets with the Ten Commandments, and then punishes those who worshipped the Golden Calf.

What is the sin of the Golden Calf?

There is a great deal of discussion by the traditional commentators about what exactly the people did wrong. Did they believe the Golden Calf was the God who took them out of Egypt or was it just a physical representation of that God? Was the calf a statue of the God of Israel or were the people looking for a new god, having felt abandoned by the old one?

The story of the Golden Calf reflects a problem inherent in religion. Idolatry is not about worshipping a statue, or even about the "false" god it represents. Idolatry is about the worshipper. Idolatry is claiming to know who God is. The worshipper who says *eleh elohekha yisrael*—this and only this is God—is an idolater. Someone who claims to know exactly what God is or what God wants is an idolater. Why? Because God is ultimately unknowable. As noted previously, at the burning bush Moses asks, *Who should I tell the Israelites is the God that will free you from Egypt?* God answers, *Ehyeh asher ehyeh*—I will be what I will be. God is unfixed. God is changing and fluid. An idol is fixed, frozen in the moment of creation. Aaron takes solid gold and melts it into a fluid form. It is shaped into an image of a calf and solidifies in that image. The first mistake of idolatry is to take that which is infinite and that which changes and freeze it in one moment and one image and proclaim that this is God or the image of God. By limiting God in this way, that person denies the truth about God. The problem isn't worshipping the statue or the wrong god—the problem is denying the limitless nature of God. The second mistake is proclaiming this and only this is God. The Jewish mystics have it right when they talk about the many aspects of the Divine.

Religion and the truth

We might think that religion is essentially about knowing the truth about existence. But we can't know that truth. As finite beings we cannot fully grasp that which is infinite. The mystics described God as *ein sof*—without end, limitless. We can get glimpses of the truth. We can describe aspects of the Divine. We can suggest our understanding of God, knowing that our understanding is limited by our very nature as human beings. But we cannot know the whole truth. This is why idolatry is not some problem that only existed in ancient times. Nor is it really about worshipping "false gods" like money or fame. Idolatry is inextricably linked with religion. Religion suggests it has the answers to the ultimate questions. People then believe they know exactly what the truth is about God, about life and death, about suffering, about any of the times we are uncertain or afraid. Thinking you have the truth isn't worshipping God; it is idolatry. Judaism is about asking questions, searching for insights, finding partial truths for ourselves. We live not in the Garden of Eden, but in the real world, filled as much with disappointment as with joy. We strive to live by the ideals of Torah but we often need to choose between less-than-perfect options.

Idolatry is believing that you have an exclusive hold on the truth. Jewish fundamentalists who claim that their version of Judaism and only their version is Torah-true have made a serious mistake. By their very act of limiting God to one name, definition or doctrine, they deny the very nature of God, who is unlimited and cannot be circumscribed by words of description. The midrash says that every Jew at Mount Sinai heard the word of God at the same time as every other Jew but it claims each one heard it differently (Exodus Rabbah 5:9). Humans cannot speak different words simultaneously, but God can. If God is everywhere and in everything, then God is the many that is one.

Seeking an unfolding truth

We have seen a different definition of the God of change: *I will be what I will be*. It rests in a changing notion of the perceived truth of God. Liberal Judaism suggests that Torah comes from the encounter of the human and the divine. It is a difficult task to hear clearly what the voice of Sinai is saying amidst the thunder and lightning of life. It is challenging to acknowledge that each person hears the voice differently. It is difficult to continue to ask what the Godly response is to the social and political issues before us. It is challenging to advocate strongly for what we believe is right while acknowledging the possibility that we may be wrong. We do not have the assured belief of the fundamentalist. We stand on seemingly shakier or at least less easily discernible ground. I remember my yeshiva teachers arguing that without the Torah as the word of God, people only had a subjective standard for what is moral. They said: Look at Nazi Germany where the murder of millions became legal. Torah is absolute morality because it comes from God—everything else is relative.

For me, the problem is not that I don't believe that Torah is the word of God. The real problem is that the word of God has been used over and over again by religions to kill people in God's name. Wars in the name of religion have been a feature of religion right from the beginning. The word of God doesn't prevent people from misunderstanding or misusing it. It is hard to disagree that it is just as likely for a person motivated by a religious belief to be immoral as someone who lacks any religious belief. It might even be more likely because of the notion of idolatry. If you believe that you have the whole truth, then there is no reason to question your course of action. Compromise seems beyond the bounds of possibility.

There are no easy answers. Those who think there are simple answers are practicing a form of idolatry. The limitless God cannot be confined within a set of doctrines or in a series of texts. Idolatry is an ever-present danger to people who are religious. The fundamental mistake of most religions is when people worship the false god of the absolute truth of their religion.

Sacrificing life for God

Nowhere in the Bible is this point made clearer than in its most challenging text known as the *Akedah*/the binding of Isaac. God tells Abraham to sacrifice his son, Isaac. Many traditional commentators see it as a story of Abraham's ultimate faith because he is willing to sacrifice his son to God. I want to suggest that this story, like some other Genesis texts, is teaching us how *not* to act. In this reading, Abraham completely fails the test of the binding of Isaac. The story of the *Akedah* is actually a cautionary tale about religion. It suggests that believing you know what God wants is a mistake. It is at the moment of the *Akedah* that God realizes that fanaticism is a significant danger in religion. When you believe you have the absolute truth, nothing can dissuade you from that belief. I imagine God weeping as God tells Abraham not to sacrifice Isaac, for God can foresee all the *Akedahs* still to come. There will be many holy crusades in the name of God. Many "unbelievers" will be killed to save their souls. We all are aware of the misuse of religion, not just in the past, but in our time as well.

Similarly, we learn from the story of the flood that the answer is never to kill everyone. God commits the first genocide, only to promise never again to commit genocide. It never fixes anything. How do we know which parts of the Torah are cautionary tales about how not to act and which ones are models of a call to action? Are we just making it up as we go? What's the point of religion if we still have to figure it out ourselves?

The Torah contains a lot of wisdom, debated by Jews over the centuries. It also contains some basic principles. The most basic of these principles is that every human being is created in the image of God. Everyone. It should therefore be obvious that you can't kill another image of God in the name of that very same God. It can't be right, though clearly there are other principles that may apply in specific circumstances—the most obvious being self-defense.

Judaism calls for questioning

Thinking life is simple is a mistake. Life is complex. Making moral choices is difficult. But Judaism's starting premise is that life is sacred. The *Akedah* makes clear that, as much as the Torah encourages a commitment to the tradition of

Judaism, it does not ask for unquestioning compliance. Right from the beginning, it recognizes the danger of fanaticism and rejects blind obedience. Questioning is an important practice in Judaism. Abraham knows that full well. When God decides to kill all the inhabitants of the town of Sodom because of their evil behavior, Abraham challenges God. He speaks truth to power, wondering whether the Almighty is condemning the innocent with the guilty. It is the pre-eminent example in the Torah of what it means to follow God's way. The prophets will carry on this tradition of challenging authority when they criticize the kings of Israel and Judah when they break God's law. Yet it is not only leaders who ask challenging questions. Children are expected to ask questions, as we see in the Passover Seder. While clearly an effective pedagogic tool to keep children engaged, the key here is that even the most marginal participants at the Seder, the children, are supposed to challenge what is being said. Questioning authority is freedom in action. Even the so-called wicked child has a seat at the Seder table. Questioning authority and questioning ourselves are key tools in the journey of life.

Our very name—Hebrew—reflects the importance of challenging the status quo. Abraham is called a Hebrew, *ivri*, but in a midrashic play, the rabbis link the word to *ayver*, which means opposite. They suggest that Abraham was on one side and the rest of the world was on another (Genesis Rabbah 42:8). While some have taken that to mean Jews are special/chosen or that the whole world is against us, there is another way to understand it. Abraham was willing to stand alone on one side with the whole world on the other. He was willing to break new ground. He was an iconoclast—smashing the idols of the accepted way to think of the world. He discovers God and thus breaks out beyond a limited way to think of the Divine. He was willing to challenge what is and even to challenge the justice of the Judge of the earth over God's plan to destroy Sodom. Abraham believed in change and possibility. To be a Hebrew is to be connected to that rich tradition. To be a Hebrew/*ivri* means to be willing both to stand up for justice and to advocate for new ways of thinking and being in the world.

> From the cowardice that shrinks from new truth;
> from the laziness that is content with *half-truths*;
> from the arrogance that thinks it knows all truth
> —O, God of truth, deliver us.
> —Mordecai Kaplan, founder of Reconstructionist Judaism

Facing loss and death: How God fails us

Perhaps the only thing more difficult than facing change is facing loss. We live our lives denying the inevitable losses, whether they occur in our personal or professional lives. Dealing with loss is an increasing challenge that comes with growing older as our bodies change, making the reality of such losses harder to ignore. The reality of death is brought home each time someone we know dies. Death is the most difficult loss because of its finality. I don't believe that God causes our death either as a punishment or part of some grand plan. Death is part of the natural process of the world. All things die.

How then do I make sense of the losses and the suffering in my life? How can I claim that this is a moral universe or a world of meaning and purpose? Can we really say it is a world of *tov*/goodness when death always wins in the end? Isn't Ecclesiastes right that life "is a vanity of vanities, all is vanity" (Eccl. 1:1)? Or Macbeth when he says, "life...is a tale... of sound and fury signifying nothing"? When we are in pain, it is very hard not to wonder, *Why me?* That question suggests that you are being punished even if you don't rationally believe that God or your deeds or the universe is striking out at you.

Responding to loss

Living with loss is the most challenging spiritual practice. I want to suggest a response to that challenge based on reinterpreting a Kabbalistic idea called *hamtakat ha-dinim*—sweetening the judgments. In Jewish mysticism, *din* is the opposite quality of *hesed*/lovingkindness. *Hesed* is free-flowing openness. One traditional way to understand *sweetening the judgments* is that in the face of physical suffering, we should overwhelm the judgment with lovingkindness (*hesed*). In so doing we might be able to reverse the judgment.

While the traditional translation of *din is* judgment, I prefer to translate it as limitations. I want to understand sweetening as acceptance of what is. It is like the phrase about averting the severity of the decree that ends the Unetaneh Tokef prayer on High Holidays. The decree cannot be averted, but we can change its impact on us. We can lessen the bitterness of unwanted limitations through a process of gaining clarity.

Seeing our limitations

The first step in this process is to remind ourselves that we are imperfect people. We were born flawed and raised by flawed human beings. Perhaps you lost your job or have a difficult relationship with your daughter. There is usually a role you played in these difficulties. There are other losses in which you had no role, like chronic physical pain. In either situation, you are not suffering because you are a bad person—at worst, you are a flawed person, just like everyone else in the world. Humans are by definition limited.

We continue the process of sweetening our limitations by seeing what they are and how they factor into the situation. We are in some ways defined by our limitations. They are who we are. We were born with them or raised with them. Sometimes we worked hard on our own to achieve these qualities, mistakenly thinking they were a useful path for us. Seeing our limitations, we can blame ourselves and pile on all the other things that challenge us. Or we could say that blaming ourselves for the way we are is not useful. How can we free ourselves from the patterns that lock us to our past?

Regret and guilt get in the way

Regret and guilt are factors that can confuse our reality. Your mother dies after a long illness. Could you have done more for her? I have rarely met anyone who felt he had done enough for his dying parent. A man once came to me for pastoral counseling about two months after his mother died. He talked about sitting in her hospital room with his father during her last days. He told me he left the room for a few minutes to buy some food for lunch and by the time he came back his mother had died. He said to me, *I can't believe my mother died all alone. I feel like I abandoned her in the last moments of life.* We sat quietly and then I asked, *I thought you said your father was with you in the hospital?* He looked at me startled and then said, *You're right. My father was in the room when she died.* For two months, the son had been living with deep guilt about a reality constructed only from guilt. How was it possible that he had forgotten his father was in the room? It was a powerful example of how guilt can distort the truth.

It is hard to see clearly through the veil of pain, whether that pain is physical or emotional, but that is what is called for during ordinary moments and critically important at challenging moments. I need to see what is happening clearly—to see what is true and what is just a story. His mother's death was real. That she died alone was false. Pain and loss are real. Suffering is the story that elaborates on the pain. It is catastrophizing what happened, thinking that it is not just this moment but my whole life that is filled with failure or loss. It is not just this relationship that has ended but no one likes me or cares about me.

In those moments of distorted reality, we have trouble believing that things could be different. I could get another job. I still have some friends. I could take up another hobby now that my failing eyesight doesn't let me do needlepoint anymore. It could be different, except that in the bleakness of my vision, nothing feels possible.

Making a difference

How can it be different? It's not helpful to believe that things can go back to the way they were. Too often, we think change requires a major shift. We want to be able to say *I am a new person.* This is overly ambitious thinking that often keeps us stuck where we are. What can be helpful is to focus on small changes in our behavior that may have contributed to losses and disappointments in the past. Be prepared to respond to the familiar voice that likes to make us feel bad by belittling our efforts to change. We should reply like in the Passover song *Dayyenu*—it is enough. The idea behind *sweetening the limitations* is not that it removes them, but that it is possible to lighten our burden one small step at a time. Each act is sufficient in itself. *Dayyenu.* Each act of kindness matters.

It is not some amazing insight that makes loss okay. It is the still small voice of truth that says it is not only people who are imperfect; the world is imperfect. It had to be for humans to have real choice—to be able to choose good or evil. With choice you can find the love of your life or have your heart broken. You can be anxious or euphoric. While we can strive to improve that which limits us, the world itself is imperfect. The world is filled with delicious food and stomach aches. There are flowers and floods, amazing vistas and terrible diseases.

Accepting the way the world works

It is not so simple to change the limitations found in nature. It can be done by accepting the way the world works. People get cancer and die. No one lives forever. Accidents happen. All of this is part of the rules/limitations of the world. Sweetening comes from understanding this. Most diseases are not our fault. Aging is a universal experience. It is what it is. We can all wish it was different. We can be jealous of people who seem to be healthy and successful and aren't losing their minds, but it doesn't change the fact that many people will get Alzheimer's. Here is a perfect example of the *din*/rules of this world. The current medical understanding seems to be that more people get Alzheimer's these days because people are living longer. Scientists suggest that our bodies weren't made to live this long. Perhaps over time some of these limitations will be eliminated, not just sweetened, if a cure for Alzheimer's can be found. In the meantime, the wonders of modern medicine mean that more people will live longer and be healthier. It also means that those same wonders will keep them alive longer even as they suffer a slower painful death. There are blessings and curses that come with modern medicine. The blessings and curses were always part of this world—we humans have added new blessings and new curses as we have continued the unfolding of creation.

Of course, no one would choose pain or disease. Our fantasy of death would be to live to a ripe old age with the health and body of a thirty-year-old and to die as if someone flipped off the light switch of our being. Instead, the reality of *din/* limitations is that life is a package deal. We get birth and growth and also aging and death. *Sweetening the limitations* doesn't ask us to accept that fact. There is no reason to appreciate the pain in your knee. *Sweetening the limitations* simply acknowledges that the pain in your knee is a reality of life.

The support of others makes a difference

A sweetening of the limitations can also come about from friends and loved ones. While it is true that no one can really feel your pain, it is also true that people can really care about you and empathize with your suffering. Friends can help you feel less alone in this experience because they care about you and what happens to you. This is why visiting the sick is such an important practice in Jewish tradition. The Talmud (*Nedarim* 39b) says visiting the sick takes away 1/60th of a person's pain, thereby acknowledging that it really can't significantly ameliorate the pain, but that it can make people feel better by reminding them they are not forgotten and alone. It is a form of accompaniment (*levayeh*). So far, we have not been successful in solving all the problems of the world, but there is no reason we can't make those struggling feel accompanied on their journey rather than abandoned.

Looking back over life

There is one other aspect of the still small voice that may be able to pierce the fog of pain and loss. We can remember to look at our lives in perspective. It is true I am not as physically flexible as I once was, and that my hearing is declining. Yet it is also true that I can still see, and I am able to enjoy my grandchildren. The practice is to enjoy what I do have because I may lose my sight or be unable to walk. There will also come a time when I will die. Losses and blessings co-exist until near the end. It is also true that I should place the reality of the decline that is part of aging in the larger context of my whole life. All of it is the reality of my life. Let me remember to see even as my eyes dim; to communicate even when it seems easier to sit alone in my room. I can smell and taste. I can touch and be touched. Neither the great moments nor the sad moments alone are the sum total of my life. This realization too can help sweeten the limitations.

We have contrasting examples from Genesis of people looking back over their lives. Upon Jacob's arrival in Egypt, Joseph presents his father to Pharaoh who asks him, "How many are the years of your life?" (Gen. 47:8). Jacob responds: "The years of my sojourn [on earth] are one hundred and thirty. Few and hard have been the years of my life..." It is most striking that as an old man, he looks over his life even now, after his whole family is together and prospering in Egypt, as *ra*—hard or bad. Jacob has spent his life angling for more and yet remains disappointed with what he has received. One could imagine, as he looks back over his life, that Jacob wonders what it all meant. He feels overshadowed by his illustrious forebears, Abraham and Isaac. He focuses on his failures and losses. Despite the moments of vision when he sees more clearly the possibilities of being connected to God and the opportunity to wrestle with what is in order to create a better future, he summarizes his life as short and bad. This tendency to view one's life negatively in retrospect is a common mindset. Jacob summarizes his life as one of suffering. He comes to the end of his life without a sense of purpose.

In contrast, Joseph has the ability to look back over his life, including its bitterest moment when he is betrayed by 10 of his brothers, and see it as part of God's plan. When he reveals himself to his brothers, he can see the worry on their faces that he will now take revenge. After all, he is the powerful viceroy of Egypt. He tells them, "Now, do not be distressed or reproach yourselves because you sold me hither; it was to save life that God sent me ahead of you" (Gen. 45: 5).

Joseph's story is of a different spiritual path than that of Jacob. Joseph's life story is as challenging and just as filled with setbacks. One could argue that being betrayed by his brothers is worse than anything that happened to Jacob. It is Joseph's response that is so markedly different. Jacob looks back on his life and sees it as bitter and purposeless. Joseph sees his life as purposeful. The contrast in how they see their lives is striking and rests not on the facts but how they chose to understand them.

Getting old

Abraham was now old, advanced in years, and God blessed Abraham *ba-kol*, in all things. (Gen. 24:1)

What does it mean to be blessed in all things—*ba-kol*? After all, Abraham's life, like that of all human beings, was filled with triumph and tragedy. His wife of many years, Sarah, has just died. Why now is Abraham described as being blessed in all things?

Despite everything that had happened to him in life, he experienced his life as filled with blessings. Abraham is the person of faith who is willing to leave everything behind in order to journey to an unknown land. His faith carries him throughout his life and brings to him, near the end of that life, a sense of years well lived and a life blessed with everything.

You might ask, *Isn't there a truth about your life? Isn't one's life objectively hard or easy?* The Hebrew word for truth is *emet*. The word *emet* is made up of three Hebrew letters: *aleph* (the first letter of the alphabet), *mem*, and *tav* (the last letter of the alphabet). Truth encompasses everything from *aleph* to *tav*, or as we would say, from A to Z. Truth is all-inclusive. Sometimes we bring forth only the good parts of ourselves. Other times, all we can focus on is how terrible we are, how much of a failure we have become. Yet, the truth about us is not just the extremes; it is everything. It is both what we proudly display and what we try to hide in the shadows. It is not just the extremes; it is the extremes plus everything in between. The everything in between is represented by the other letter of *emet,* the letter *mem.* An oft-repeated homiletic interpretation of *emet* is that it is made up of the first and last letter of the alphabet and the middle letter *mem.* I can't tell you how many times I've seen this interpretation by different teachers. The only problem is *mem* is not the middle letter of the alphabet! What is the middle letter of the Hebrew alphabet? Since the alphabet has 22 letters, it actually has two middle letters and *mem* is neither of them. (It is the 13th letter.) The middle letters are *khaf* and *lamed,* the two letters that make up the word *kol,* everything.

At the end of his life, Abraham has achieved the blessing of *ba-kol,* of everything. In fact, his whole life is framed by the letters of *lamed* and *khaf.* At the beginning of his life, with those two letters he is told, *lekh lekha,* "go forth." At the end of his life these same two letters are reversed; he is blessed with *kol,* everything. The blessing of *ba-kol* means that Abraham has achieved a clarity of vision to see all of life as a blessing from God. He has an equanimity about life. While we may never achieve that level, we still strive to come close to an understanding of the truth about ourselves, a truth that validates who we are, in our failures and our successes. Yet, we desire to move beyond the acceptance of our present, flawed reality to strive to be one of the children of Abraham. We seek nothing less than to be blessed with *ba-kol* and then, like Abraham, we too "shall be a blessing... and all the families of the earth shall bless themselves by you."

A follower of the Kotzker rebbe complained about not getting a prayer shawl (*tallit*—a four-cornered garment worn during morning prayers) from his in-laws—a traditional wedding present. The Kotzker replied: "Then wrap yourself in the four corners of the world and pray!" (*Emet mikotzk titzmah* source #50). The teaching of that story is you can lack many possessions and have many physical limitations but that doesn't stop you from being able to feel embraced by the universe as you wrap yourself in its wonder and in the memories of your life.

I got out of bed
on two strong legs.
It might have been
otherwise. I ate
cereal, sweet

milk, ripe, flawless
peach. It might
have been otherwise.
I took the dog uphill
to the birch wood.
All morning I did
the work I love.

At noon I lay down
with my mate. It might
have been otherwise.
We ate dinner together
at a table with silver
candlesticks. It might
have been otherwise.
I slept in a bed
in a room with paintings
on the walls, and
planned another day
just like this day.
But one day, I know,
it will be otherwise.
—Jane Kenyon

Death

Death is a loss different from all others because of its finality. Your loved one
will never again walk into the room and speak to you. It is impossible to believe
that and yet you know it is true. In the face of death of loved ones, the notion
of *sweetening the limitations* needs to be suspended. The one thing that trumps
Judaism is death. According to Jewish law, between the time of death and the
burial of the deceased, we are not obligated to fulfill such commandments as daily
prayer. Why? One explanation is that you need time to make all the preparations
for the burial which traditionally should take place as soon as possible. This takes
priority over the regular daily practice of observant Jews. Another explanation
is that in the midst of grief and sometimes shock you don't have the attention to
focus on saying prayers. I want to suggest an additional explanation. The Talmud
refers to the period between death and burial as *meito mutal lifanav*—literally the

corpse is lying before you. Death is a challenge to faith. In the face of the death of someone you love it is hard to affirm that the world is *tov*—a world of goodness. It is difficult to believe in moments of great loss that we live lives of meaning. It can be impossible to affirm a belief in a benevolent God or universe. It is hard not to feel bereft and alone. How can we be expected to say prayers that affirm God's goodness and caring when our loved one lies before us? None of those qualities seem present—only grief and death are in the space. Before the burial, we are in a world disrupted. In the fog of the unreality that the person is gone forever, we struggle to plan the funeral and just try to get through the day. Regular Jewish observation is suspended.

The practice of shiva

There are a variety of reasons that Jewish tradition requires burying the deceased as soon as possible. One explanation is that it enables us to move to the next stage of grief. The funeral service and the actual burial help make the unbelievable feel believable. Reality begins to set in. In the first stage, the focus is on the deceased—arranging for the funeral and the eulogies that will bring to life the person who has died by describing them in vibrant colors. After burial the focus shifts to comforting the mourners. Traditionally, when visiting a shiva home you enter and sit down and wait silently for the mourner to begin the conversation. We can't make things alright as much as it pains us to witness the suffering of someone we care about. There are no magic words to make it all better. People's desire to comfort too often leads them to say the wrong thing: *At least she died quickly and didn't suffer. He was really old and lived a full life. She was out of it for so many years, it must be a relief.* Those things might be true or it could be the mourner feels the opposite: *I know she lived to 95 but I wish she could have lived a few more years.*

How do we sweeten the loss for mourners? We show up and remind them they are not alone even at this moment when they may feel most alone, having lost a parent, become an orphan, or lost a beloved partner and realize that they will be sleeping alone for the first time in years. We listen to them tell stories about the deceased. We feel the love that the mourners express. We respond with love and caring, metaphorically holding hands in the face of the loss. The traditional phrase said to the mourners is: May God comfort you among the other mourners of Zion and Jerusalem. I was struck that the name of God that is used in this phrase is *ha-makom*—literally *the place*. Rabbinic Judaism used that word as one of the names of God. I understand its use here to mean *May this space be a measure of comfort to you at this time of loss.* This space still echoes with the words and stories and deeds of the deceased. The people who knew the person best are gathered in this room. Others have come to uphold the mourners in this difficult time so they will feel connected to life by caring friends and relatives. This space, this *makom*, is a living representation of the lives of the mourners and of the deceased. The deceased lives on in the community of those who have come to this space. Those who have died are no longer reflected in mirrors, but we can get glimpses of them in the hearts and memories of those who knew them.

I urge people who lost a loved one after a long illness not to think of them as they were in the last year of their life. Don't picture them as they looked in their hospital bed. Remember them instead in how they spent the majority of their life active and vigorous. Remember the fullness of their personality with all their strengths, weaknesses, and quirks. Remember their oft-repeated stories, their jokes, their sayings, their flaws, their principles—their being.

Facing our mortality

The Talmud (*Ta'anit* 30b) says that the 15th day of the month of Av was one of the most festive days of the year. Clearly there was a tradition of celebration, but already in Talmudic times the reason wasn't clear. Though there are six explanations offered, I want to quote only one.

> Rabbah bar bar Chana said that Rabbi Yohanan said: This was the day that those destined to die in the desert finished dying. For Mar said: So long as they hadn't finished dying God didn't speak to Moses.

It's a strange text. The context goes back to the book of Numbers, when the Israelites sent 12 spies to check out the Land of Israel. They reported on the abundance of the land but 10 of the spies said the local inhabitants were too powerful to defeat. God punished the people's lack of faith by condemning the whole generation of the desert to die over the course of the next 40 years. The midrash says that every year on the ninth day of Av the Israelites would dig graves and sleep in them. Each year some of the Israelites would die. In the 40th year, the last Israelites of the desert generation dug their graves, certain that they were to die. The next morning, they discovered no one had died. They assumed they had miscalculated the date. The next night the same thing happened. Finally, on the fifteenth of the month they could see the full moon and knew they couldn't have miscalculated. They realized that they had been spared the punishment of dying in the desert.

This is a remarkable, even terrifying midrash. Imagine lying in a grave each year knowing that this would actually be the grave for many of your fellow Israelites. Each year the odds of your dying increased. In the last year, you were sure this would be your last night alive. Equally remarkable is that there is a whole group of people who are spared the punishment and presumably will enter the Promised Land. This midrash thereby contradicts the biblical text that states, except for Joshua and Caleb, the whole generation that left Egypt died in the desert.

The second line of the text is perhaps even more stunning. "For Mar said: So long as they hadn't finished dying God didn't speak to Moses." What?! Isn't the Torah filled with many times that God spoke to Moses? Isn't Moses's prophecy described by the tradition as extraordinary because God spoke to him directly? The commentators are troubled by this statement. One suggested solution is that there is an intimate quality to God speaking to Moses and it is that quality that is absent during the 40 years of wandering. With this death sentence hanging over the Israelites, the relationship with God had to have been affected. There can't be real communication between God and human beings. Humans are created in the image of God, but death is a stark reminder that we are also different from God. The gap seems unbridgeable in the face of death. Like the suspension of prayer between death and burial, the 40 years becomes an elongated period when death is ever-present, and graphically rehearsed each year on the ninth of Av. I wonder whether the people had no interest in talking with a God who had no compassion for their fears about the unknown Promised Land. Perhaps looking down on the terrified remnant as they dig and then lie in what they are sure will be their graves, God finally acknowledges their limitations and flaws and relents on the punishment. Now the remnant lives like every human being—in our world of uncertainty where death can happen at any time. We mostly ignore our mortality, making it easier to be in the moment and celebrate the blessings and potential despite the limitations of our existence. This frees us to act more like images of God and thereby connect to the holy and even to the Holy One. In this world of limitations, we ignore that ultimate reality by proclaiming about each day of life—*dayyenu*—it is sufficient.

Find love in loss

> To live a meaningful life, each of us must step outside the familiar, confining walls of ego defenses and enter our own wilderness, our own charnel ground, to face honestly the truth of impermanence and loss. In the strange cemetery of imagination, mourning ourselves, we suddenly stumble upon what's most essential. Facing loss, we find love.
> —Lorne Ladner, from *The Lost Art of Compassion*

Core Principle #8:
Working On Our Inner Qualities

Maimonides, the 12th-century philosopher and rabbinic scholar, has an unusual commandment among his list of 613 commandments: "The commandment is to imitate God as much as we are able. As it says: walk in God's ways (Dt. 28:9) ...just as God is merciful so you should be merciful, just as God is compassionate so you should be compassionate, just as God is righteous so you should be righteous and just as God is loving so should you be loving... This means to imitate the good deeds and honorable qualities of God..." (*Sefer ha-mitzvot* commandment #8).

The Talmud (*Sotah* 14a) asks how it is possible for a mere mortal to imitate God. The answer is found in the notion that we are created in the image of God, which means we should act as God does in the world. The tradition understands this to refer to specific acts of lovingkindness such as visiting the sick or burying the dead. In the view of the midrash, the Torah begins and ends with such acts by God, who clothes the naked Adam and Eve and buries Moses.

According to Maimonides, these Godlike qualities should become ingrained into a person's daily life. This can only be done by paying attention to the qualities that need work and then fixing what is broken. Maimonides has a particular approach based on his belief that we want to find the golden mean for every quality and then adhere to it. We should not be stingy, but we should also not be overly generous, either. We should practice over and over again until we rid ourselves of the extreme version of any quality. Maimonides makes an exception to his golden rule for the qualities of anger or pride. These qualities are to be avoided rather than trying to find, for example, the golden mean between anger and patience.

The rabbis realized that it is possible to observe all 613 commandments and still not be a very nice person. Ramban, 13th-century Bible commentator, had an expression for this: "a scoundrel who doesn't violate the Torah" (commentary on Lev. 19:1). You could be nasty and unkind without violating any of the Torah laws. There has been a strand within traditional Judaism that has tried to correct for this possibility by stressing good character traits. This strand produced works of *Mussar*, moral instruction. One of them says:

"If you do not possess refined character traits, then neither do you possess Torah and *mitzvot*, for the entire Torah depends on the refinement of character traits." (*Orchot Tzaddikim*, 15th century).

Mussar/ethical qualities

Over the centuries, many texts stressed the importance of cultivating good qualities as a form of ethical self-improvement. In the 19th century, Mussar became more than just a genre of ethical Jewish literature; it became a movement within Jewish life. Founded by Rabbi Yisroel Salanter, it encouraged Jews to focus on self-criticism of their character traits. The Mussar movement found its home among those who were studying in yeshivot—schools of advanced Jewish learning whose basic curriculum was Talmud. In those yeshivot that encouraged Mussar, its teachings were added to the Talmudic curriculum. Just as you studied Talmud with a study partner (*havruta*), so you had a Mussar partner with whom you shared your struggles over improving your character traits. The movement and its adherents were decimated during the Holocaust but the Mussar movement has recently been revived by teachers such as Alan Morinis, founder of the Mussar Institute and Rabbi Ira Stone of the Center for Contemporary Mussar.

A "new" category of commandments

I want to elevate the importance of the practice of Mussar. In the rabbinic understanding, one group of commandments focuses on our relationship with God (*mitzvot bein adam le-makom*), while another group concentrates on relations between human beings (*mitzvot bein adam le-havero*). There is a little-known third category in the traditional literature that refers to commandments between a person and themself (*mitzvot bein adam l'atzmo*). In this new understanding, there are now three prongs of religious life: our relationship with God and/or the universe, our relationship with other people, and our relationship with our inner qualities. This emphasis on the self seems particularly appropriate in the modern world, which has been so profoundly transformed by psychology.

Promulgating this category of commandments between a person and themself seems a vital way to reconstruct *halakha*. Although most traditional Jews have never heard of this category, I first heard it mentioned during a lecture by Rabbi Hershel Schacter, a contemporary Orthodox Talmudic scholar. The one commandment clearly associated with this category is walking in God's ways. But it is also clear that cultivating inner qualities can have a broad impact on our practice of Judaism and on our being. In a previous chapter, I quoted two traditional authorities that encouraged us to cultivate kindness as an important component for our social justice practice. Let us focus on another inner quality as an example: openheartedness or generosity.

Openheartedness

In the rabbinic imagination, Abraham and Sarah are considered the models of hospitality. "God appeared to Abraham by the terebinths of Mamre. Abraham was sitting at the entrance of the tent as the day grew hot. Looking up, he saw three men standing near him. As soon as he saw them, he ran from the entrance of the tent to greet them" (Gen. 18:1-2). From this we learn that welcoming others is an important spiritual *midah*/quality to cultivate.

In one reading of this biblical text, Abraham is having a conversation with God when three visitors approach his tent. Abraham leaves God in order to offer the travelers hospitality and food. It seems a surprising choice on Abraham's part. The rabbis teach the following on this verse:

> Hospitality is greater than a visit to the House of Study; it is greater than welcoming the *Shekhinah* (God's indwelling presence) (Shabbat 127a).

According to the midrash, Abraham and Sarah's tent had door flaps on each side so that visitors could enter from any direction (*Midrash Tehillim* 110). They would not wait for guests to "knock." They would rush out to greet strangers and invite them to wash off their traveler's dust. It is striking that the first Jews in the world would be known particularly for this quality, of all possible good qualities such as patience, humility, or equanimity. Abraham and Sarah become the models for hospitality.

Hospitality

Why? Why is hospitality greater than greeting God or visiting the House of Study? Perhaps because it is too easy to become isolated from the world and retreat into the world of study and intellect, or to retreat into the world of contemplation of the holy. Hospitality requires interaction between people, bringing together souls and hearts, opening up and getting to know one another better, by making a connection to a world beyond ourselves.

To be hospitable is to make space for others. According to Jewish mystics, the infinite God created the world by contracting God's self (a process called *tzimtzum*) to create a space for the finite world to exist. Inviting guests is a form of *tzimtzum*—contracting to make room for others. This contraction does not create a vacuum, but rather a space that suggests welcome; that makes others feel at home, that crosses across the walls in our lives and connects our souls to others. In that space both learning about others and ourselves occurs. God's presence is there whenever we are really present with each other. In that contraction, making space and welcome, we create new worlds as God did in that original *tzimtzum*—worlds of connection, meaning, stories, food, laughter and sharing. This, then, is why hospitality is greater than study or even welcoming God's presence.

This teaching is another way of saying that the Jewish way involves acting with compassion, not only in circumstances of great injustice but also in daily acts of kindness. We have a responsibility to ease the journey of others by being an oasis of hospitality on the road. Here Judaism suggests that it is a misunderstanding to think that religion is all about God. What religion is about is helping us to live a life of meaning. This text reminds us that travel is often strenuous. It can mean quite a lot to see a friendly face waiting with a ride for you at the airport or to have a chance to rest in the shade of a tent in the desert. It is a form of accompaniment, as I discuss in "Core Principle #4: Engaging in Social Justice." The rabbis saw the intersection of the Divine and the human in the seemingly simple act of hospitality. When we greet the stranger, we greet the *Shekhinah*—the presence of God. After all, each human being is an image of God. Even more important, the point of Judaism isn't to worship God or to observe Jewish ritual. It is to continue to strive to make this world a place of *tov*/goodness. It is to open our doors and our hearts to those who need a kind word, a cool drink, or a helping hand.

You will find explorations of other inner qualities throughout the book. Let's look at two other important spiritual qualities: gratitude and satisfaction. We will examine them in the context of food.

Food is a vital component of life. While food insecurity is still a challenge for millions of people in the world today, most of the people reading this book have enough to eat. Even so, food remains central to our lives, influencing our body image and health while providing a sense of being nourished and satisfied. Food can also serve as a specific focus for expressing gratitude.

Blessings as a gratitude practice

Traditionally, Jews say a blessing before and after eating food. There are specific blessings before and after eating fruits, vegetables, bread, cake, and wine, and a general blessing for any food that doesn't fit under those categories. All these blessings thank God for food, acknowledging that the food on our table doesn't come there solely by our efforts. Fundamentally, these blessings are a gratitude practice for a basic element that sustains our life—food.

Having a gratitude practice is fundamental to a spiritual life. It is too easy to take the blessing of food for granted, especially since most of us don't go to bed hungry. We can create a simple gratitude practice by using the traditional blessing formulas, expressing gratitude in our own words, or even just pausing for a second before eating. This practice can take place throughout the day (whenever we eat) and doesn't take up a lot of time. It is easy to integrate even on the busiest days. If you find it too difficult to remember to say a blessing every time you eat or drink, you might try to say a blessing or take a moment before each daily meal. Some people use the tradition of saying blessings as a way to be thankful for many aspects of life. Before eating, they reflect: *Thank you for all the gifts of life—food and breath, love and laughter, connecting with another person and the wonders of nature.* Cultivating a sense of gratitude is an important practice whether we direct that gratitude to God or use it as a moment of intention for its own sake. Being grateful and feeling nourished are essential for spiritual health.

It is also important to have a practice around something so fundamental as what we eat. The first practice we know of in the Torah focuses on eating. Adam and Eve are told they can eat anything that grows in the Garden of Eden except for the fruit of the Tree of Knowledge of Good and Evil. They eat of the tree and are banished from the garden. The first diet in the world is immediately disregarded. From this story, we learn that eating is not a simple thing. Since Adam and Eve react to this forbidden eating by making clothes to cover their nakedness, we see the link between food and self-perception. How we appear to others is a fundamental aspect of being human. This is only intensified now when many of us have access to an abundance of food. Many people pay special attention to how much and what they eat. More choice can often mean making bad choices about what we eat.

Jewish law forbids certain foods, such as pork or shellfish. It also requires that kosher (permitted) animals be killed in a certain way. Finally, it also prohibits the eating of milk and meat together. These basic rules are found in the biblical text and were subsequently interpreted and elaborated by the rabbis into many additional rules.

The meaning of the biblical laws about food is unknown. The text simply says that you should keep them to be holy (Lev. 11:45). This could mean that there is something taboo about these particular animals or the practice of mixing milk and meat. Some contemporary Bible scholars suggest that milk and meat can be understood to be symbolic: mother's milk represents the sustaining of life, while the meat of slaughtered animals represents death. Mary Douglas, a 20th-century anthropologist, suggested that the ancient world tried to create categories to give order to the chaotic world around them. Animals that didn't fit neatly into the categories were seen as problematic. While most animals have cleft hooves and chew their cud, those that don't, such as pigs, were seen as prohibited. As interesting as these ideas are, we have no real way of knowing the purpose of these commandments. The laws did make it complicated for Jews to eat with people who did not observe kosher rules. In America, that aspect of keeping kosher has been largely rejected by the liberal Jewish community. The vast majority of liberal Jews, including liberal rabbis, will eat in a restaurant that is not under rabbinic supervision. They want to be able to eat with friends who are not Jewish, whether at a business lunch or a night out. As discussed in the chapter "*Minhag America,*" liberal Jews have redrawn the traditional *halakha* in a number of areas—most strikingly regarding kosher rules.

This change may reflect a sense that there isn't an obvious rationale for observing the laws of keeping kosher. Without an apparent purpose, there is not much in the way of positive energy pushing for its observance. Certainly, some people still have kosher homes to enable family and friends who keep kosher to eat in their homes. Others continue to observe the kosher laws since this is "the way Jews eat." Some even argue that it is a good spiritual discipline to do something that has no rational reason. While each of us will decide which aspects of Jewish tradition in regard to keeping kosher we will observe or ignore, you may want to consider cultivating a spiritual practice around what you eat. Eating is a central human activity. Today, people may choose to become vegetarian, vegan, organic, locavore, and more. Each has a clear rationale based on health, attitudes about eating other life forms, and/or impact on the environment. Some of these practices, such as vegetarianism or veganism, make the laws of kosher irrelevant since without eating meat or fish, they have no real application. Using the apparent precedent in the Torah that assumes that humans were vegetarian before Noah's flood, some argue we should return to that practice. Given the environmental and health issues raised by the large-scale raising of animals for food, some argue it is time to change our eating practice. Whether you choose kashrut, new practices or a combination, it is important to have a practice around food.

Satisfaction and desire

The first food practice focuses on expressing gratitude before eating. The second focuses on what we eat. This third practice asks what our response should be after we eat. This involves cultivating the quality of satisfaction. Like gratitude, satisfaction can be found in situations other than eating. Feeling satisfied with what we have, or, as some call it, "enoughness" (Mussar calls it *histapkut*), is a useful quality to cultivate for a healthy spiritual life.

Let's begin our exploration of satisfaction with its opposite quality: desire. The last of the Ten Commandments states: "You shall not covet your neighbor's house, you shall not covet your neighbor's wife, or his male or female slave, or his ox or his donkey, or anything that is your neighbor's" (Ex. 20:14). The language of this commandment suggests that coveting comes from envy. After all, it doesn't say that you should not have too many cars, tools, or appliances. To covet is to want what your neighbor has. It suggests that this desire comes not simply from an ad pitching a product that you never knew you were missing. The desire comes from a comparison with others.

Samson Raphael Hirsch, a 19th-century rabbinic scholar, maintained that it is not intrinsically bad to want things. Desire has led humans to settle the world, build cities, and create culture. While animals desire only what they need to survive, humans are created with desires beyond survival. Yet these desires can also lead to unrestrained yearnings. Hirsch wrote:

> Unspeakably frightful are the consequences of *ta'avah* (desire) when it exceeds the bounds of the necessary and good. It destroys all happiness in life...What you have has no value for you; only what is not yet yours attracts you, and this, too, loses its value on being acquired.... Where *ta'avah* (desire) rules, mitzvah must give way, for the latter binds you not for your own benefit but for that of others; and *mishpat* (justice) also must give way since it sets up the rights of others as the limit to your pursuit of wealth...Value your life not according to possessions and enjoyments, but according to good deeds... It is not how much or how little you have that makes you great or small, but how much or how little you are with what you have, how much or little you utilize what has been lent to you for action in the service of God—that is what makes you great or small. (*Horeb*)

Yet such traditional teachings often feel like a call to live a life of austerity. There are those who believe a life of simplicity is a better way to be in our world, particularly when we experience the damage to the environment by the overuse of the earth's resources by an ever-burgeoning human population. It is appropriate to question how much we really need even as we acknowledge that each of us would answer the question differently. The tradition sees the world as God's gift to us. One Talmudic teaching states:

> In the world-to-come a person will be asked to give an account for that which, being excellent to eat, she gazed at and did not eat. (Jerusalem Talmud, *Kiddushin*, end).

We are supposed to enjoy life, but lusting for or coveting something suggests that enjoying the object or pleasure is secondary to our sense of ownership. It is the difference between enjoying a delicious piece of fruit and enjoying being the only one who has such a fruit; or perhaps, even worse, enjoying that we have the fruit and someone else doesn't. While the Talmud teaches that the world is to be enjoyed, it also teaches that the world belongs to God. We are only temporary tenants. Our sense of ownership distorts the truth that being mortal means that at best we may have a long-term lease on our property. But every lease comes to an end.

Cultivating satisfaction

There is a verse in Deuteronomy that might suggest how to achieve satisfaction. "You shall eat, be satisfied and bless God (ve-akhalta, ve-savata uvei'rakhta)" (Deut. 8:10). The verse suggests that we should enjoy the pleasures of this world, feel satisfied with what we have, and then bless God, the creator of the world. Through partaking and feeling sated, we will feel blessed. Satisfaction comes from enjoying the world, not from refraining from all the world has to offer; but it is important to come to a place of feeling satisfied. This does not come about by measuring what we have as compared to our neighbor. What they have doesn't detract from the apple we ate or the beautiful sunset we saw. Satisfaction comes from appreciating the apple and the sunset or the beauty of a flower, or its fragrance. The fact that there is always more should not distract us from what we have experienced through our five senses. Satisfaction is a great gift that only we can give ourselves. No one can give it to us.

Being present in the experience of this moment can lead to satisfaction and a sense of being blessed. Or we can hold back from our own satisfaction and hunger insatiably for more. We have all experienced unconscious eating. We eat a whole bag of potato chips or a quart of ice cream and we have no real recollection of the experience. There is an automatic quality to the eating. This usually has nothing to do with being hungry. We are trying to satisfy some other need. It could be feeling unnourished because friends or family don't seem to care for us. Or it could be feeling all alone. We are depressed and think that somehow, we can eat our way to happiness. It usually only makes us feel worse. What we seek can never be found in that bag of chips. It is the opposite experience of treating ourselves with a delicious dessert to celebrate a special occasion.

In the Middle Ages, there was a great deal of emphasis on asceticism. Maimonides suggested that one should always eat less than needed to feel full. Many of us have the challenge of living with abundance. Our lives are increasingly driven by more than a need to sustain ourselves. We are searching for personal meaning and purpose. We are also looking for what humans have always longed for—connections to other human beings. We may think that we can achieve satisfaction by acquiring things. Filling our homes with "treasure" can give us pleasure, but so too can an evening spent with friends, or a beautiful vista. It all depends on our attitude.

Shlomo ibn Gabirol (11th-century poet and philosopher) wrote:

> Who seeks more than he needs, hinders himself from enjoying what he has. Seek what you need and give up what you don't need. For in giving up what you don't need, you'll learn what you really do need. (*Mivhar Hapeninim*)

The Gaon of Vilna (18th-century Talmudic scholar) wrote in *Even Shelei-mah* that there are three levels of satisfaction.

The first is not to pursue something bigger and better. In this first level you retain a sense of something missing, but you push yourself to let it go.

The second level is based on a rabbinic saying: "Who is wealthy? Someone who is happy with what he has" (*Pirkei Avot* 4:1). Alan Morinis, a contemporary Mussar teacher, suggests that satisfaction is not to get to a place where you are resigned with what you have, but to be happy with what you have. Looking back on my life, I think I often convinced myself that I was happy with what I had by first determining that I didn't need more. It was of course a way to prevent myself from being disappointed when I didn't get it. An Israeli friend used a Hebrew expression to describe this mindset: I was satisfied with too little. It can be hard to know whether we are really happy with what we have or if we just force ourselves to that mindset because the alternative is too disappointing. The goal is to be truly happy with what we have.

The third level is "I have everything—*kol.*" Even when we are happy with what we have, there can still be a sense that something is missing. This level conveys a sense of completeness. I feel satiated. I feel full. (There is a fuller teaching on the quality of everything/*kol* on p. 174.

In the Shabbat morning liturgy, we read that those who observe Shabbat enjoy satisfaction and delight/pleasure (*yisbe'u ve-yit-angu*). The word for delight is *oneg*, which has come to describe the reception after services—oneg Shabbat. You would think that the order of the words should be reversed. First you taste the delights of Shabbat and then you have a sense of satisfaction amidst the special experience of rest on Shabbat. Instead, the order of the words reminds us that only when we have a real sense of being satisfied can we really enjoy the *oneg*—the pleasures and delights of Shabbat or, more broadly, the world.

"You give it open-handedly, satisfying every living being to its heart's content" (Ps. 145:15). I never understood this verse from the daily liturgy. There seem to be a lot of people who are not content. There are also a lot of people who do not have the basic necessities of life. I now see that it is not an absolute statement. For the most part, we are created with what we need: the ability to love, a mind for understanding, a means to communicate, a body that enables us to enjoy the pleasures of the world, hands with which to create, and so on. We have all we need if we would only see it that way. Happiness comes from seeing all that we have. Sharon Salzberg, a contemporary spirituality teacher, writes: "A loving heart will give you more happiness than anything you crave." Satisfaction is the key to happiness. The Psalmist maintains that God has given each of us enough to make our heart content. If you think what you need is always just beyond your reach, then no matter how much you manage to grasp, all you will have is a discontented heart.

A simple satisfaction practice is to end each meal with that phrase from Deuteronomy. You shall eat, be satisfied and be blessed (*ve-akhalta, ve-savata uvei'rakhta*).

Core Principle #9:
Turning and Returning: *Teshuvah*

You must be the change you wish to see in the world.
—Mohandas K. Gandhi

The Sefat Emet, a 19th-century Hasidic master, taught that the Oral Torah is what we add by our deeds to the Written Torah. Each of us tells defining stories about ourselves. Some stories are embarrassing ones, like the time my third-grade teacher told me to stand in the corner. These are stories that last longer than they should. I can't remember the teacher's name but I can still remember feeling embarrassed before the whole class.

Being shy

Our most important stories, the ones we tell others and ourselves, define who we are. My story, like all human stories, is complex, and has multiple components. One of the key threads in my story is that I define myself as shy. While children are often less self-conscious about their identity, as we grow up we become more reflective. We begin to ask ourselves: *Who am I?* We compare ourselves to others and others compare themselves to us. We begin to care about such things as appearance. We notice that when the school class divides into two teams to play baseball, certain people get picked first and some always get picked last. It also becomes clear pretty quickly who the smart kids are and which children struggle academically, which kids are popular and which are not.

I was mostly in the middle of these characteristics, except for being pretty smart (but not the smartest). My day school class graduated with 19 students, a larger than average class at the time; but because we spent so much time together, we knew each other pretty well. One of my teachers, an Israeli with typical Sabra candor, once remarked that he thought I was stupid since I never spoke in class. Then he saw my first test results and changed his opinion.

The home I grew up in was pretty quiet. With an older sister and a younger brother, our family was very nuclear. Almost all of my father's extended family was murdered during the Holocaust. My mother had only one brother, who never married. We rarely had guests for Shabbat meals because my mother was an anxious entertainer. I have a strong memory of my family sitting in the living room on Shabbat afternoons, each of us reading books to ourselves (we lived across the street from a branch of the Boston Public Library). I had few male friends in school and even fewer in college.

I got married at an early age. My wife was outgoing and, in the division of roles in our marriage, she managed our social life. I would be silently present at our Shabbat table, content to let others fill the room with conversation. One evening, we were invited to a party of some friends. Near the door was someone I had known for years. He asked me if my wife was coming as he looked right past me for her. I realized that he had little interest in talking with me. Suddenly the absence of friends struck a chord. I realized the inadequacy of my story. I could no longer say I was just shy.

Being an introvert

I began to say that I was not good at casual conversation. It was a skill I never learned at home. I think I was looking for a positive reason for my lack of friends. I wasn't a big gossiper. I liked to talk about Jewish matters, not make small talk, but I still felt badly as I became increasingly aware that while I had many acquaintances, I had very few friends.

I began to write books. I would sit for hours at a time doing research on a book called *The Jewish Holidays* in the old reading room of the library of the Jewish Theological Seminary. Eventually, I decided I couldn't make a living writing Jewish nonfiction and decided to look for employment in educational and cultural programs in a Jewish setting. I got a job at Congregation Ansche Chesed on the Upper West Side of Manhattan. But after a number of years, I realized I didn't want to just organize opportunities for other people to teach or speak about Judaism; I wanted to do the teaching. In some ways I had found my voice. I decided to go to rabbinical school. At the age of 39, I began commuting to the Reconstructionist Rabbinical College in Philadelphia. It was a difficult time juggling school, my job at Ansche Chesed, and a family with three children.

The thing I was most worried about the rabbinate was pastoral counseling. I was terrified at the idea of being alone in a room with an individual or a couple and being asked for advice on how to deal with death or loss. The one course I took in pastoral counseling was not very helpful. Week after week I hoped for some wisdom to be able to respond to tragedies. I didn't hear anything inspirational, until the teacher remarked that it is a big mistake to think you are supposed to have answers. Many times there are no answers. Just listen.

Being a good listener

It was not only liberating to understand that I didn't need answers to the unanswerable, but it turns out I am a good listener. All those times I sat at dinner tables or in meetings not talking made me a practiced listener. There was a real positive aspect to my not talking—I learned how to listen. You have probably noticed that in the middle of a conversation, some people are rehearsing in their heads the point they want to make—which means they are not listening carefully to the person who is talking. Since I rarely spoke, I was not distracted by thinking of what I was going to say and was thereby free to focus my attention on listening.

This ability to listen frequently allowed me to discern the real concerns of my congregants. Often something from my own experience seemed useful to share with them. Listening to their vulnerability enabled me to be vulnerable, especially as I no longer felt pressured to come up with an answer that would make everything all better. Often it was just the conversation—the person speaking and feeling heard—that brought them a measure of comfort.

My worst nightmare still remained being in a room full of strangers, or even congregants I didn't know very well. It turned out that even in such settings being a rabbi helped. Every Shabbat morning after services, we would have Kiddush (the blessing over wine followed by some food) in our social hall. It was not challenging for me to make conversation because each week lots of people wanted to talk with me. I rarely got a chance to eat since the food was long gone before the wave of people wanting to talk to the rabbi receded. Being reactive in this weekly format was easy and even enjoyable for me. I never had to initiate a conversation.

Looking at the trajectory of my work life, I moved from the solitary nature of writing to creating programs for others. I came to be even more engaged with people by becoming a rabbi—a totally people-centric profession. Like Kiddush, there is a structure to that social interaction. One of the unique things about rabbis (and clergy in general) is that they are not really members of the community. On one level, every congregant was my boss, making real friendships complicated. While each rabbi treats the idea of friendship with congregants differently, every rabbi knows this is not simple. I wondered whether being a rabbi was a perfect role for me—I could be in relationships with lots of people but there would always be a boundary to the relationship. I thought it analogous to being a rock star who wants the adulation of their fans and yet remains on the stage, separate from the audience. There is a clearly demarcated line.

Being home alone

This new understanding about me and my relationships worked until my divorce. After 26 years my marriage came to a mutually agreed-upon end. I moved out and began to recreate my life. It required a lot of attention and work just to put my new home together. It took a while before I realized that very few people called me to see how I was doing. It took a little longer to realize that most Friday nights I was home alone having Shabbat dinners by myself. Over the course of that first year, I received less than a handful of invitations. In part, that could be explained by my quiet demeanor. I did not exude neediness. When I was an undergraduate, I was asked to be an advisor to the Orthodox national youth group I had been involved in as a teenager. At a regional convention, I overheard a young rabbi remark to someone else, "Strassfeld has a real *savoir faire*"—the last words I would have used to describe myself. I think it probably said more about that rabbi's own insecurities. One of the interesting things about being so quiet is how people interpret my silence—assuming I was either stupid or super cool.

Sitting alone week after week became increasingly troubling. After all, you shouldn't have to express neediness for people to want to have a social experience with you. Was I so disliked or thought of as so uninteresting? It wasn't just social invitations. I noticed I was rarely asked to speak on panels or to teach at conferences on subjects in which I had expertise or experience.

These feelings ebbed and flowed over time. I remarried. I left Congregation Ansche Chesed and became the rabbi of a Reconstructionist synagogue, the Society for the Advancement of Judaism (also on the Upper West Side of Manhattan). I had changed the story about why I had so few friends over the years, but that didn't change the reality of my experience. The feelings of hurt from that year of eating alone on Friday nights lingered. Was this the way it was going to be for the rest of my life? Years passed. As I neared retirement, I pondered my professional legacy but I increasingly wondered about my personal relationship legacy. I debated with myself whether I was successful as a congregational rabbi, but increasingly felt there was little doubt that I was seriously flawed in the friendship department. Interestingly, I didn't feel that way when it came to my relationship with my wife or with my children. I felt deeply connected to them.

Talking about *teshuvah*/change

At High Holiday services, like most rabbis, I usually spoke about *teshuvah*/ change and repentance. I often mentioned that Jewish tradition is remarkably optimistic that people have the capacity to change their lives. I also knew that most people faced the same challenges year after year. The basic rabbinic notion about *teshuvah* could be summed up as, *Just say no!* Faced with the temptation to do something you know is wrong, you should stop yourself. About to lose your temper and say hurtful things? Count to 10 and speak wisely. Needless to say, this is a hard path to follow. If it was easy, these wouldn't be temptations in the first place. After all, Adam and Eve could eat any fruit in the Garden of Eden. There was only a restriction on the fruit of one tree in the whole garden. Maybe the fruit of the Tree of Knowledge was better fruit or maybe it was just the fact it was forbidden that made it so tempting.

Teshuvah as transformation

The Hasidic tradition suggests a different path to *teshuvah,* rooted in the theology that no place is empty of God's presence; Godliness is everywhere. Where is God when we do a misdeed? One answer (*Likktum Yekarim* 83) is that the moment we understand we have done something wrong is the moment we have the opportunity to change our behavior. Meditation teachers say the same thing: The moment you realize your attention has wandered is the moment you have the opportunity to return your focus to your breath. When your mind is lost in its wanderings you don't realize that you are not paying attention. Similarly, as long as you don't realize or won't admit that what you are doing is wrong, you aren't able to fix it.

In Hasidism, there is another level of Godliness in the misdeed or impulsive anger, found in an unusual doctrine about the *mahshavah zarah*/the distracting or alien thought. For the rabbis, the distracting thought during prayer was challenging. You are praying and suddenly you are thinking about your to-do list. Perhaps someone walks into the synagogue who you are either happy to see or with whom you recently had an argument. The rabbis of the Talmud urge you to stop thinking about what has distracted you and bring your attention back to your prayers. In Hasidism, because prayer is so important, the problem of distractions during prayer is an even greater challenge. Instead of advocating the worshipper stop thinking about the distracting thought, Hasidic teachers suggested that there was a purpose to the distracting thought. The Degel Mahaneh Ephraim, an 18th-century Hasidic master, commenting on the Torah portion *Ekev,* used the classic analogy of a servant coming before the king at his court. Surely, while the servant addressed the king, no one else would interrupt. If someone else did dare to speak to the servant, it must be that the person interrupting is doing so by the order of the king. How else would he dare interrupt during the court session? In such a way, the distracting thought during prayer is not just some random idea that popped up in the person's head. It must have come because God wanted it to come to the person. This rather startling and complex idea could be understood as Hasidism's version of a Freudian slip. There are no slips of the tongue; they are purposeful and come from the subconscious. In Hasidism nothing can happen without God letting it or making it happen. Therefore, God must have sent the distracting thought.

The second part of this doctrine is just as remarkable. If the distracting thought has a purpose, the response to it isn't to stop thinking about it. Rejecting the distraction isn't an appropriate response to this "messenger" from God. The distracting thought is actually an opportunity to reflect on why it is arising and what kernel of holiness can be found within it. Hasidism calls for the worshipper to transform the distracting thought by looking for the Godliness disguised in that thought. The most common example is a lustful attraction toward another person. How do you transform this attraction? For Hasidism the love of God is the basic impulse in the universe. All other love is derived from that highest form of love. Inappropriate or lustful attractions are distorted impulses of that love. Lust is a distorted form of love that forgets or ignores that the other person is a person and an image of God, not an object to be used. If the worshipper understood how much greater it was to love God, he would want to put aside the baser forms of that love to experience the "real thing." If you understood the pettiness of the feelings that are distracting you—jealousy, anxiety, annoyance—and returned to the more essential truths like gratitude for the blessings of your life, loving relationships, and health, wouldn't you want to focus on those "truths" rather than the distractions?

This radical doctrine has obvious dangers. You might just stay focused on the distractions and never get around to transforming them. After the first few generations of Hasidism, this practice was limited to Hasidic masters. For me the idea underlying this practice has become a powerful way to think about *teshuvah*/change.

Imperfect: The truth about us

I want to take this Hasidic teaching one step further. If everything comes from God then all of me comes from God, including the aspects of my personality that make me proud and those that embarrass me. If, for example, I am a generous person, I can trace that tendency to God but the same is true if I lack the attribute of generosity. We are born with certain characteristics, and being human, we are all born flawed. Our bodies are flawed and so are our personalities. There is no such thing as a perfect person. The rabbinic notion that we should just say no to those things that tempt us or challenge us in some ways denies the truth of who we are. I think Hasidism is suggesting that change can come about by acknowledging those feelings and accepting that they are part of the truth about ourselves. You may be an envious person. You might lust for sex, money, power or fame. You can be an ungenerous person. You may get angry easily. Instead of fighting these flaws, we first acknowledge that they are issues with which we struggle. We probably have done so our whole lives. It is probably true that at least some of these ways of being are innate. Others we may have acquired during our upbringing. They represent the truth about ourselves.

The truth about who we want to be

The deeper truth, however, is we would rather not be this way. We don't like the person we see in the mirror after we have mistreated a friend. We don't really want to be the angry person we seem to be, or the one whose first impulse is to answer every request with a no. For me it meant acknowledging a deep truth: If I want to have friends, I need to be open and vulnerable.

Hasidism suggests that change comes about when we encounter the distracting thought not as an outsider but as an annoying roommate who has lived with us for too long. Evicting him never seems to work. Seeing him (actually ourselves) clearly, and reflecting on how this is not the person we really want to be, just may allow us to change.

How do we do the hard work of changing who we are? The tradition believes strongly in our ability to choose. But we know how hard it can be to choose when our present reality feels so familiar and change feels so frightening. Hasidic teaching suggests that transformation comes about not by saying no but by acknowledging the truth about ourselves. Acknowledging that truth means admitting that we really want to change this aspect of who we are. It is that process that can lead to change. Thomas Moore (the contemporary psychologist and author) talks about *care* of the soul, not *cure* of the soul. We cannot radically change who we are but we can move closer to our best vision of ourselves. Hasidism talks about love of God as the basic impulse in the world. I would suggest that being caring, compassionate, and connected to human beings is a vision all people share.

Aren't most of the stories we tell ourselves distortions of the truth? In my case, I was often exaggerating the bleakness of my situation, ignoring any evidence to the contrary. Whether it was self-pitying or self-aggrandizing, the distortion was a mechanism for not facing the truth. Either the situation was hopeless or it was close to perfect—in either case there was nothing for me to do. Instead, I could realistically assess the situation, acknowledge my part in creating it, and then attempt to improve or resolve it.

It doesn't have to be love of God that helps us transform our treatment of a person as an object into treating them with a real and mutual emotional connection. Wouldn't we prefer a deep relationship with someone we care for and who returns that love? Our search for a connection in love or friendship is a universal desire. As God says in Genesis: It is not good for a person to be alone. Shouldn't we devote our energy to creating and maintaining those relationships? I could continue to be angry at people who didn't invite me for Friday night dinners and "enjoy" my martyrdom, or I could try to create such relationships.

Discovering the real truth

I eventually realized a truth that had always been staring me in the face. The reason nobody invited me to dinner was because I hadn't created the kind of relationships where people would care or even think about me. The people I knew weren't wondering whether they should invite me. They were not rejecting me. I simply wasn't on people's radar. The worst part of this realization was that it wasn't their fault. It was mine. I never put the time and energy into making friends. I certainly wasn't willing to be open and vulnerable in order to have relationships based on real sharing. It struck me that whenever people asked me what I was working on, I would answer in a vague, general way and quickly change the subject by asking them about their work. As long as I was reluctant to talk about myself, why would anyone want to be my friend?

Making friends is not simple. I realized this a decade earlier when I had tried to become friends with a few people I liked. They were the opposite of me in terms of personality—very outgoing, and fun to have at a party. Looking back, I understood why that effort wasn't successful. I always held back and after a while people gave up trying to penetrate my wall.

Too late to change?

This all came to a head around the time I decided to retire from the congregational rabbinate. Retirement is a moment of real transition from the world of work to a totally new way of being in the world. It is also hard to miss the reminder that "The End" is no longer off in some distant time zone. I knew I wanted to write this book. I also knew I would be sitting alone at home and the phone would rarely ring. There would be no more interaction with the other people at work, or meetings or congregants calling for information or advice. I like quiet, but was this going to be too quiet? Would the lack of friends be too overwhelmingly obvious to me? Was it too late at this stage of life to make friends?

With my new sense of responsibility, I decided to take my fate in my hands. I called a half a dozen people suggesting that we have lunch sometime. Guess what happened? No one called back. I decided to keep trying. There are no rules for a good friendship. Some people I see regularly, while others I only meet once in a while. Some I know will never call but I like them enough that it doesn't matter that I have to put in the work to make the friendship happen. It's still early in this process but I learned that it is possible to change the patterns that shaped my whole life. This is doing *teshuvah* at its essence. I will never be the life of the party. I still find large social gatherings painful. Yet, I hope I have changed just enough to create new friendships and deepen the ones that I have.

This feels like the kind of transformation that Hasidism teaches. Though it took me a long time, I realized the truth about myself—that I found friendship challenging. I could actually recognize that there was a silver lining here. I was a good listener. Qualities are problematic when they are extreme, but there is some benefit even to challenging qualities. We all struggle with aspects of our personalities that limit our ability to be in the world the way we would like to be. I have lost much in these many years of having very few friends. There is nothing like the depth of decades-old friendships. Yet, my "new" friendships still are a rich source of connection in my life. It is certainly true that "*lo tov*," it is not good to be alone.

The status quo is an obstacle to change

One of the challenges to change is that those around us have become used to the way we are. Even if people are unhappy about your deficiencies, they have expectations. They may complain or joke about how you are always late, but it is part of your identity. Human beings find chaos overwhelming. We strive to bring order and structure to our lives. We like our relatives and friends to act in mostly predictable ways. That's true even if those ways disappoint us. It is true even in couples. As much as one partner expresses a desire that their partner change in specific ways, when the other person actually begins to change it can destabilize the system. I know of a number of cases where couples have broken up because one person changes even though the change embraces what the other person has long criticized in their partner. What might this change mean? Is this still really the person I married? Is the glue that held us together, however unhealthy, now melting away? Even if change is not a direct threat to the relationship, the deeper truth is that the couple is actually comfortable with the division of roles between them. Having someone play the role of naysayer is useful to the partner who always says yes. Similarly, the role of being subordinate is useful to the partner who likes to be in charge, despite all his complaints to the contrary. Destabilization can be frightening to the supposed status quo. Change is very difficult. We can be helpful to people trying to change or we can subvert their efforts by reminding them that we expect them to continue to be exactly who they have been.

Nahman of Bratslav, a Hasidic master (1772-1810), creatively reads Psalm 37:10: "Just a little bit more (*od me'at*) and there will be no wicked one; you will look at his place and he will not be there." The usual understanding of this verse is that prayer can cause God to remove the wicked from the earth. Instead Nahman reinterprets the words *od me'at* to mean that we should focus on "the little bit." He says when we encounter someone we don't like, we should focus on the little bit of good in the person. He suggests that everyone has some good in them. By focusing on their good aspects, their wickedness will be gone. How? When we focus on people's goodness, they are able to change. The old personality that was difficult or annoying will have disappeared from our view (*Likutei Moharan* 282).

Nahman here points to the key role others can have in the process of change. I return to my story one last time. If no one responded to my efforts to make friends, I certainly would have fallen back on my old excuses, that I was shy or have some personality flaw or there's something wrong with them. The fact that some people responded enabled me to at least partially change my story. Nahman continues his teaching by saying that now that you have discovered some good in other people, you must apply the same process to yourself. It is also true that there is some good within yourself. Sometimes it is harder to believe in your own goodness than in that of other people. Once you find that bit of good within yourself, the task is to see if you can expand your sense of goodness within you. He ends this teaching with this image: Each good deed is a musical note and when you string them together you create the unique *niggun*/melody of your life.

Our individual Oral Torah

In telling this tale of *teshuvah*/change, I gained an insight into the importance of the Oral Torah. Each of our stories is composed of a written Torah and an Oral Torah. The written Torah is what happened in our lives—the failures and successes of life. My divorce and my remarriage. The job I quit and the job I got. The facts of my life. We each also have an Oral Torah that explains each of the events and their significance. It is useful to think of them as Oral Torah not just because our interpretation includes subjective elements, but because anything that is oral can change over time. It is not as fixed as something written down. Over our lifetime we can gain new understandings of the facts of our stories. My understanding of my shyness shifted over the course of my life; maybe it will shift again. Perhaps that is a particular gift of getting older. We have a longer perspective to look back over our lives. The passing of time may allow us to feel less engaged in the emotions of that moment. We find an interesting example of this in the book of Numbers, when God tells Moses to send spies to scope out the land of Israel. The spies return with mostly negative reports. In response, the people despair of being able to defeat the "giants" living in the land. A disappointed God then decrees 40 years of wandering for the Israelites so that this untrusting generation will die in the desert. Strangely, when Moses retells this story in Deuteronomy as part of his final words to the Israelites, the spies are sent not at God's request but rather at the people's demand! One way to understand this is that when Moses tells the story in Numbers, he is embarrassed by what happened and so places the blame on God. But now in Deuteronomy, Moses does not feel it's critical to protect his reputation or that of the people, so he tells the true story—that it was the people, not God, who wanted the spies.

Sometimes, we too can look back and be more ready to acknowledge our responsibility in the events of our lives. Maybe I played a role in the way a job had badly ended. Maybe it wasn't just my unreasonable boss. Sometimes we can look back and say taking that job was a mistake, but I was young and inexperienced. Looking back now, it was an obvious mistake but at the time, given who I was, I did the best I could. Perspective can allow us to be more forgiving of others and even of ourselves. Retelling our story gives us a chance to see it more fully. Our understanding can be more nuanced and complex and can more easily allow us to move forward. We don't bury the "old" story, but instead appreciate the way we can compose new notes in the still unfolding melody of our lives.

Rabbi Joseph Soloveitchik, a 20th-century Orthodox theologian, teaches that when we say the *Shema*—"Hear O Israel, the Lord our God, the Lord is One"—the word "one" means unique. God is unique in the world. Soloveitchik goes on to say that being created in the image of God means each human being is also unique. Humans are not just created equal; they are unique. Each of us has the ability to create and innovate. The challenge is for each of us to discover what we have to enrich the world. It is a difficult challenge because too often we listen to those who disparage and criticize us. Just as God is described as having glory (*kavod*), each of us has glory that enables us to make an impression on this world. Referring to the midrash that says God created many worlds before this one and then destroyed them because they weren't right, Soloveitchik suggests that we shouldn't give up in the face of failures. We should try again.

High Holidays: A season of change

Judaism's faith in our ability to change is so important that a whole season is devoted to the process of *teshuvah*/change. We start in the month of Elul, which precedes Rosh ha-Shanah, the New Year. Rosh ha-Shanah celebrates the creation of the world and begins the ten days of repentance that climax with Yom Kippur—the Day of Atonement. It is a long period because this process of *teshuvah*/change is difficult.

Wouldn't it be more logical for Yom Kippur to precede Rosh ha-Shanah? Shouldn't we first review our deeds from the past year and then welcome the New Year with a resolve to do better? There is a reason we begin with celebrating the creation of the world. It reminds us of the important lessons found in the beginning of the book of Genesis. We live in a moral universe, not just a mechanical one. We continue the work of creation by striving to bring *tov*/goodness into the world. We create our world through deeds and speech just as God spoke the world into being. Life is about our interactions with other people, each of whom is another image of God.

This is why we start with Rosh ha-Shanah—a celebration of the new—before we begin to reflect on the past year. Without the focus on the new year, we would have difficulty believing change is really possible. Aren't we struggling with the same personal issues this year that we have struggled with our whole life?

A changing world

We live in a world of change. God is a God of change. The status quo is an illusion. Judaism is a tree of life to those who hold it dear and use it to navigate the modern shoals of Scylla and Charybdis, holding desperately onto the past and equally fearing to move into the unknown future. Judaism deeply believes in the possibility of renewal. The midrash says that one of the things created before the world was created is *teshuvah*—the ability to change (Gen. R.1:4). Beginning with a sense that we are all human and therefore imperfect helps us avoid becoming mired in a feeling of failure. Instead of beating ourselves up, we can move forward by acknowledging that we want to change. Rabbi Larry Kushner, the contemporary rabbinic teacher, suggests instead of observing the traditional ritual of beating our chest with a fist when we recite the list of mistakes we have made during the year, we use an open palm to embrace ourselves in all our complexity.

Making the New Year new

There is a line repeated in the High Holiday liturgy based on Ps. 71:9—"Do not cast me aside in old age, when my strength fails, do not forsake me." The Degel Mahaneh Ephraim, an 18th-century Hasidic master, understands this to mean that we shouldn't allow our lives to become old and routine. "Spirituality that is old and ancient does not have enjoyment, great vitality or novelty. This is what is meant by make every day as new in your eyes" (*Degel Mahaneh Ephraim,* Ekev). How do we make the New Year new? Often expectations get in the way. We expect things to be the way they were. The routine is familiar and feels comfortable. We can be paralyzed by fears of traveling into the unknown. We can't control everything that will happen, but we can try to control our attitude as we journey. Are we overwhelmed with anxiety? Or can we hold on to the truth that worrying about what could happen doesn't change the future? Worrying only changes our present by making us unnecessarily mired in anxiety.

Newness practice

We have no real idea what the new year will bring. Any next moment is always unknown. We can be anxious about it or rest in unknowing. Just as we wish others a sweet new year, we can express these wishes for ourselves for the new year:

I acknowledge that I am an imperfect person.
I am also anxious about the unknown future.
Yet, I welcome the new year with its possibilities for renewal.
In this New Year:
I hope to be more compassionate to others and to myself.
I hope to be more patient with myself and with others.
I hope to be more open to renewal (*hithadshut*).

The practice of imperfection and change

> Imperfection is not our personal problem; it is a natural part of existing.
>
> —Tara Brach

> Without imperfection, neither you nor I would exist.
>
> —Stephen Hawking

We learn from the stories of Genesis that we live in an imperfect universe. Humans are not created perfect. The story of the Garden of Eden is not that we were perfect and fell from that status, but that we were born with the ability to choose and will inevitably make unwise choices. We don't live in a garden that provides for all our basic needs. We live in a world in which we struggle to get by. It is also true that no human body is perfect. I am not talking about a subjective judgment of our appearance, but rather every aspect of our bodies. That imperfect body is a physical manifestation of the even more important truth—that no one is a perfect person. If there are a few people who are saintly, they achieve that state through lifelong work. No one is born a saint.

We begin the ten days of repentance by acknowledging that we are imperfect. This is not an excuse for what we have done. Rather we are to see the truth that we are born imperfect and then raised by imperfect people. Both nature and nurture make us imperfect. Now we need to figure out what we will do with the helpful qualities and the problematic qualities that make up who we are. How will we change in the coming year? Are there ways to turn some of the problematic qualities into positive ones? What illusions about ourselves prevent us from seeing the truth?

The shofar calls us to change

This challenging practice of change is very much an internal one. There are few rituals associated with these holidays, most of which involve synagogue attendance. Why? Even though change is an individual process, it is useful to engage in the process knowing that everyone around you is involved in the same introspection. It reminds us that everyone is flawed, and also creates a context for the experience different than if we engaged in it by ourselves. One High Holiday ritual is the blowing of the shofar, a ram's horn. Maimonides, a 12th-century philosopher and rabbinic scholar, describes the eerie sound as an attempt to rouse us from our spiritual slumber. In "waking up," we might welcome the New Year by making ourselves "new" people. Awakened by the shofar on Rosh ha-Shanah, we can begin a process of change that climaxes with the intensive effort of Yom Kippur's fast day.

Embracing imperfection

A central theme of the traditional liturgy is that we are judged on Yom Kippur, when God determines whether we deserve to live or die in the coming year. This notion is given concrete expression in the metaphor that we are being written in the book of life. From a liberal perspective, we are being asked what we shall do with this gift of another year of life. The new year is pregnant with the possibilities for change. As the central prayer of Yom Kippur (the *unetaneh tokef*) states, each of us writes the book of our life with our own hand by the deeds we do. Can we bring increased awareness into the new year and inscribe additional goodness in the book of our life?

There is a verse from Psalms: "The stone rejected by the builders has become the cornerstone" (*even ma'asu ha-bonim hayta le-rosh pinah*, Ps. 118:22). Even as we recognize our imperfections, it is possible to see that those imperfections can sometimes be useful or even good. Someone who struggles with anger can better stand up for what is right than someone who is averse to confrontation. Similarly, someone who avoids confrontation might be better able to find a compromise between the warring factions in a meeting.

A blessing

Blessed are You Adonai our God, source of the universe, who creates innumerable beings and their imperfections (*ve-hes-ronan*). For all that You have created to enable the life of all beings, we praise You, the giver of life to all existence.

This is a traditional short blessing, (*borei nefashot*), recited after eating a snack. It recognizes and validates our imperfections. In fact, it suggests that the imperfections enable us to live in the world. If we were all perfect, the world of human choice and freedom couldn't exist.

Forgiveness and Compassion

The tradition sees Yom Kippur as a time when God judges us. We might see that it is God alone who judges us. The One who knows all things can fairly judge what my motives were when I did something. God knows what is in my heart when I ask someone to forgive me. As a human, it is close to impossible to know what other people's motives are or how sincere they are. One of the ways we are not like God is that we struggle to understand our own motives and those of others. In this understanding of Yom Kippur, we are encouraged to leave judgment to The One who knows the truth. Too often for us, judgment is really only judgmentalism.

There is a way that we are to be Godlike in the context of Yom Kippur. Our goal is to be compassionate. Just as we seek forgiveness for what we have done wrong, we should also strive to forgive others. We should do this for their sake, but also for our own sake. Each of us suffers from the way we act in self-destructive or simply hurtful ways. Each of us is disappointed in the ways we fail to live up to the person we truly wish to be. Yet, others are affected by our actions and words. Part of the practice of this period is to try to mend relationships. This can involve approaching friends and family and asking forgiveness for things we have done.

According to tradition, we are supposed to ask someone for forgiveness up to three times. At that point, if the request is sincere, we are forgiven, even if the person themself refuses to forgive. This feels too mechanical to me. While it is always difficult to know when a person is genuinely sorry for what she did, the tradition is wise to lean on the side of forgiveness. Too often, we carry grievances for years and years. Isn't it healthier to let them go, accepting that we are all flawed people? We all say and do unwise and hurtful things, often in the midst of an argument or crisis. One of the difficult dynamics in couples is when one asks the other why he can't be, for example, more patient? In truth, patience may come easily to the one asking, but is much harder for the one being asked, which is why it is an issue between them. As a therapist of mine once said to me, "I finally gave up being angry at my mother for not being able to show me love when I realized that no matter how many times I opened that refrigerator door, I would never find hot food there."

Wrongs too hurtful to forgive

There are wrongs that are so hurtful that they cannot easily, or perhaps ever, be forgiven. I disagree with the tradition that says if we ask for forgiveness three times that we must be forgiven. I have been asked a number of times whether a person is required to say mourner's kaddish for a parent who was abusive. While encouraging making amends even after death, there are rabbinic sources that would support not saying kaddish. Reciting kaddish is understood as honoring the deceased and in extreme cases the person is not deserving of honor.

> Love isn't finding a perfect person. It's seeing an imperfect person perfectly.
>
> —Sam Keen

> Have patience with all things, but chiefly have patience with yourself. Do not lose courage in considering your own imperfections but instantly set about remedying them—every day begin the task anew.
>
> —Saint Frances de Sales

> It doesn't matter how long we may have been stuck in a sense of our limitations. If we go into a darkened room and turn on the light, it doesn't matter if the room has been dark for a day, a week, or ten thousand years—we turn on the light and it is illuminated. Once we control our capacity for love and happiness, the light has been turned on.
>
> —Sharon Salzberg

Kavanah to begin Yom Kippur

On Yom Kippur we probably say more words than any other day. We begin with the Kol Nidrei prayer, acknowledging that in the past we used many words to make promises that we left unkept. So much of what we said last year was just idle chatter, or wasn't really true, or was badly said, or was meant to hurt. Many of the promises we made last New Year were not fully kept. As we acknowledge the power of words, we are called to imitate God and create our world through speech. What words do we want to leave behind, and what words do we want to carry into the New Year? To paraphrase the poet Robert Frost, we have miles to go before we sleep and have many promises to keep. We seem to be lost in woods that are dark and deep.

There is a verse we recite on Yom Kippur that can serve as an intention throughout the holiday: *Khu imakhem devarim ve-shuvu el Adonai* (Hosea 14:3): Take with you words and turn to God, or take with you words and turn to the good that is within you. Find the words that will help you change and move forward into the New Year.

Who shall live and who shall die?

The *unetaneh tokef* prayer sets out in detail the themes of life and death through a series of questions: Who will live and who will die and how? The climax of the prayer asserts that repentance, prayer, and charity can avert the severity of the decree. Traditionally this is understood to mean that if you repent during the High Holidays the decree of your death can be reversed. A more liberal theological interpretation understands that death comes to us all and is not a punishment for the errors of our life. The decree of death cannot actually be averted, but we can lessen the severity of the decree by living a life infused with the values of striving to change (*teshuvah*), engaging in spirituality (*tefillah*), and acting with lovingkindness (*tzedakah*). In other words, we avert the severity of the decree by living a life of purpose.

Core Principle #10:
Be a Lifelong Learner

Existential unknownness

The measure of a life is not how much you have accomplished—it is not the money, or the awards, or the fame, though it is natural to seek those things. A Jew is to engage in one thing: the study of Torah. And it is not how much Torah you know that is the measure of a Jew. The study of Torah is a lifelong enterprise. There is no graduation when you have "mastered" Torah. It is not how much you have eaten of the Tree of Knowledge but how much you have eaten of the oft-forgotten second tree in the Garden of Eden, the *eitz hayy-im*—the Tree of Life. Every week in synagogue as we return the Torah scroll, we sing *eitz hayyim hi*—it is a tree of life to those who grasp it.

Twentieth-century German Jewish philosopher Franz Rosenzweig suggested that creation, revelation, and redemption are the three central activities of God. The rabbis taught that we are to walk in God's ways, meaning that we are to imitate God. Clearly, we are called to bring redemption to the world. In the modern world, the notion of humans as co-creators has become ever more evident even as we struggle not to bring destruction to this planet. We easily understand how acts of compassion and connection can bring redemption to the world. However, what could it mean to say we humans should bring revelation into the world?

Perhaps it is that we deepen the storehouse of human knowledge as we discover more about the world, whether it is our bodies, our minds, or our universe. But reflecting back on my life brought me to an insight about people and revelation. The voice of Sinai goes forth every day, not just constantly revealing Torah but calling each of us to join in the act of revelation by revealing ourselves to the world. It is not how much you know but how much you are known. How well, in your daily interactions, did you connect with the other divine images disguised as human beings? Were you open or hidden?

Understanding this, I finally understood why I became a rabbi. It gave me, an introvert, a forum to reveal myself as each week I taught Torah, which is always both the Torah of the plain meaning of the text, and also the meaning reflecting my inner concerns and values. I became a rabbi as a way to be known and as a way to know myself. I now understood that I was a connection not just between Jews and Torah but also between me and you. It is not existential aloneness that is the challenge of our modern world—it is a sense of existential *unknownness*. Each of us wants to be known. Each of us is afraid to be known, afraid that we will be considered lacking or foolish or unsuccessful. Or we try to conceal our deepest selves. We think we can control what we show the world. Freud argues that we are always revealing and concealing, either consciously or unconsciously. Revelation is an ongoing process for each of us. We each stand again and again at Sinai, receiving and creating Torah.

It could be argued that the single most important core principle in Judaism is the study of Torah, which includes learning how to practice Judaism as well as understanding its values and teachings. For centuries the study of Torah, and more specifically the study of Talmud, has been central to Jewish religious life. It should be noted that until recently this practice was reserved for men. Various movements in Jewish history prioritized other choices. For Hasidism, prayer was more important than study. It is also true that the study of Torah has meant different things to different Jews. For some it had a more academic, theoretical quality. Mystics looked for the secret hidden meaning of the Torah. For others, the focus was on learning the details of halakhic practice. Torah study is also a spiritual practice because these texts create an opportunity to encounter God, holiness, or wisdom about the deepest questions of life. In its fullest expanse, Torah is the 3,000-year-old discussion of these questions by the Jewish people. It contains narratives, law, philosophy, theology, poetry, midrashic imaginings, history and myth. It is written from different perspectives both religious and secular, and is gathered from many historical periods, adding to its diversity.

Central to my rabbinate, despite the many responsibilities that come with serving a community, has been to set aside time to continue to study Torah. Despite a strong Jewish background, I felt my continued learning was critical to my Jewish life. It wasn't only that I needed to continue to look for new things to teach and preach about; it was essential to my ongoing growth as a Jew. I quickly discovered that studying on my own wasn't effective. It was too easy to put it off in the face of many other priorities. I found it helpful to have study partners, usually other colleagues with whom I would meet weekly for an hour. Most years I had two different study partners. For the last few years, I've been studying Talmud with one colleague and Hasidic texts with another. Sometimes we talk about work or our lives and do little study. Not infrequently, one of us has had to cancel because of a funeral or a meeting. Even so, it is amazing how much you can learn over the course of 40 years. (I've recently had the unique pleasure of studying online with my son, who teaches Jewish and Gender Studies at the University of Arizona.) I share this with you for two reasons. First, many people look at the vastness of Jewish literature and feel overwhelmed. They especially feel that way if they didn't have a strong Jewish education as a child. It is important to remember that it is impossible for anyone to learn everything about Judaism. Torah study is about engaging in learning, which gives you resources to enrich your life. It is also true that over the span of a life you can acquire a fair amount of knowledge.

Suggested method of study

There is a value to studying with a partner. It is not only that you have made a commitment to study with someone on a regular basis. It is also not just that your partner may be able to figure out something that puzzles you in the text or have an insight that makes the teaching a memorable one. Studying with a partner is the traditional way to learn Talmud. It is called *hevruta* study from the word *haver*, meaning friend or partner. Specifically, one of you reads the text out loud to the other, explaining what it means. You discuss it and then switch readers. The most important part of this study technique is that it forces the students to read the text word by word and explain it. I find reading out loud forces you to move more slowly and thereby makes you focus more carefully on the text, often enabling you to see meanings you might miss in a rapid reading.

Study as a spiritual practice

At Havurat Shalom, the intentional community in which I was a member in my 20s, the study of Torah was a spiritual practice. While there were elements of all the various ways the texts had been studied by Jews, central to what was happening was a spiritual encounter with the texts of the Jewish people. The manner of study was ostensibly borrowed from the world of the *yeshiva*—advanced academies of Torah learning. What distinguished the *hevruta* study in Havurat Shalom from the yeshiva was that it was not about mastering the page but encountering the text. Or to put it another way, it was a meditative reading of the text.

To use the language of Martin Buber, a 20th-century philosopher, our study was, at its best, an I-Thou experience. For Buber, most often this meant a real and deep encounter with another person or with God. For us, it was an encounter with a text and with the ongoing conversation of the Jewish people about the text. It was an encounter with the other people in the room. Most of all it was an encounter with ourselves through the prism of the text and our discussion of it.

Some of you may wonder what can be gained by two people studying together who don't know very much about Judaism. Isn't that the uninformed leading the uninformed? While there were members of Havurat Shalom who had a great deal of knowledge, the distance between the teacher and the student was less important. We were all students. It wasn't about how much you knew. It was all about being open to learning in each encounter with the text.

Prayer, study, and community were the three pillars of Havurat Shalom. We viewed study as a spiritual practice about the search for meaning rather than the acquisition of knowledge. This way of understanding a core practice in Judaism has spread throughout the Jewish world. I would encourage you to make time to study Torah. While for those whose formal study ended in college or graduate school, where the focus was on grades, the study of Torah has no such pressure. It is learning for its own sake.

Where to begin

There are a variety of Jewish texts you can study, some more difficult than others. There is plenty of material to study in translation that requires nothing more than an occasional online search to find the meaning of a term or the identity of someone quoted. You shouldn't think of texts or Torah in the narrowest definitions. Contemporary fiction and poetry are examples of non-traditional texts. Nevertheless, the traditional texts remain important as a way to become acquainted with Judaism.

A good place to start is the Bible. You could begin in Genesis 1 and continue straight through. If there is a section that does not appeal to you, either skip it or read through it quickly without discussion. There are many translations of the biblical text. The Jewish Publication Society (JPS) translation is the most authoritative. Robert Alter has translated the whole Bible, and includes explanatory notes that can be helpful if the translation seems unclear. One way to study, especially if you don't know Hebrew, is for each of you to have a different translation. Comparing the difference between the two translations may help clarify the meaning. If you want a modern running commentary on the text, you can use *Etz Hayyim*—it has the Hebrew text, the JPS translation, an abbreviated version of the JPS Bible commentary, and some additional commentary. JPS also has a five-volume Torah commentary with more extensive notes than the one volume *Etz Hayyim*. Each volume also has a number of essays that go into detail on a specific subject.

Each week a portion of the Torah is read aloud in the synagogue. Traditionally, the whole Torah, from the beginning of Genesis to the end of Deuteronomy, is read over the course of a year. Each Torah portion is divided into seven sub-portions (*aliyot*). There is an old tradition (not widely observed today) that encourages reading one aliyah each day so that you will have read the whole portion on your own. If you are studying once a week with a partner, it is unlikely that you could study a whole portion each week within your study time frame. One alternative is to follow the cycle of some synagogues, which read only a third of the Torah portion each week. In the first year of the cycle, they read the first third of each portion. Over the course of three years, each Torah portion is read in its entirety. You might not even finish a third of the Torah portion in your weekly study. Try to leave the last ten minutes of your study time to finish reading that week's portion without discussion. That way you will have at least some familiarity with the whole Torah. Doing it this way will take three years; alternatively, you can just read the Torah in order, letting it take as much time as you need even if that means it is a multi-year project.

There is also a relatively new project that encourages the study of each chapter of the whole Bible. Begun in Israel, Rabbi Adam Mintz has edited the English version, which can be found at www.929.org.il. Each posting includes a wide variety of commentaries on a chapter in the Bible. It begins in Genesis and goes all the way through to the end of Chronicles. It derives its name from the number of chapters in the entire Bible—929.

Talmud and Midrash

Sefer Aggadah is an anthology of rabbinic texts arranged by subject matter. There are sections about biblical and rabbinic personalities. Most of the collection focuses on such topics as the nature of human beings, good and evil, and character traits, selected from rabbinic literature. These are midrashic texts, meaning they are not legal in nature but concentrate on moral exhortations, stories, parables, or wisdom. The collection was first published in Hebrew by the Israeli poet Hayim Nachman Bialik and Yehoshua Hana Ravitzky and translated into English by William Braude with the title *The Book of Legends* (Schocken, 1992). Inevitably you will come across texts that will leave you puzzled and some that you will find offensive. There are many more interesting and striking texts that will evoke thought and discussion and will give you access to the rabbinic tradition. I would suggest starting with the sections that look interesting to you.

Another, more challenging way to study Talmud is *daf yomi*. This practice, begun in the Orthodox community in the 20th century, includes the study of a page (*daf*) of Talmud every day (*yomi*). Those who do this finish the entire Talmud over the course of seven-and-a-half years. Recently, some people outside the traditional community have engaged in this practice. There are a number of online guides in English to assist people in this study, since it is not easily accessible for those who have never studied it. The Talmud includes legal texts as well as the non-legal texts found in *The Book of Legends*.

The website Sefaria (sefaria.org) is a great resource of traditional texts. Anyone with internet access can now find most of the traditional library through this resource. Some of the texts are translated into English. Sefaria enables people to create and then share source sheets on topics that interest them. You could create a learning program for yourself by choosing topics that look interesting and using the source sheets.

I've also created a study guide to this book to study more closely many of the texts, often in fuller versions than are quoted in my book. You can find the Judaism Disrupted Study Guide at sefaria.org/sheets/457706.

Blessing for Torah study

There are traditional blessings for Torah study near the beginning of the morning service. They are recited then under the assumption that you will be engaged in Torah throughout the day. You can also recite them to frame a time you have set aside for Torah study:

> Blessed are You Adonai, our God, Source of the universe, who has made us holy through your *mitzvot* and commanded us to occupy ourselves with words of Torah.

> Adonai our God, let the words of Torah be sweet in our mouths and the mouths of the Jewish people, so that we and all who follow after us, will all be knowers of Your name, and learners of your Torah for its sake alone. Blessed are You, Adonai our God, who teaches Torah to Your people Israel.

Our role in creating Torah

After 40 days together on Mt. Sinai, God gives Moses the tablets. When Moses comes down from the mountain and sees the Israelites worshipping the Golden Calf, he smashes those tablets. Eventually, God invites Moses to return to the mountain and tells him to write a second set of tablets. I used to understand this text as another example of the failure of human beings to accept God's gifts to them. Despite all the miracles that God performed for us in Egypt and on the way to Sinai, we can't go 40 days without doing the wrong thing, worshipping the Golden Calf. We only deserve the second-rate set of tablets—written not by the hand of God but by mortal Moses.

I now think that the point is the opposite. The world needs to be built by human hands, guided by laws and wisdom developed and written by human beings. We are seekers of truth, not guardians of the truth. We create the truth and question it over and over again. The midrash tells us that when the Ark of the Covenant was completed, the second set of tablets was put inside as well as the broken pieces of the first set (*Bava Batra* 14b). We strive for a vision of the broken tablets made whole. We may attain pieces of that vision, but for now, the Torah we live with is the human interpretation of the encounter with the divine at Sinai.

We have the written Torah and the Oral Torah. Our task is to continue to study the written Torah. As we bring our insights and our questions and challenges to the text, we create the Oral Torah, which changes in each generation. We live in the tension of the written Torah and our contemporary understanding, each of which challenges the other. That is the task of all those who are students of Torah. It is why we need two Torahs—the written and the oral. One without the other would be incomplete.

Each one of us is needed

Who is engaged in this extraordinary process? The wisest scholars of our time? In fact, all of us are participants, each adding the piece of our lives to the Torah until it is complete. According to a mystical tradition, each Jew has one letter of the Torah, our own special letter that we learn and develop and raise up to the Holy One (see the Hasidic master Me'or Einayim on *Va-Yelekh*). This notion is based on the tradition that there are 600,000 letters in the Torah and there were 600,000 Jews who left Egypt (neither count is really accurate). Each person's Torah is unique. This vision, that each of us has our own special letter of the Torah, is empowering, but also frightening. It means that with so many Jews distant from Judaism, whole parts of the Torah are being left unread. According to Jewish law, if even one letter is missing from a Torah scroll, it is *pasul*/not kosher and can't be used in the synagogue. Lacking even one Jew, one letter, the Torah scroll is incomplete. Our task is to invite everyone to find their place in the Torah scroll. Adding their "Torah," their understandings, to ours and to those who came before, will help complete the Torah.

Shavuot and Simchat Torah

Shavuot commemorates the giving of the Torah at Mt. Sinai. There are no biblical commandments like eating matzah or sitting in the sukkah to give it a unique character. The mystics of Safed (16th century) instituted a custom of staying up all night studying on Shavuot. The source of this custom, called *Tikkun leil Shavuot*, was attributed to a midrash that said the Israelites overslept the morning of the revelation at Sinai and had to be awakened for the big event. To ensure that this insult to Torah doesn't happen again, the all-night study vigil was instituted. For the mystics, the anniversary of this great event was a propitious time for *tikkun*—repair of the world—and had mystical significance. For most people today, the *Tikkun leil Shavuot* is an opportunity to study Torah as a way to celebrate Shavuot. In recent years, the *Tikkun leil Shavuot* has been adopted by some secular Israelis as a way to engage in the study of the variety of Jewish texts.

For years, I have wanted to try a Torah study marathon during the day of Shavuot. This would be in fulfillment of the verse: "You should meditate on it day and night" (*ve-hagita bo yomam ve-layla*) (Joshua 1:8).

Shavuot is an opportune time to create or review your Torah study goals. How much did you accomplish during the past year? What would you like to attempt in the coming year? Do you like studying on your own or with a partner? Do you need to switch study partners?

A *kavanah* for Shavuot: When the Temple in Jerusalem existed, we were commanded to bring the *bikkurim*/first fruits of our crops and offer them to God. The Sefat Emet, 19th-century Hasidic master, suggests that with the destruction of the Temple, we offer first fruits every day as part of our prayers. It seems particularly appropriate to offer them on Shavuot. Our first fruits can be the best of our selves and reflections on our growth and learning in the past year as we prepare to receive the Torah of this Shavuot.

Simchat Torah

Simchat Torah comes at the end of the fall holiday cycle. It marks the end of the Torah reading cycle as we finish the book of Deuteronomy and immediately start Genesis. This is accompanied by singing and dancing with the Torah scrolls and is the most spiritual joyous occasion in the festival cycle.

Embodying Torah practice

Why do we have two holidays of Torah—Shavuot, which marks the moment of receiving the Torah, and Simchat Torah, a time to rejoice as we finish and begin the Torah reading cycle anew? The Sefat Emet sees an answer in the sequence of events that occurred at Mt. Sinai. Moses spends 40 days receiving the rest of the Torah. On his way down Mt. Sinai, he sees the Israelites worshipping the Golden Calf and, in anger, he smashes the tablets. When God agrees to forgive the people, Moses goes up on the mountain again for 40 days and nights and brings down a second set of tablets. The Sefat Emet asks: Why did Moses have to stay up on the mountain for another 40 days? After all, he had just received all of the Torah. It should have taken only enough time to make a new set of tablets and maybe a quick review! He answers that actually it is not the same Torah. The episode of the Golden Calf had happened in between. In one of the blessings we recite when being called to the Torah, we say: "...who has given us a Torah of truth and planted in us eternal life." The Torah of truth is not the ideal Torah given at Sinai. The Torah of truth is the lived Torah of everyday life. It is affected by the imperfect people who live their lives in the light of Torah. It contains hopes and visions and mistakes and stumbles.

On Sukkot, we gather together the four species and the strands of our lives and with them we circle around the synagogue in whose center is a Torah scroll. On Simchat Torah, we take the Torah scrolls and circle around the synagogue, leaving space for the holy or the Holy One to be at the center. We literally grasp the Torah in our arms, expressing what we recite as we return the Torah to the ark each Shabbat—it is a tree of life to those who grasp it. It isn't enough to study Torah, as we do on Shavuot. We need to plant it inside us. We strive to embody Torah by dancing it with our feet. In that way, we learn how to walk in the path (*derekh Adonai*) that God sets out for Abraham. This journey began in the Garden of Eden. Adam and Eve tasted of the Tree of Knowledge of Good and Evil. Exiled from the Garden, they did not eat of the second forbidden tree—the Tree of Life. Humans became mortal. Yet, the Torah is referred to as the Tree of Life/*eitz hayyim*. It is not because if we observed it perfectly, we would live forever. The Torah allows us to partake of eternity by engaging in a life of purpose and meaning.

Core Principle #11:
Living in an Open Society

The universal and the particular

"In the beginning God created the heaven and the earth." Surprisingly, the Torah doesn't start with Abraham, the first Jew. It doesn't start with either the Exodus from Egypt or the revelation at Mt. Sinai—two critical moments in the Jewish people's story. We begin at the moment of the creation of the world. In fact, the first eleven chapters of the book of Genesis are universal in their scope.

While Judaism is a particularistic take on life, it exists in a universalistic context. Its most fundamental "truths" are true of all people or of the universe, not just Jews. This is why the Torah begins with the creation of the world. Too often we forget about this beginning and only focus on a particularistic vision of the world. Our most sacred text tells of a world where for many generations there are no Jews. Apparently, Jews aren't essential for the world's existence. It is a humbling lesson.

Every person is a unique individual. Because we are human, we see the world with a perspective limited by the nature of our being. We are shaped by our genes and by our environment. Each of us is unique, but we are also like every human being who has ever existed or will exist. Our bodies are more alike than not. We communicate not only with the humans around us but with the human past. We strive to create a legacy for the human future. Most of all, the boundary of our concern lies not with the small circle of our life but with the whole universe.

It is a common mistake to think that the particular is paramount and the universal is secondary. The Torah begins with the universal before we get to Judaism to ensure that we understand that the particular exists within the universal. My being and body don't let me forget my particularity. I need to remember that which is universal.

In our time, some people look at the particular and see it as a source of much of the conflict in our world. They wonder why we don't simply embrace the universal aspect of the world and be all-inclusive. Why should we be limited to one particularistic tradition? Why not take a teaching from one religion and a practice from another religion? Wouldn't a boundary-less society be the ideal?

A newborn baby sees the world as undifferentiated. The baby and the mother are one. Life is about the process of differentiation. We can't live in the universal. Quickly we move to the particular. The baby will become an "I." Still, we are not to forget that we are part of the universal. Despite our experienced sense that we are alone, Judaism's most fundamental teaching is that we are connected to the whole universe.

While after the opening chapters of Genesis, the story will turn to Abraham and the Jewish people, nowhere does the Torah say that God is only the God of the Jewish people. Monotheism proclaims that there is only one God, who is God of the whole world. Nor does it suggest that God only speaks or has a relationship to the Jewish people alone.

This first lesson is critical. I am a citizen of the world and I am also a Jew. Increasingly today, there are those who believe that we must choose one identity or the other, as though they are in conflict. I reject the notion that the only option is to choose one. I strive to be both. I am deeply interested and involved in Judaism and I love America. My favorite books are about the Civil War and I like American folk art. The woods of New England remain the landscape of my soul. This has much to do with the environment in which I grew up, both in my family and the old Jewish neighborhood of Boston. It also has to do with my belief that Judaism and America are not an either/or proposition. But most importantly, it is not just that I am choosing both America and Judaism. I think the teaching of the beginning of Genesis is important to our understanding of our place in the world. It is true about every human being, not just Jews. We are universal and we are particularistic. We need to remind ourselves that we are part of the weave of the whole universe. We are not a people who stand alone. I am a person like every other. We are all images of God.

Alike and unique

Yet, I am also unique—I am a person who is not like anyone else who was, who is, or who will be. I am unique, particular. The two perspectives are essential to see the world and my place in it clearly. My particularity helps me feel rooted. It helps connect me to a tradition and a vision of the future. You cannot be just a universalist. You cannot choose everything; that's the whole point of choice. You come from somewhere and have a set of experiences that no one else can fully share. Particularism gives a sense of place and a sense of identity, even if that identity has become more multifaceted in our increasingly diverse modern world. Each of us, as well as all of us, is on the journey of our lives.

The question of the balance between the universal and the particular has always been present in Jewish life. During much of our history as a people, we were shaped by our minority status and for much of the pre-modern period, the majority culture was ambivalent at best about the Jews living in their midst. Jews were restricted in law or in custom in how much they could participate in the larger society. Modernity has torn down the ghetto walls and Jews have eagerly embraced both the economic and social opportunities available. This change didn't come about easily. Some believed that we needed to give up aspects of Judaism in order to be fully welcomed into the modern world. Even as late as the 1920s and 30s, Jews were not accepted everywhere in American society. There were those who said the chosen people doctrine proved that Jews hadn't really accepted modernity and remained a clannish group who regarded themselves as superior to people who are not Jewish. Over time the issue of chosenness has faded away as Jews have become accepted in American society. Instead of being regarded as unassimilable outsiders, we have been broadly accepted. The question has flipped. Are we so welcome that we will disappear in the melting pot of America?

Intermarriage

The issue of intermarriage is emblematic of the potential assimilation of Jews. In the first half of the 20th century, a Jew who married someone who was not Jewish was making a statement that either their Judaism was unimportant or needed to be rejected. Similarly, there were Jews who changed their names because they sounded too Jewish. Now, we live in an America where a Jew can marry the child of a president (so far two presidents). Jews and Judaism are part of the fabric of American life and culture. We are so accepted in American society that we no longer feel the need to hide our identity or change our names. It has become a totally legitimate part of a person's heritage. Whether Judaism is a significant or insignificant piece of that heritage may be a question for each Jew but is a matter of indifference to most Americans.

Not surprisingly, this has created challenges for the continuity of the Jewish people. There are no signs stating that Jews are not welcome here and most of the old ethnic neighborhoods have disappeared. Intermarriage is a natural outcome of this open society. People meet and fall in love and want to marry. An intermarriage isn't necessarily a statement of indifference to Judaism. How should the Jewish community respond to the increasing rate of intermarriage?

Much of the organized Jewish community decried the rate of intermarriage. The Conservative movement doesn't allow their rabbis to officiate at intermarriages, while the Reform and Reconstructionist movements do. All the liberal movements have tried to make intermarried couples welcome, with varying success. The rate of intermarriage has continued to climb. The truth is when the organized Jewish community talks about intermarriage as a threat to the future of Jewish continuity, the message that all are welcome rings hollow. To be told that your marriage is helping to bring an end to Judaism but we still want you to join our synagogue is more off-putting than welcoming to many people.

There is conflicting data on the efforts that have been made by the organized Jewish community to address this challenge. The Jewish community has supported a variety of efforts to encourage young Jews to meet and marry each other, including Birthright Israel (a free trip to Israel for young Jews). Other initiatives, like Base Hillel, Moishe House, and One Table, are startups that have been designed to offer opportunities for individuals and couples, many of whom are involved in interfaith relationships, to engage in Jewish life outside of the synagogue. Time will tell whether these efforts will have a significant impact on the rate of intermarriage or connection to Jewish life.

Shifting identities

Our open society has created other challenges as well. We live in a time when peoples' identities are fluid and shifting. Perhaps because we are living longer, or because time is now measured by how fast the processor in our computer can run, or because the internet has made the whole world accessible at the touch of a keyboard, our identities are not formed and fixed at one period of our life. We change jobs, residences, even partners with increasing frequency and we have a much more fluid sense of identity, moving in and out of aspects of that identity as changes occur in our lives. These changes are not only triggered by lifecycle moments, like having children or retiring, but are sometimes simply a redirecting of priorities or focus. As Americans, we have inherited the legacy of the frontier, that vast wilderness of newness where each American can recreate their identity into new versions of themselves. It is not just computer programs that come in successive versions; many of us do as well. We are constantly hoping to upgrade.

American ethos and intermarriage

Obviously, marriage is a very personal decision. When Jewish parents try to make the case for marrying another Jew, we run up against a striking counter-argument. America believes in the equality of all its citizens. We hold these truths to be self-evident, that all people are created equal. If we think there is nothing wrong with Americans of Italian descent marrying Americans of Puerto Rican descent, why are Jews different? Does the survival of Jewish culture in America have significance in a way that other people's culture does not? If we suddenly say that being Jewish is more about a religion than an ethnicity or a culture, would we tell a Protestant not to marry a Catholic or a Buddhist? Some parents try to convince their children that the survival of the Jewish people is more important than love—a claim undercut by the fact that there are increasing numbers of intermarried couples who raise their children with a Jewish identity.

In the face of the overwhelming value of equality, we can only respond with emotion and gut feelings, and, I would add, with some reluctance. I have noticed that one of the things that has changed over the last few decades is the willingness to pressure people to convert. It was not uncommon in the past for a Jewish partner to ask his or her future spouse to convert as a condition for getting married, perhaps for the sake of parents or grandparents. Nowadays, when I work with people interested in conversion, I don't have a sense that anyone is being pressured. That has changed in part because the Jewish partner often feels it is wrong to ask someone to convert for any other reason than their own choice. What has changed is that Judaism is increasingly viewed as an attractive life choice.

Living in a world without borders

Fundamentally, we are caught between an embrace of the open society and the danger that society could just swallow us up in its welcoming vastness. In response, we turn to the old paradigms that are frankly ineffective and are undercut by our deep commitment to the freedoms of the open society. This Core Principle is called "Living in an open society" because I believe that is the world young Jews inhabit these days. While we may live in unprecedented times, the story of a minority group negotiating its relationship with the much larger surrounding culture begins with Abraham. Today, most liberal Jews do not hold negative stereotypes of people who are not Jewish. We don't think they are all anti-Semites or, in the classic stereotype of eastern Europeans, that everyone who isn't Jewish is a drunkard. We believe that people are people. When it comes to marriage, we may be more concerned with class differences than ethnic background.

The challenge of the moment

Our challenge, then, is different than it was in the past. Instead of viewing our open society as a threat to Jewish peoplehood, we now have an opportunity to create a Judaism that can thrive in a world without borders. In such a world, Judaism competes with all the other choices people make about their identities. In such a world, even the most basic aspects of identity cannot be assumed. It is not only sexual orientation, but gender itself that is no longer clear-cut. If the rabbis understood the Torah of Sinai to be focused on distinction and separation, today we need a new Torah that helps us live in a world that seeks wholeness instead of separation. We need to find holiness not in the rejection of all the world has to offer but in the discovery of the holy within everyone and everything. Let us be clear: we still need to differentiate between the good and the bad or the helpful and the hurtful, but we now redefine Judaism by declaring all humans are created in the image of God. No group of people is, in its essence, better than any other group.

The Jewish wedding ceremony sanctifies the union of two people. The word for this is *kiddushin*, which comes from the Hebrew root meaning holy or sacred. This couple now becomes sacred and committed to each other from both a legal and emotional perspective. While some rabbis omit the language of *kiddushin* when officiating at interfaith ceremonies, isn't the coming together of any two people in marriage a holy act of commitment? Isn't it just as holy for two people of any faith to be married as it is for a Jewish couple? Isn't this a universal holy moment even if it is celebrated in different ways by different religions and ethnic traditions?

Holiness is everywhere

It is not only in relationships of many kinds where we find holiness; it can appear in the most unlikely of places as well. In the book of Genesis, we learn that Jacob fled his father after having tricked him into getting the blessing meant for Esau. On his way back to the old country, Mesopotamia, Jacob came upon a place (*va-yifga ba-makom*) and decided to stay there for the night as the sun set. He lay down in that place and dreamt. In his dream, Jacob saw a ladder set on the ground and reaching up to heaven. There were angels going up and down the ladder.

How does Jacob respond upon awakening? He proclaims: "Surely God is present in this place and I did not know it...How awesome is this place! This is none other than the house of God and this is the gateway to heaven" (Gen. 28:16-17).

Is there something special about this place? I think not. Jacob stopped at this site because the sun was setting and he needed a place to stay for the night. It was just a *makom*—a place. The point is, any place has the potential to be a special, even awesome, place. It is simply a matter of realizing the true nature of existence. We find the holy in the unexpected and in the ordinary, not just in the extraordinary.

This is suggested by the description of the angels who are moving up and down the ladder. As heavenly creatures, we might expect the angels to be seen as descending and ascending, not the other way around! But holiness begins with the human; it first rises and then descends. Ultimately, it is Jacob who makes this a holy place. In a moment of real existential aloneness, he has a vision of what his life can be about. Any place and any moment can be a gateway to heaven, that is, a gateway to all that is beyond our individual selves.

This episode is another lesson about the potential mistakes of religion. Too often, religions proclaim that a particular space is holy and imply that other places are not. Too often we define Godliness in one way and consider that only that way is true and correct. Here we are told that anywhere you stop for the night can be nothing less than a gateway to heaven. In the Torah, things and places are not intrinsically holy. The only thing that is intrinsically holy is God. God can ascribe holiness to things. We first see this when God sanctifies the seventh day, turning it into Shabbat. Jews also can make Shabbat holy. *Kiddush,* the prayer over wine that begins every Friday night, is a ritual that makes the day holy. It is also true that holiness exists outside of Judaism. The love that is expressed at weddings is one of the most universal experiences of holiness.

Halakha's treatment of non-Jews

Suspicion of the *other* has existed since almost the beginning of time. Rabbinic Judaism regulated dealings with people who weren't Jewish as part of its halakhic/legal system. Today, this is the area of Jewish law that has most fallen into disuse, even in the traditional Jewish community.

Simply put, the tradition viewed those who weren't Jewish as idolaters. On the one hand, Judaism did not maintain, as other religions did, that salvation can only come to those who believe in the one "true" God. The Talmud says that righteous Gentiles can attain the world to come. On the other hand, being an idolater meant you worshipped false gods. The rabbis of the Talmud thought that for a Jew to worship idols was one of the three worst violations of Jewish law; the other two were murder and adultery. Therefore, the rabbis were concerned that Jews shouldn't even indirectly engage in idol worship. Buying goods from an idol worshiper right before a pagan holiday was forbidden lest the seller use the money to buy a sacrifice for his idol. This was a challenge in the Middle Ages because in the Christian calendar, saints' days occurred frequently throughout the year. If strictly followed, this would have made economic relations with people who weren't Jewish difficult, if not impossible. The Meiri, a 14th-century rabbinic scholar in Provence, solved the problem by creating a new category that declared that Christians and Muslims were no longer considered idolaters and therefore traditional legal strictures did not apply to them. This not only allowed for economic trade; it also was a fundamental shift in the way Jews understood other monotheistic religions. (For more details, see *Exclusiveness and Tolerance* by Jacob Katz, p. 114).

In the modern period

With the beginning of the Enlightenment, the notion that individuals had equal rights allowed those on the margins of society to become full members. As the preeminent outsiders in Europe, Jews were the focus of much of the debate about implementing the principles of equal rights. The modern fight for equality for all people has been a long and often slow process. It would take until the beginning of the 20th century for women to be allowed to vote in the United States. The struggle still continues here and around the world. Yet, now in America, people are free to marry or partner with whomever they want.

Prejudice in the Jewish tradition that we need to renounce

This is the current context for the question of intermarriage. What is our relationship with people who are not Jewish if we no longer consider them as *other*? We certainly do not see them as idol worshippers. Nor do we say that they are all anti-Semites. Truth be told, we need to acknowledge that there are remnants of prejudice in traditional Jewish texts toward those who are not Jewish. Orthodox Jews are still forbidden to enter a church sanctuary because it is defined as a place of idol worship. The Talmud, especially the tractate of Avoda Zara (Idol Worship), has statements about people who are not Jewish that are too horrible to repeat. The mystical tradition in Judaism is a particular offender in this regard. While Hasidism is an important source for my understanding of my spiritual life, its adherents, along with earlier Jewish mystics, maintain that the spiritual redemption of the world is a task that only Jews can perform (and probably only Jewish men). There are texts that suggest that someone who is not Jewish has a lesser form of soul than do Jews. Such a statement is the definition of racism. Like every other religious tradition, Judaism needs to repudiate some older traditions, just as Vatican II repudiated the slander of Jews as Christ Killers. Most liberal Jews have no idea that these texts exist. Their attitudes toward people who are not Jewish reflect notions of the equality of all people. Even here the Jewish community has work to do. The assumption that all Jews are white and of Ashkenazi origin is at best a form of blindness to the increasing numbers of Jews of color who are part of the community.

Intermarriage is a sign of our time, not the problem of our time. The world has advanced to a place where the particular and the universal live together in creative tension. We can live in our Jewish skin even as we embrace a universal outlook. We can welcome the diversity of existence. In the interconnected world of the internet, it is as though the people who live on the other side of the world actually live just across the street. The world enters electronically into our homes. Similarly, the world also enters into our intimate lives through those we marry. We have chosen an open world. For most of us, this is a settled idea.

There are some obvious benefits to such a world. It is not just the freedom and expanded sense of choice. Our lives are enriched. We can learn about anything we want through a search engine or listen to an extraordinary variety of music through YouTube. I am not minimizing the problems of this digital age; we need to devote considerable effort now to combat the spread of hate that comes from inappropriate use of this technology. Every step of progress also has its challenges.

In many ways it was simpler to live in a world without choice. The outside world and the Jewish community both agreed on our identity as Jews. We don't want to live in that world—not only because it was a world of prejudice and persecutions, but because it was a world with limited choices. If, as the Sefat Emet teaches, Torah is all about freedom, then the world in which we now live is closer to that ideal. Yet, with more freedom to choose comes additional responsibility to choose wisely. In this open society, there are and will be new challenges as well as new possibilities. The only good way forward is to embrace the challenges, even if that way looks to be a harder path.

Judaism as a dynamic tradition

This book is my attempt to explore what it means to live in an open society. As someone who is deeply rooted in the Jewish tradition, I am also interested in the changing spiritual landscape of our world. I believe we need to radically change the Judaism we have inherited even as we remain rooted in the wisdom of the more than three-thousand-year discussion of what it means to live a life of meaning and purpose.

Jews have been a minority for most of our history. Even when we had our own state, whether in biblical times or today, we have never been a major world power. We have always adapted to and adopted from the surrounding cultures. That is actually part of the "secret" of the success of Jewish survival. We have been able to absorb from the world around us even as we maintain our Jewish identity. By definition, therefore, that identity has been ever changing. The metaphor of Torah as a tree of life means the Torah continues to grow. It is a dynamic rather than a static tradition. Judaism remains vibrant because of this dialogue with the world. Whether it was Hellenism or Aristotle in the past or egalitarianism today, Judaism has had an ability to interact with rather than simply reject the modern world, making it possible to be a particularistic tradition rooted in the past while embracing the present moment. The open society may be a more encompassing challenge than Judaism has ever faced but it is also just a contemporary version of the challenge of a minority tradi-tion. Overall, Judaism has been enriched by these encounters over time with the world. It is also true that some Jewish paths that resisted that encounter or embraced it completely became historical dead ends in the ongoing story of the Jewish people. The open society offers the gift of a world without borders, which doesn't mean that there are not fundamental challenges that come with this new reality. I believe our current moment is the culmination of centuries of a slow movement to a more open and inclusive world. This is the world in which we want to live. Martin Luther King said, "I have a dream that my four little children will one day live in a nation where they will not be judged by the color of their skin, but by the content of their character." Sadly, we know how much of his dream remains unfulfilled, but we have also made more progress toward its fulfillment than at any time in history. Instead of seeing intermarriage as a problem or even as a demographic fact of life we just can't change, we should see it is a reality of this new world without borders. We should see it as an opportunity to increase Jewish wisdom in the world. We want to embrace a world with less persecution and discrimination.

A porous Judaism

How do we create a Judaism that welcomes the stranger into our core and yet remains a vibrant Judaism? What has Judaism to offer in an open society when the whole world of choices lies at our fingertips? What is the value of a particularistic tradition, Judaism, in this world without borders? How can Judaism benefit from this new world to better respond to the contemporary moment?

Each particularistic tradition has something to add to the world's wisdom. An open society makes it much easier to offer that wisdom to the world. Jews have brought the idea of a day of rest, a Sabbath, to the world. That concept is more crucial today than ever before. What else do we have to offer the world as we strive to live lives of value and purpose?

In the face of the destruction of the Temple, rabbinic Judaism created a system of meaning that Jews could carry with them wherever the winds of misfortune would blow them. Today, much more than we need a portable Judaism, we require a porous Judaism. We face the challenge of the disrupted new world of our time. We need to engage in creating a Judaism that can live creatively with the universal, not live separate from it.

There is a verse from the book of Isaiah that is often quoted when looking for the universal element within the Jewish tradition. "I shall bring them to my sacred mount and let them rejoice in My house of prayer...For My house shall be called a house of prayer for all peoples" (Is. 56:7). This is a vision of a future where Judaism and the universal live together in a harmonious whole. What is not often quoted are the verses that precede this verse, which gives it its context. "Let not the foreigner, who has attached himself to God, say: God will keep me apart from God's people; ... I will give them, in My house and within My walls, a monument and a name" (Is. 56:3, 5). Basically, these verses say that those who are not Jewish shouldn't think they are unwelcome. The opposite is true. They will be welcomed by God and brought by God to the house of prayer for all peoples. After all, this verse makes clear that God's house of prayer isn't just a synagogue, or a church, or a mosque—it is wherever God's name is called upon, for there is only one God.

The midrash on this verse says: God doesn't disqualify any person. The gates are open at all times and anyone may enter. The descendants of the stranger will one day even be priests (See Ex. Rabbah 19:4). If nothing else, this midrash understands the verses to mean that God is connected to all people, not just the Jews. Today that vision of a house of prayer for all people may be closer to reality (though still far off) than at any time in human history.

A different midrash says that God used the Torah as a blueprint to create the world (Genesis Rabbah 1:1). What does it mean that the Torah existed not only before there were Jews but before there were people or the world itself? It is a remarkable image, that a specific book that tells stories and is filled with details about rituals and laws is a blueprint for the world. It suggests that the text we have is one attempt to take that "blueprint" and make it into a structure—a structure called Judaism. It is a Judaism not separated from the world but inextricably linked to the blueprint, the DNA of all existence. Torah is embodied in the world. The world is Torah and the Torah is the world.

Community: Context for the present

I have described how I think Judaism can enrich each of our lives by providing meaning and purpose. I have set out practices that can be done by individuals to evoke an awareness of particular spiritual themes. Yet Judaism isn't just about individuals. Central to Jewish life is community, both in its ideal and in practice.

One might imagine that prayer should be private. Each of us expresses individual needs to God not necessarily shared by the person sitting next to us. Instead, the preferred manner of prayer is in a *minyan*/a group of at least ten people. Most traditional prayers are written in the plural, not in the singular, asking God to give *us*, for example, wisdom. What is the value in community? Is it only that we would be lonely without it? When God says in Genesis that it is not good for the human to be alone, what is "not good" about it?

Community is the context in which we live our lives. We live on this planet and we live with other people. We live in many different kinds of communities, which range in size from small to very large. Community exists in time as well as space and is part of the context of our past. From where and whom did we come? As much as this book is a break from Jewish tradition, I continue to feel deeply rooted in that tradition. I believe I am actually fulfilling the tradition by helping it to respond to the contemporary moment. By suggesting innovations, I am joining the many innovators that began with Abraham, who the midrash portrays as smashing his father's idols.

I also have tried to show how many of these innovations are suggested by ideas and texts that are part of the broad Jewish tradition. It is important to me to know that I didn't just make this all up. There are, of course, some ideas that are drawn from the contemporary moment, but I feel fully part of the community of Jews that stretches back 3,000 years and has engaged in the ongoing conversation about what it means to live as a Jew in the world. Perhaps this rootedness in a community with a long past is even more important in the rapidly changing world of today. For most of human history, the vast majority of people lived their whole lives no more than a few miles from where they were born. Today people move more frequently and over greater distances.

Our country and our society are also communities. If we are not hermits living alone in the woods, we interact with people every day—people with whom we live, neighbors nearby, and people with whom we work. Only together can we even begin to attempt to address the societal problems we face. It might be easy to love your neighbor if you didn't have any neighbors or not to gossip if you had no one with whom to gossip, but the reality is that we live with other people who are human just like us.

The challenge for each of us is to understand the world is bigger than us. It is not all about me. We all struggle in similar and different ways to bring goodness into the world. This is a critical perspective to integrate into our lives. We are in this together. We are encouraged to pray in a *minyan*/a group of ten to remind us that we are more alike than different in our needs. While Judaism stresses community, particularly when it comes to prayer, it is part of the whole weave of Jewish life. Shabbat and holidays are celebrated through shared meals with friends and family. Joyous occasions and sad ones include more than immediate family.

Sitting shiva after the death of a loved one is a powerful example. Because the tradition requires that we say the mourner's prayer (*kaddish*) in a *minyan*/a group of ten, people will make an extra effort to ensure there are enough people to make up the quorum. In many synagogues, people attend a house of shiva even if they don't know the deceased or the family well in order to help make a *minyan*. Countless times a mourner has said to me: "I can't believe so many people from the synagogue came, even people I barely knew." The mourners are touched because, at a moment of grief, instead of feeling alone with their loss, they felt embraced by their community.

It isn't only at important life cycle moments that community is important. During the Torah service on Shabbat mornings, people are honored by being called up to the Torah. It has become standard in many synagogues that anyone who is marking the anniversary of a loved one's death (*yahrzeit*) in the coming week or wishes to offer a prayer of healing receives an *aliyah*. People may be called up for their upcoming birthdays or anniversaries. In this way, the community can share events in people's lives. The experience is different from having your birthday announced by Facebook or even having it in the synagogue bulletin. On Facebook, the exchange will be electronic and too often routine. It requires effort to respond to the news in the synagogue bulletin. At services, the response is immediate and personal. People will congratulate you or share a memory from your loved one's funeral. They will shake your hand as they wish you well.

People who don't belong or attend regularly miss the one thing that many synagogues do well: create natural communities. If you attend services over many years, you see children grow up, become *b'nai mitzvah*, go off to school and become adults. You experience people getting older and losing their parents. Natural communities are ones that grow over time. When we spend enough time with others in community, we are able to share the important moments in their lives just as they share ours. While the service itself may not resonate, the sense of belonging frequently can. The old adage may be truer than we think: *Chaim goes to shul to talk to God; I go to talk to Chaim.* The highlight of Shabbat morning for many people is Kiddush—the food after services are over. Here people reconnect with their synagogue friends and chat with synagogue acquaintances and newcomers.

It is not the food that is important; it is the casual conversations that make the community come alive. Many people have remarked that during the pandemic, even when they were able to come to services, what felt particularly hard was not having Kiddush, since most synagogues required masks and didn't allow food. They missed the opportunity to connect over a bagel.

New models of communities

There is one other element worth mentioning here. The current model of synagogues is challenged by a number of factors including both the decline of interest in religion and the high costs associated with synagogue membership. There is a small but increasing number of groups that are informal, led by lay leaders, have a limited number of activities, and don't own any real estate. This means that they can operate on a very small budget. Some have Shabbat services. Some are families who want to create a group for their children to experience Judaism together. Some focus on social justice or on study. They can be more participatory than synagogues, which have financial responsibilities like salaries and building maintenance that require members to support the institution even though only a minority attend events regularly. The sense of community can be stronger in a small group than a 1,000-family synagogue. It will be interesting to see how this model develops over time. Most of these groups are made up of like-minded people, like those who want programs for their children. While people with young children will naturally be mostly of the same age cohort, there is no reason for that to be true for a group focused on prayer or social justice. Yet, most of these groups have participants of the same age cohort. This is partly because these groups tend to be formed organically from within one's network. There is an advantage to a certain amount of homogeneity, which allows for a broad agreement on goals, but there is something lost as well. Diversity can broaden our horizons. Much has been written about the divisions in America today. It is not just that we are separated from those who don't share our religious or political views. Increasingly, we hang out with people just like us. Synagogues offer a different model. Anyone can join. Synagogues strive to have people of all ages. Thereby, people are encouraged to find ways to work together despite differences.

There is an unspoken desire for synagogues to outlive their members. Real estate alone suggests that synagogue leaders must work not only for the present but for the future. They are always building for the future, even a future that will not include themselves. Some of the havurot of the 1960s that were comprised of people of similar ages now find themselves unable to sustain their groups as people become sick and die. This is a natural life cycle. Synagogues, hoping to live beyond the founding generation, work hard to be multi-generational communities, which is a rare phenomenon in the American social landscape. Both models should be part of Jewish life in the 21st century. The havurot of the 1960s rejected rabbinic leadership, making the claim that all Jews can lead services and teach. This came at a time when young people were rebelling against authority in general, but it was rooted in a belief that Jews need to create their own Jewish lives and not outsource the work to the clergy. As important as this idea was and is, there is still something lost by communities without rabbinic leadership. It's not only that people often have limits on the amount of time they can volunteer. It is also that clergy can provide a perspective on the entire community that individual volunteers often lack. We clearly need new models of rabbinic leadership that encourage more participation and lay leadership and also realize the value of expertise, learning, and spiritual modeling.

Larger communities

Jewish community also includes groups of Jews larger than any one institution. It could mean the community of Jews of a town or city. In the tradition, there are a number of commandments that must be observed by the larger community. They didn't fit easily in the traditional halakhic structure of obligation. If a commandment was a responsibility of the community, who was actually obligated to fulfill the commandment? The leadership of the community? Everyone in that community? Such *mitzvot* include creating a judicial system or an educational system. One way to understand this category is to imagine what structures a Jewish community needs in order to be a just and thriving community. It needs communal institutions to engage in spiritual life, to educate children and adults, to advance social justice, *tzedakah*, and kindness, and to maintain those institutions to make all of that happen. Some of these institutions serve the community itself or its members. Some serve the world. It is important to realize that individuals alone cannot create these necessary institutions. To have a just, caring and thriving Jewish community, many people need to feel committed to creating that community.

Finally, the community can create a context for the future. This is most obvious in multi-generational communities that provide continuity into that future. Just as community connects us to the Jewish past, it is also an expression of our hopes for the future. It may seem as though a belief in a messianic era, where everyone lives in peace, is no more rational than believing that there is a God. Yet don't we all hope that the world can be and should be a better place? What if religion in general and Judaism specifically became more of a force for good in the world? Isn't every religious tradition essentially about that—to live closer to the ideals of that religion? Can Judaism change the world? Can it move us closer to the vision of the prophets that every person will sit under their own fig tree and none shall make them afraid?

I think it can, if we believe its essence is to bring good into the world. That process begins with the individual but must also be happening on the level of a community. How do we build such a world? Perhaps the most important building project in the Torah has some wisdom to teach us.

Mishkan/Sanctuary

The Torah describes the creation of the world in 34 verses. The second half of the book of Exodus has over 450 verses describing in great detail the building of the *mishkan*—the portable sanctuary—and the making of the priestly garments for those who will officiate there. Why? What is the purpose of all this detail? It is not as though we are commanded to rebuild the sanctuary in each generation!

I think the building of the *mishkan*/sanctuary is a lesson on how to move from the extraordinary moment of the revelation at Sinai to living in the real world with its everyday challenges. Our life is not lived in extraordinary moments such as Sinai or the special celebrations of life cycle moments like a wedding. Certainly, we should cherish such moments. However, life is lived in the everyday. We need to build the structure of our lives. Each of us is asked to build a *mishkan*. Our lives are shaped and realized by the details. Small acts, the kind word, the expression of sympathy, and the friendly smile build the *mishkan* of our lives. We hope that in that sanctuary godliness and good will dwell more often than not.

God dwells in community, not in buildings

Many commentators point out a striking feature in the verse when God commands the building of the sanctuary. God says: "Make for me a *mishkan*/sanctuary and I will dwell in their midst" (Ex. 25:8). God doesn't say make for me a *mishkan* and I will dwell in it. The *mishkan* isn't really God's house. The building of it will lead to God dwelling amidst the builders, the people of Israel. The verse doesn't even instruct the Israelites to build God a *mishkan* so that God can dwell within you (singular). Judaism isn't about your own religious experience. Judaism is about building a life whose wisdom helps us interact with the people around us, in our community and across the globe.

God dwells in the *mishkan* created by a community because ultimately God dwells in community, not in buildings or sacred spaces. The Book of Exodus ends with the building of the *mishkan*. Its language echoes the first chapters of Genesis, which describe the creation of the world. In Genesis, we are told that God completed (*va-yikhal*) the work of creation. At the end of Exodus, we learn that Moses completed (*va-yikhal*) the work of building the sanctuary (Ex. 40:33). When we build the *mishkan* of our lives, we fulfill a vision of holiness and wholeness. As the co-creators of the world, we carry forward the work of creation begun by God during the first week of creation. The real answer to the Israelites who clamor for a God they can see is found in the experience of living a religious life. God is revealed when we fully live our lives.

The other point of building the sanctuary is that the people take on this task. Until that moment, the Israelites have experienced their lives through the deeds of others. As slaves, they were dependent on Pharoah. Their liberation is achieved by God and Moses, not by themselves. At this moment the people finally step forward to actively make the sanctuary a reality. They have become builders, not just in completing the project but in the way it is done. It is the only building campaign in history where they raised more than was needed to complete the project. Moses tells them to stop giving! What is remarkable is not the quantity of the gifts, but how they were given. God tells Moses to accept gifts from every person whose heart so moves him (*asher yidvenu libo*, Ex. 25:2). The gifts come from a place of generosity rather than obligation. Everyone contributes what they can. Everyone contributes whatever skill they have to participate in the actual building.

Even more than a structure, it is this process that creates community. While the tradition values the worth of each individual created in the image of the Divine, the practice of Judaism takes place in community.

Building the Tower of Babel

This building project at the end of the Book of Exodus stands in contrast to the building of the Tower of Babel, which is recounted earlier in the book of Genesis. The Tower of Babel story suggests the danger of unity. Following the flood in Noah's time, the people of the Babel story must have been worried about another flood, despite God's promise. A tower that would rise to heaven will surely save them from a flood, no matter how catastrophic. The problem is that in response to the chaos of the generation of the flood, they wanted absolute unity, where everyone spoke one language and worked on one project. Their hope was to prevent people from scattering. As bad as the chaos that led to the flood, so too was the uniformity of the tower generation. When there is only one language and one vision, there is no room for other ways of looking at things. There is no outside critic. Leon Kass, the contemporary scientist and educator, writes on this story:

> Awareness of the multiplicity of human ways is also the necessary precondition for the active search for the better or best way. Discovering the partiality of one's own truths and standards invites the active search for truths and standards beyond one's

making. (From *The Beginning of Wisdom*, p. 238).

People often understand religion as being about eternal truths, but its purpose is actually the opposite. Religion reminds us that we, humans, do not have the truth; only God does. We live in a world of partial truths and of conflicting subjective truths. The response to the chaos of the world of the flood is not to have a world of lockstep unity. It is not only that lockstep can too easily become goose step. Diversity encourages criticism and challenges the way things are. While it would be easier to live in a world where everyone spoke the same language, it would also create a sameness to life. Imagine the nuances of different languages that would be lost if there was only one language in the world. Different languages, different races, and different countries all lead to notions of multiple truths. Diversity allows individuals to be individuals rather than be forced to conform to one collective vision of the world. The answer to the challenges of life isn't that we should all be the same, but that we all be fully our unique selves, while able to appreciate all the human beings who inhabit this planet. How? When we accept that each of us is an image of God, we acknowledge the essential sameness of every human being and that we all are connected to the underlying unity of the world called God.

Indeed, unity is realized when we embrace the diversity of the world. Genocide comes about when we reject that diversity. Here is the point. Judaism doesn't want the whole world to be Jewish. The whole world is God's creation. That world is filled with endless species, reminding us that diversity is the basic paradigm of our world, not sameness. The building of the *mishkan* brings people together—in such a place God dwells.

> True Godliness does not turn men out of the world but enables
> them to live better in it and excites their endeavor to mend it.
> —William Penn,
> 17th century founder of the colony of Pennsylvania

Creating the world, the *mishkan*, or your life, is an act of generosity. You build by giving away. You give love and you offer caring and support. It is not a matter of self-interest—I'll help you today so you will help me tomorrow. Hasidism taught that God created the world as an act of *hesed*/generosity, based on the verse *olam hesed yibaneh*—the world was built through lovingkindness (Ps. 89:3). We want to live in a place of openheartedness. Too often we are afraid, and live in a place of clutching, of anxiety, or even with a sense of deprivation. The heart is limitless in its capacity to love and to give. It is one of the ways that we are created in the image of God—the ability to love. The well of love does not run dry. Even if God is not in the details, redemption certainly is. It is small acts that help make the redemption of the everyday and the rarer moments of societal redemption come to pass.

Value of work

Finally, the building of the *mishkan* was an affirmation of the value of work. The Talmud talks about the 39 categories of work, from planting to dyeing to sewing, which were involved in building the sanctuary. Life isn't just about spiritual work like prayer and Torah study; it is about working with your hands. The six days of creating are as much a part of the week as resting on Shabbat. The building of the *mishkan* demonstrates that any work can lead to God dwelling in our midst. The ideal vision of Jewish life is not to spend all of our time learning Torah. It is to continue the work of creation. We are to work six days and rest on the seventh.

In Avot deRabbi Natan ch. 11, Rabbi Tarfon says:

> The Holy One did not cause God's Shekhinah/presence to rest upon Israel before they did work as it is said: "Let them make Me a sanctuary that I may dwell among them." (Ex. 25:8)

The portable sanctuary that accompanied the Israelites during their wanderings in the desert reminds us that wherever we go, God is there. The whole world is the house of God. Wherever we find ourselves we are to continue the work of creation. We are the ones who are responsible for what happens in this world.

When the Israelites camped in the wilderness, the *mishkan* was at the center of the encampment. There were three tribes on each side. At the center of a people's journey are the history, the values, and the vision that connects them to the past and carries them into the future. Without that they will only be aimless wanderers in the desert, a place of shifting mirages that can deceive people into drinking sand.

Holy communities

What transforms individuals into a community? Is it numbers alone that make the difference? The rabbis read Psalm 82:1 as: *God stands in a holy assembly.* The Hebrew word, *edah*, is understood to mean *ten* because it is used to refer to the spies who were sent to explore the land of Israel. Twelve spies were sent and ten returned with a negative report. Having a community doesn't ensure that it will act in good ways. The rabbis understood the verse in Psalms to mean that God is found in a group with good intentions. What is special about a group? Individuals come together and in so doing act with an element of unity. In such a space, the unity that underlies the universe, God, is present, even if unacknowledged. Being in community moves us beyond ourselves. A sense of connection to others can help each of us go beyond the perspective of our individual needs to the larger question of what the community needs.

A traditional term for synagogue communities is *kehillah kedoshah*/a holy community. Communities have the potential for holiness. For the rabbis, even groups smaller than ten can have an element of oneness. In the tractate *Berakhot*, there is a chapter entitled "three that ate as one." (*shelosha she'akhlu ke-ahat*). This means that if three people share a meal together, they recite a special introduction to the grace after meals (*zimun*). It is clear that two people don't make up a group. Three is the minimum number. Yet, the number is only the first step. To be a group, there has to be a sense of oneness—in this case a shared eating experience—hence "three that ate as one."

While recognizing the holiness of people coming together, we should acknowledge the pitfalls as well. It is not only that communities can exclude others or disparage those who are outsiders. There is often the pressure to conform lurking in communities and a tendency to minimize individuality. There is a tension between individualism and collectivism in every society. Too much individualism is often accompanied by rampant narcissism. It is an ongoing challenge for each of us and the groups in which we belong to balance community and the individual. Yet, community remains an important way we appreciate the diversity in life and continually remind ourselves that we are all flawed people with a similar goal—to live a life of purpose and happiness.

> It is only by becoming builders that we turn from subjects to citizens. We have to earn our freedom by what we give. It cannot be given to us as an unearned gift. It is what we do, not what is done to us, that makes us free.

> —R. Jonathan Sacks, Chief Rabbi of England, 1948-2020

Israel

I have chosen to live in the United States rather than live in Israel and the focus of this book is about creating a Jewish life in North America. Israelis need to create a vibrant Jewish life in Israel, which will, by definition, share common aspects with what we are creating and yet be very different. I have visited Israel many times in my life, but I don't have the ability to reconstruct Jewish life in Israel because I remain a visitor. Israelis are the only ones who can possibly create a renewed form of Judaism for themselves. While the critiques and problems of traditional Judaism that I have discussed are equally true for liberal Jews in Israel, the context is radically different there. In Israel, the chief rabbinate makes important decisions about Jewish status and lifecycle events such as weddings and burials. In America there is no central religious authority and many rabbis and synagogues operate independently, even within their denominational structures. While in America the liberal denominations outnumber the Orthodox, in Israel, the opposite is true; the liberal denominations remain small, though growing. Perhaps most importantly, living in Israel means that the most secular Israelis speak fluent Hebrew and are familiar with the Bible and Jewish holidays. While I think a secular Jewish identity is impossible to sustain over generations in America, I think it is possible in Israel—though there is a danger that it will become an Israeli identity and not really a Jewish identity. Nevertheless, the same question applies: What can help give life meaning? Life, loss, and inner struggles are universal challenges. Yet, the cultural context as well as the real-life circumstances of Israeli Jews are different enough that an Israeli liberal Judaism needs to grow from native soil.

The challenge of Israel for American Jews

The Jewish community has been diverse since its beginning in America. Unlike in Europe, there has never been a rabbinic authority for a city or for the country. While individual synagogue communities might have rules for membership, they mostly are about paying dues. What you did or mostly did not do at home was your business. You could eat pork publicly on Yom Kippur and not be banned from the Jewish community.

As the community grows more polarized regarding the conflict between Israel and the Palestinians, support for Israel has become a litmus test in the organized Jewish community. There is an obvious challenge trying to determine which criticisms of Israel's policies are legitimate and which are anti-Israel or anti-Zionist positions. The Jewish community is operating with a short historical memory on this issue. Modern Zionism began in the late 19th century, arising as a response to the persistent anti-Semitism in the modern world. The Zionists claimed that in a world of national identities, Jews would never be fully accepted living in other people's countries and needed their own national identity in a nation state. Theodor Herzl and others thought that only then would Jews be "normal" and anti-Semitism would fade away. It should be noted that until the Holocaust and the founding of Israel, probably the majority of Jews did not support Zionism. There were many Jews who felt an allegiance to the country in which they were living. Some Jews were worried that there would be accusations of dual loyalty if they supported Zionism. There were groups that thought a socialist revolution would solve the problem and that anti-Semitism was part of the oppressive class structure of society. In America, despite figures like Justice Louis Brandeis, who gave credence to American Zionism, there was a great deal of opposition to Zionism. The opposition in the Reform movement is often cited, but it was true in different degrees of every denomination except Reconstructionism.

With the founding of the state and the increasing awareness of the horror of the Holocaust, more Jews came to support Israel, especially as a refuge for persecuted Jews, but it was only the Six-Day War in 1967 that brought the overwhelming majority of the Jewish community to identify as Zionists. This period lasted for perhaps 20 years before it began to erode over questions of how to bring peace to the Middle East. It was a relatively brief period of history that the claim that we are all Zionists was mostly true. Even that claim can be made only by ignoring the Hasidic community, many of whom still believe that the return to sovereignty in Israel should only take place when God brings the Messiah. Many feel that is not for humans to create a sovereign state and especially not Zionists, most of whom were anti-religious secularists. Over time, some Hasidic groups have shifted their position, but most ultra-Orthodox Jews are non-Zionist. They don't oppose the state but they don't support it because of its secular nature. Satmar Hasidim, which is the largest group of Hasidim in the world today, remains ideologically anti-Zionist.

This is important to note because these days, there are those calling for certain Jewish groups on the left end of the spectrum to be considered outside the consensus of the Jewish world. People argue that they shouldn't be given platforms to speak in the Jewish community. While Satmar has been sharply criticized for its position, no one in all these years suggested that Satmar be banned from the Jewish community. (Satmar should not be confused with a small fringe group called Neturei Karta, who oppose the state and who are seen as outside the Jewish consensus.) For most Jews, Satmar and much of the ultra-Orthodox world operates under the radar. Some would say the ultra-Orthodox are clearly committed to Judaism and therefore are different than the left-wing critics of Israel. I remain unconvinced by that argument.

Recently non- or even anti-Zionism has begun to appear among young Jews who are critical of Israel's policies, especially with regard to the treatment of Palestinians in the West Bank. I was recently at a Shabbat service made up entirely of young people. The services were lay-led and spirited. Their commitment and enthusiasm for Jewish practice was apparent. Speaking to a member afterward, she mentioned that the only rule they have for the person giving the sermon/teaching during services was that Israel couldn't be discussed. In this group of young committed Jews there were people who were non-Zionists as well as pro-Zionists and they decided such conversations on Shabbat morning were only divisive. The established Jewish community laments the absence of young Jews from their institutions. Here were exactly such a group of young Jews that should give hope to the established community, but as committed as they all were to Judaism, a significant number of them did not feel committed to Zionism. Too often the organized Jewish community believes that it needs to draw lines regarding who is in and who is outside of community. The assumption that you have to be pro-Zionist will inevitably wind up excluding too many committed Jews, whether they are Satmar Hasidim or left-wing ideologs.

How to sit together with people with whom you have fundamental disagreements about an important matter is a challenge in the tribal nature of today's American society. Judaism can ill afford to be divided into small groups, each claiming to be the only authentic form of Judaism. We need to embrace diversity with all its challenges. Are there any positions that put someone beyond the pale? There are always lines but we should strive to make the circle of inclusion as wide as possible. Let us err on assuming the best intentions of others even when we believe their actions are not helping Israel but are detrimental to Israel's future.

Israel's role in American Judaism

Finally, and most importantly, what role does Israel play in the religious life of American Jews? From the beginning of Zionism, the question of its relationship to Judaism as a religion has been an issue. Secular Zionists rejected religion and saw Zionism as a replacement for religious Judaism. Among the different forms of early Zionism, religious Zionism emerged, which basically grafted Zionism onto Orthodox Judaism without changing Orthodoxy very much. A notable exception was Rav Kook, the first Ashkenazic chief rabbi of Palestine, who saw Zionism as a fulfillment of Judaism's connection to the land of Israel. For him, the secular Zionists were doing God's work in settling the land and should be appreciated for this. In this way, he stood opposite those ultra-Orthodox Jews who saw nothing good in secular Zionists or their efforts.

With the founding of the state in 1948, the question of what it means to be a

Zionist changed. If Zionism was about creating a Jewish state, what does it now mean to be a Zionist? For those living in the state, it meant continuing to build the fledgling state and deal with its challenges. There were Zionists like David ben Gurion, the founding prime minister of Israel, who argued that now that the state existed, to be a Zionist you must move to Israel to join in that enterprise. He criticized American Jews and their "Zionist" organizations as not real Zionists.

Despite Ben Gurion, most American Jews did not make *aliyah*/move (literally *go up*) to Israel. American Zionism promoted the support of Israel both financially and politically. This worked for the first decades after the founding of the state, when Israel desperately needed the funds to build a country and absorb the thousands of Jews emigrating, especially from Arab countries, to Israel. Zionism provided a larger purpose for American Jews and strengthened the existing Jewish federations of philanthropy. American Jews took pride in Israel's success and in its victory in the Six-Day War. For Israeli Jews, there was a mixture of gratitude and disappointment that diaspora Jewry didn't join them in their grand enterprise of building the Jewish state. The relationship was mostly one-sided; that is, American Jews felt connected to Israel. After a time, some Israelis came to resent the "rich uncle" who visits with money and advice and whose children don't risk their lives serving in the Israeli army. It is also true that it has been years since Israel has been a poor country.

For American Jews affiliated with the religious denominations, their connection to Israel was like their secular brethren. They supported Israel financially, they visited, and they took pride in Israel's accomplishments. Israel's impact on Judaism as a religion was minor. The observance of Israel Independence Day is a perfect example. It is celebrated for the most part in synagogues by showing an Israeli film, eating Israeli food, or doing Israeli folk dancing. While some synagogues may add a prayer for Israel to a regular service, the religious significance of Israel is left unexplored.

Following the Six-Day War, there was a discussion of the meaning of the victory. For some, it was a miracle that Israel won and was able to recapture Jerusalem and the West Bank. Disciples of Rav Kook built on his teachings on the importance of settling and building of the land. This led to a form of religious Zionism that deeply integrated Zionism and Judaism. Central to this Judaism was the task of settling the land of Israel, specifically the newly conquered West Bank. The power of this religious Zionist ideology could be seen during the evacuation of the settlements in Gaza in 2005. The school year hadn't ended in the schools of Torah learning in the Orthodox world. Many students opted to remain in school because of the primacy of Torah learning as a value. Others left to join the protests against the Gaza evacuation because they believed that settling the land was an even higher priority than studying Torah.

The paradigm for Israeli engagement of American Jewish support for Israel has become increasingly tenuous in the last decade. This is mainly due to an increasing sense of alienation from Israel's policies, which go beyond the conflict. Because of the nature of Israeli society, where religious life is controlled by the Orthodox rabbinate and there is no separation of church and state as it exists in America, liberal Jews have felt increasingly alienated from a country that doesn't recognize their Jewish practice or identity. They have tried to focus on such specific issues as egalitarian prayer at the Kotel/Western Wall, or lack of recognition for liberal rabbis, to limited success. The disparaging comments from some Israeli religious leaders conveys real contempt for liberal Jews. Even more important is a sense that Israel's government policies are not consonant with liberal American Jewish values. Whether it is Israel's treatment of refugees, the passage of the nation state bill that can be understood as making Israeli Arabs second-class citizens, or the treatment of the Palestinians in the West Bank, these policies increasingly alienate many American Jews.

What is the paradigm for American Jews' relationship to Israel and its Jews? The old paradigm was of Israel at the center and the diaspora at the periphery. A few years ago, I imagined a paradigm based on a strange verse we recite during the Torah service in synagogue. "From out of Zion will come forth Torah and the word of God from Jerusalem" (Is.2:3). Doesn't the Torah come from Mount Sinai? What is the Torah of Jerusalem? I developed the notion of two Torahs—the Torah of Sinai that we have wrestled with for 3,000 years and the Torah of Jerusalem, which is a Torah of sovereignty that is being written at this very moment. (See the chapter in my book *The Book of Life: Embracing Judaism as a Spiritual Practice*.) I developed this paradigm at a more hopeful time. It was after the Oslo accords when it felt that peace might be around the corner. I began with the question: If there was real peace in the Middle East, what could be the paradigm for diaspora Jews and Israeli Jews? It is a much less hopeful time these days. The problems seem intractable.

What connects us to Israel

What continues to hold us together is what has held the Jewish people together from the beginning: an unrolling of Torah. We are always challenged to discover what Torah means for us at this moment, but some moments are harder than others. This is such a time. We live in a rapidly changing world, which some welcome as more inclusive and more democratic. Others see this change as destroying tradition, chaotic and less democratic. Across the globe, the basic notions of modernity and of democracy are being challenged from the left and even more from the right. Yet, the questions remain the same: *Ayekha*—where are you? Are you your brethren's keeper? Which path is the path of doing good when the choice is very unclear? In *Rise and Kill First: The Secret History of Israel's Targeted Assassinations,* Ronen Bergman tells the story of the ongoing choices made by Israel's secret services in the ceaseless war against its enemies. Whether or not one agrees with their decisions, it illustrates the difficult choices Israel was forced to make. As a sovereign state, Israel is challenged to develop the "Torah" of the use and abuse of power.

While Jews in America as a group do not get to make such decisions, as individuals—and as a community—we too are challenged to build a caring society and live lives of meaning. While Israeli Jews and diaspora Jews live in very different contexts, what we share is the challenge to continue the Torah's vision: to create a world of *tov*/goodness. Having a shared joint project that rests on the ongoing conversation of the Jewish people for over 3,000 years can be the link that binds together the Jewish people all over the world. It requires a shift in viewpoint—there is no one way that is Torah-true nor is one locale the only center. Judaism can exist in very different forms that are vibrant and purposeful. Those in Israel cannot claim that the Jewish project is only taking place there and that those who live elsewhere are at best mostly vicarious supporters. Those living outside Israel cannot ignore the project of building a Jewish homeland despite all its imperfections. We begin by acknowledging that each of us makes a choice of where to live. Whether that choice is pragmatic or idealistic, the choice has been made. The diaspora is not moving en masse to Israel. The real question is whether we will grow farther and farther apart until we are just distant cousins who can barely trace their joint ancestry.

This sense of a joint endeavor is the way forward, provided we can find mechanisms for each of us to know each other. While diaspora Jews have been focused on Israel for decades, Israeli Jews in general know very little about the lives of diaspora Jews. We need to explore our common Jewish heritage, however differently we might express that heritage. While some American Jews might find Israeli culture too secular, it is clear that that culture is infused with Jewish texts and values. *Rise and Kill First* takes its title from a Talmudic principle (*Sanhedrin* 72a) that legitimates self-defense. Israel used that Talmudic principle as the starting point for an ongoing discussion of how that might apply to the real-life situation of Israel facing terrorist attacks. It was not because Israel feels bound by *halakha*/Jewish law, but because the Jewish tradition is seen as a source for a Jewish state to think about the issues it faces. There has been a growing trend in Israel for secular Israelis to study traditional texts beyond the Bible. For a long time, those texts were seen as coming out of the experience of living in exile. Like

Yiddish, forms of the exilic period were to be rejected by a "new Jew" who worked the land and was ready to defend it. But increasingly, Israelis have come to see that the diaspora is not disappearing and that the 2,000 years of the diaspora should not simply be erased. Jewish history cannot skip from the Bible to modern Israel, leaving out everything that happened in between.

This is the challenge. How do we create interactions that lead to a sense of a common history and a shared destiny even while recognizing the substantial differences between living in Israel and living elsewhere? In biblical times, Jews were supposed to come up to Jerusalem three times a year for the pilgrimage festivals of Pesach, Shavuot and Sukkot. It is unclear how many Jews came on pilgrimage and how often they came. It was a long trip by foot or mule from Northern Israel. We do have evidence from Second Temple times that pilgrims did come to Jerusalem. With the destruction of the Temple, this practice has ceased. What if this notion was revived, and as a matter of practice, Jews took a pilgrimage not to the ruins of the Temple, but rather to the land of our ancestors, the land of the patriarchs and matriarchs, and of kings and prophets? I had an unexpectedly powerful moment a number of years ago at the valley of Elah, where the battle between Israel and the Philistines took place. The battle climaxed with the defeat of Goliath by David. I had been to many historical and mythical sites in Israel, in such places as Bethlehem, Hebron, Megiddo, Masada, and of course Jerusalem. Looking over the valley of Elah, I could imagine the rival forces gathered on opposite sides of the valley awaiting the battle to come. Jewish history, particularly of the biblical period, is alive in Israel in ways that it cannot be elsewhere in the world. We should go on pilgrimage to reconnect to our story and to literally walk in the footsteps of our ancestors. Whether you go once in your life or more frequently, it is an opportunity to see the land where the Torah unfolded. It is also an opportunity to encounter the modern state of Israel with all of its amazing accomplishments and its difficult challenges.

A small example of Israel/diaspora contact

Finding that discussions about Israel in my synagogue usually generated much more heat than light, I chose to engage in aspects of Israeli culture as a more effective way to make a connection to Israel. For a number of years, the Marlene Meyerson JCC Manhattan brought a variety of Israeli artists for a week of Israeli culture and encouraged synagogues to host some of the artists for the Shabbat before the festival started. In response, my synagogue invited Vertigo, a modern dance company. After services, they performed two pieces, the first of which was called Power of Balance, and was performed with dancers on crutches and in wheelchairs. The second was called *Chatuna*/marriage, and featured a female dancer standing center stage, while another dancer moved her arms and legs in different positions as though she was a puppet. The text of the *ketubah*/Jewish marriage contract was chanted in a staccato manner.

The members of my synagogue were very taken by the dancers. After the performance people asked questions of the directors of the company. Someone then asked them if they had any questions for us. One of the directors asked, "I don't really understand who you are. Is this a synagogue? We have never been in a synagogue before." The gap between these secular Israeli artists and my congregants was suddenly clear. The truth is the gap went both ways. I loved the second piece, which I understood as a critique of the subordinate role of women in traditional Judaism. It wasn't just the passivity of the bride. It was the way the marriage contract was chanted with a frequent emphasis on the word *kesef*/money. The truth is there is nothing romantic about the traditional text of the marriage contract; it is a legal transaction. Yet many of my congregants, not fluent in Aramaic and Hebrew, missed that part of the critique. The language gap for most American Jews is a barrier to access Israeli culture. Even secular Israelis have enough familiarity with the text of the Jewish marriage contract to understand the point of the piece. The afternoon then was both a powerful example of how people can connect through culture and a demonstration of how far apart these two worlds are.

We do share a vision of Zion that is articulated by the prophets in the Torah. It is a vision of peace where we will sit under our own vine and none shall make us afraid. Rabbinic scholars have debated what the prophets' vision of the messianic future meant. Is it a time when the world will change—a world without darkness and only light? Or do we accept the view of Maimonides, the 12th-century philosopher and rabbinic scholar, who believed that the messianic era will not be radically different. It will be marked by a return of sovereignty for Jews in the land of Israel.

In the early 20th century, there were many competing visions of Zionism. One major vison was socialist Zionism, which held that the State of Israel would not only be a homeland for the Jewish people but would, through such institutions as the kibbutz, fundamentally change the nature of its society. It was to be a socialist experiment that emphasized the collective over the individual. In the end, what might be called practical Zionism was the vision that was most successful. David ben Gurion proclaimed that the goal was to be a state like every other state, no better and no worse. It was a Zionism that was seeking normalcy. The kibbutzim and the socialist vision faded over time.

It is not unreasonable to want a state that is like every other. We don't want the world to hold Israel to a different standard than it holds Great Britain or France. Yet, we, the Jewish people, also want to engage in *tikkun olam*/repairing the world and help Israel move closer to the vision of the prophets. We have a higher expectation for Israel. In the most significant way, we both share a vision for a better world.

Elsewhere in this book, I have emphasized that we are all imperfect people. In the end I believe Ben Gurion was wrong. We don't want to be a state like every other state. Just as recognizing my imperfections shouldn't be an excuse for not trying to change, so too acknowledging that any state will be imperfect is only a call to make Israel a place that more closely lives up to the visions of its founders and also of the prophets of Israel. The prophets looked at the kingdom of Judah and of Israel and saw its imperfections. In response, they spoke truth to power and rejected the notion that injustice and oppression are the necessary reality of a Jewish state.

We don't settle for "that's just the way the world is" in our personal lives or in our society. As different as it is to live as a Jew in America and to live as a Jew in Israel, we share a vision of peace and prosperity for all. The goal is the same. The prophets' call still echoes from the hills of Judah to the plains of the Midwest:

> If you banish oppression from your midst,
> The menacing hand and tainted speech,
> If you give of yourself to the hungry,
> Fulfilling the needs of the poor—
> Then shall your light shine in darkness,
> And your darkness shall be like the noon.
> God will guide you always,
> Will satisfy your thirst in desert wastes,
> Will give your bones new life,
> And you will be like a well-watered garden,
> Like a spring whose waters do not fail.
> And those among you will rebuild ancient ruins,
> Foundations long dormant you'll restore.
> You shall be called the repairer of bridges,
> The restorer of roads for habitation.
> —Isaiah 58:9b-12

Perhaps it is not an accident that some of the early settlers of America, such as the Pilgrims, referred to this new land as Zion. Zion still needs building. The different perspectives of living in America and in Israel can help with that building. Israel's experience of sovereignty and an emphasis of the collective can balance the American Jewish experience of being a minority in a country that focuses more on the individual. The inclusivity, the separation of church and state, and a focus on spirituality and the Jewish past can be an important addition to the Zionist vision. We need to increase the ways that we share our lives as we strive to make this a better world. We have to find ways to really listen to each other and not be dismissive of the possibilities and the challenges that each of us face.

> For the sake of Zion, I will not be silent. For the sake of Jerusalem, I will not be still. (Isaiah 62:1)

Final Words

Over the course of this book, we have unrolled the Torah and drawn on its understanding from the past in order to create a new understanding for our time. We used the story of creation to learn about the nature of human beings and the world. As we conclude, it would seem appropriate then to study the last verses of the Torah, which describe the death of Moses. The Torah describes him as the greatest leader of the Jewish people. It says of him that there never arose a prophet like Moses in Israel chosen by God to perform signs and portents before Pharaoh in Egypt. The Torah concludes with this verse (Dt. 34:12):

> And in all that mighty hand and awesome power that Moses displayed before all Israel.

The Hebrew of "mighty hand" is *ha-yad ha-hazakah*. In the very last verse of Torah there is an amazing switch. It is no longer God's mighty hand and awesome power—it is the hand of Moses. What is this mighty hand of Moses? Is it a fist? Is it when Moses smote the Egyptian taskmaster or hit the rock? Rashi, the 11th-century Bible commentator, writes that *ha-yad ha-hazakah* means that Moses received the Ten Commandments in his strong hand, either because the weight of the tablets required strength, or perhaps what made his hands strong was the Torah itself. Either way, to receive Torah, or anything for that matter, you need not a fist, but an open hand.

The verse concludes by stating that everything that Moses displayed was "before the eyes of all Israel/*einai kol Yisrael*." What did Moses display before all of Israel? Rashi says this refers to one specific moment. "Before the eyes of all Israel—this refers to the fact that Moses' heart inspired him to shatter the tablets before the people," referring to the time Moses descended from Mount Sinai to see the people worshipping the Golden Calf and smashed the tablets in anger. Rashi continues: "and we know God's opinion of this deed because in Ex. 34:1 God said of the tablets *asher shibarta*—literally which you broke—is to be reread as *yishar kohakha sheshebarta*—congratulations that you had the strength to break them."

In this interpretation, the tablets needed to be broken. In his very last comment on the Torah, Rashi says that Moses, not God, has a *yad ha-hazakah*—a mighty hand—a hand that is mighty because he accepted Torah with it but also mighty because he had the courage to smash the tablets when necessary. It is an amazing concluding statement by Rashi: that we must receive the Torah, but there are times we must break the tablets of that Torah. It is a fundamental statement about Judaism with which Rashi ends his commentary and therefore how he understands the greatness of Moses, the preeminent leader of the Jewish people. It is also the first example of Judaism disrupted.

To be disrupted is to experience a break with the past and simultaneously reconnect in a new way to that past. This is what this book has been about—taking Judaism as it is being disrupted by the world around it, and engaging in a renewed examination of the tradition that has been my home all my life. I do not claim to be Moses. What I am proposing comes not from sitting at God's feet for 40 days and 40 nights. It comes from my study of the tradition and my changing understanding of it. I fully understand that in some ways it is an act of chutzpah. Only time and the Jewish people will tell whether what I have proposed here is the basis for a new Judaism. I believe—and in fact hope—that others will offer their own versions of a Judaism disrupted. The truth is that the moment of transition from biblical Judaism to rabbinic Judaism offered many versions of Judaism. It was a time of great religious ferment even before the Temple was destroyed. Many groups, like the Sadducees, the Essenes, and the Dead Sea sect, have disappeared. There were probably more that have been lost to history. Early Christianity comes out of the same moment of ferment and it too had a number of forms until certain ones emerged as the historical winners.

In the modern period, we have seen both religious and non-religious forms of Judaism. It will take decades, if not centuries, before it will be clear which form or forms of Judaism will succeed. Our task is to respond to this moment. What is the Torah that is needed for our time?

The midrash says that the Ten Commandments were put inside the Ark of the Covenant in the sanctuary. Alongside the second set of tablets that Moses brought down from Sinai, the broken pieces of the first set of tablets were also placed in the ark. The broken and the whole make up the Torah. The eternal and the temporary. The universal Torah, which served as the blueprint for the creation of the world, and the minute details of the building of the sanctuary in the desert. All of it is Torah.

How do you know what you believe isn't a distortion of Torah? You don't. Every religion is filled with distortions of its teachings. We can only try our best, guided by the understanding that God and the "true" Torah are unknowable. It is a form of idolatry to claim you know the absolute truth, as though you live in the land of certainty. We are only on the journey to the Promised Land. Like the Jewish people in the book of Deuteronomy, we never make it. Like Moses, the best we can do is see the Promised Land far off in the distance. We journey with a sense of humility even as we never cease striving to gain insights into the truth.

We grasp Torah as a tree of life that can help carry us on this journey. Despite our mortality, the tree of life enables us to touch immortality by connecting us to the universe and to God. We hold the past, we see the present, and we hope for the future. Finally, we relate to the Torah ultimately in one mode. The first letter of the Torah is the letter "*bet*" of *bereishit*—in the beginning. The last letter of the Torah is the *lamed*, the last letter of the word *yisrael*/the people of Israel. Why? One opinion is the two letters form the word *bal*, which is the Aramaic word for "not." The Torah, then, is a book of law that tells you what to do and not to do, since there are more negative commandments than positive ones. The second opinion is the two words are the essence of the Torah. Every life starts with "in the beginning." That beginning is Torah. The last word is *yisrael*/Israel. We are Israel, the ones who wrestled with gods and humans and prevailed. This is the Torah of life.

The third opinion suggests we have to imitate Moses, who in the book of Deuteronomy looks back over his story and that of the people to see it from the perspective of the passage of time. If you take the last letter and the first letter and read them from that perspective, they form the word *lev*/heart. It is not a book of *nos* but rather a book of love. We are meant to see our lives with compassion, which includes its truth—all of it—the broken pieces and the whole, the mistakes and the masterpieces, and the tragic and the joyous. The Torah is a book of openheartedness that seeks connection with the other images of God with whom we share this world. The Hasidic master, Rebbe Nahman, is supposed to have said: "The whole world is only a very narrow bridge and the essential thing is not to be afraid at all" (*kol ha-olam kulo gesher tzar me'od ve-ha-ikkar lo le-faheid klal*). His teaching is understood to mean that despite the difficulties of this world, we should not succumb to fear. But there is another way to read this. The beginning of the phrase literally means the whole world is only a bridge, meaning that all of existence is ultimately only a bridge. A bridge allows you to cross the void. Instead of being blocked on your journey you can move ahead to encounter what is on the other side. Life, then, is only about encounters: encounters with yourself, encounters with others, and encounters with the Other or the universe. These encounters don't have to be grand or transformative. Their width or depth are not critical. It is the encounter that makes all the difference.

I am struck by the unrealistic idea found in the second half of Nahman's teaching. We should not be afraid; in fact, we should not be afraid at all. Really? Is there anyone who is never afraid? But I read this differently. We are actually being told not to be afraid of the *klal*. *Klal* can mean the general rule. Don't be afraid of the common wisdom that tells you: "you won't succeed," "it is an unsolvable problem," "there is no partner for peace," or "what difference will your small effort make." We live in a world of change. Nahman asks us not to be afraid to take the path less trodden or even to make a path where none existed before. The Torah is a Torah of freedom that urges us to strive to see clearly and wisely as we encounter life on our journey.

The whole world is an encounter. Don't be afraid of the possible.

The last commandment, #613 in the *Sefer Ha-Hinukh* (a medieval work that describes each *mitzvah*), is that each person should write a Torah scroll. These days this commandment is often fulfilled by paying a scribe to write one letter in a new Torah scroll on your behalf. Writing one letter counts as if you wrote a whole scroll. The author of the *Sefer Ha-Hinukh* understands this commandment literally, but he says that even if your parents left you a scroll you should still write one. Why? "This is in order that scrolls proliferate among us and … also in order that each and every one of Israel read from new scrolls, lest their souls be sick of reading in the old scrolls that their fathers left them."

In all likelihood, in pre-modern times very few families had a Torah scroll. Books (all written by hand) were a luxury of the wealthy. This commandment must have been largely aspirational, but I am very struck by the last line. Since Torah scrolls are exact copies of the Torah text, in what way would it matter if you were reading from an old scroll or a brand new one? The idea that a new generation's soul might be sick of the old scrolls left to them by previous generations suggests a broader understanding of this commandment. The Torah of the new generation needs to be experienced as fresh by that generation. As Rav Kook, the 20th-century theologian, wrote, "the old must be renewed and the new must be made holy."

For me, a metaphorical understanding of this, the last commandment, is appropriate. In fact, we all write a Torah scroll: it is the story of our lives. We write it by our deeds and misdeeds. It is filled with hopes and disappointments. It is probably the only commandment that every Jew fulfills even if we do it without awareness. We leave the Torah we have written to family and friends to read and remember when we are gone. The author of the *Sefer Ha-Hinukh* is wrong. Those handed-down Torahs enrich rather than sicken the souls of the living. They provide comfort and ongoing connection to those who are no longer alive. These Torahs will be repeated as long as memories endure. The themes of each Torah parallel the written Torah, whose Hebrew names trace our individual lives. It contains beginnings and growing up (*bereishit*). It continues with adulthood as we are given different names (*shemot*) defined by our professions, our relationships, and the qualities that distinguish us. What becomes our calling (*va-yikra*), what has been holy about our lives? How well did we manage traveling through the desert (*be-midbar*)? Looking back over our lives, what is the legacy (*devarim*) that we leave behind?

This is a text about the Men of the Great Assembly, a legendary group of sages from the Second Temple period. The text tells how they came to be known by this designation. In the Torah, Moses referred to God as "great, mighty and awesome" (Deut. 10:17), a phrase that later became a part of the central prayer of Jewish liturgy—the Amidah. Many years later, the prophets Daniel and Jeremiah refused to call God either mighty or awesome because in their time the Jewish people were persecuted and the Temple in Jerusalem was destroyed. The Men of the Great Assembly redefined these attributes, recasting the notion of God's "might" as God's willingness to be long-suffering and God's "awesomeness" as demonstrated by the very existence of the people of Israel through its many years of exile. Because they restored God's reputation, they are called the Men of the Great Assembly. But the question then remains: How could Daniel and Jeremiah ignore the authority of Moses and omit the attributes "mighty" or "awesome" in their prayers? R. Eleazar replies: Because they understood God wants to hear the truth (Yoma 69b).

I was first taught this text my freshman year at Yeshiva University by Rav Aaron Lichtenstein, a Talmud scholar who died in 2015. He would periodically set aside the tractate of Talmud we were studying and teach about a larger issue. He used this text to respond to Elie Wiesel, who was just becoming well known at that time as a powerful advocate for remembering the Holocaust. Wiesel famously asked the question on so many peoples' minds: Where was God during the Holocaust? Rav Lichtenstein recognized that Wiesel spoke from the truth of his terrible experience just as Daniel and Jeremiah did in their times. Nevertheless, he understood the text to say that despite tragedies we ultimately should not doubt the existence and power of God. Years later, I came to understand the text differently. The text seems to say the Men of the Great Assembly were correct to restore those attributes to the liturgy. Yet I noticed that Daniel and Jeremiah get the last word in the text. God wants the truth.

There are a number of traditional texts that convey heretical ideas that are not completely refuted. Contemporary scholars argue that the rabbis are giving expression to some of their own theological doubts. I believe that saying God wants the truth, not just piety, is an encouragement, perhaps even a requirement for us to speak from the truth of our experience. I have tried to do that in this book. I think the Jewish world would be strengthened if we all tried to do that.

I have taught this text a number of times. It was in the context of writing this book that I realized the significance of the third attribute of God: God as *gadol/* great. Neither Jeremiah nor Daniel reject God's greatness. Left unchallenged is the attribute of greatness. Most of all it is striking that that is also the attribute used to describe the Men of the Great Assembly. They are not called the men of the learned, important, or wise assembly. When it is desired to distinguish them, they are called great.

Why?

What does it mean that God remains great, no matter what happens in the world? It teaches us that we, who are created in the image of God, are also great. The final meaning of being created in the image of God is that we have the potential for greatness. We are not completely limited by our mortality. We can think and create. We can open our hearts. We can encounter and embrace. That potential is what makes us images of the limitless God.

We are all part of the great assembly of human beings who seek to live our lives fully, lives brimming with possibilities. We bring connection as we assemble the sparks of holiness to be found everywhere in this world. Even as each of us experiences our own unique truths, we seek the oneness that underlies all creation—multiple truths, not one; a multitude of diversity that is ultimately one. *Shema Yisrael*/listen, you who wrestle with what you believe, God who created a world of diversity is like us, the many that is One, and the one that is Many. This is the Torah for our times.

Jewish History at a Glance

BIBLICAL PERIOD (1200-500 B.C.E.)
Abraham & Sarah, Isaac & Rebecca, Jacob, Rachel, & Leah, Joseph and his
brothers.
Moses, slavery in Egypt, Exodus, Revelation at Sinai, 40 years in the desert.
Conquest of the land of Israel, Joshua, Samson, Gideon, Deborah (period of
the Judges).
Kings: Saul, David, Solomon (circa 1000 B.C.E.) Building of the Temple in
Jerusalem.
Kingdom divides into the Northern Kingdom of Israel and the Southern
Kingdom of Judea.
It is also the period of the prophets such as Elijah, Isaiah, Jeremiah, and
Ezekiel.
The Northern Kingdom is destroyed by the Assyrians in 721 B.C.E.
Southern Kingdom and the Temple are destroyed by the Babylonians in 586
B.C.E.
Babylonian Exile.

SECOND TEMPLE PERIOD (500 B.C.E.-70 C.E.)
Transition from Biblical period to Rabbinic period.
Persian rulers allow Jews to return from exile to the land of Israel.
Last of the Biblical books e.g., Ezra and Nehemiah, and last of the prophets—
Zechariah, Malachi.
Building of the Second Temple 516 B.C.E.
Maccabean revolt 165 B.C.E. Hasmonean dynasty (another name for
Maccabees) rules.
Romans conquer the land of Israel 63 B.C.E.
Beginning of rabbinic Judaism with such teachers as Hillel and Shammai.
Birth and death of Jesus. Beginning of Christianity. Dead Sea Sect.
Revolt against Rome leads to the destruction of the Temple, the end of the
Jewish state, and the dispersion of Jews. 70 C.E.

RABBINIC JUDAISM (70 C.E.-1000 C.E.)
Rabbinic Judaism replaces Biblical Judaism. Teachers (known as the rabbis)
replace priests. Ritual and prayer replace sacrifices. Halakha/Jewish law is created.
At first it is an oral tradition, then written down. Mishna/early rabbinic teaching
(200 C.E.). Two centers: in Israel and in Babylonia. Then in the sixth century the

ongoing discussion is written down: Gemara. Together they are called the Talmud.

Besides the discussion of legal matters, the rabbis also interpreted the stories of the Bible as well as matters of theology and the nature of human beings and the world. This is called Midrash.

Rabbinic Judaism continued to develop after the Talmud's completion. The period up until the year 1000 C.E. is called the Geonic period, after the leadership of rabbinic Judaism of this time.

MEDIEVAL PERIOD (1000 C.E.-1500 C.E.)

Ashkenazic Jews lived in France/Germany. Commentaries on the Bible and Talmud. Rashi is the most well-known commentator. Flourishing of rabbinic Judaism, including codes and responsa literature. Status as outsiders. Persecutions by Christians, beginning with Crusades. Blood libels. Expulsions. Money lending.

Sephardic Jews lived in Spain and North Africa. Inferior but protected status under Islam. Golden Age of Spanish Jewry. In addition to rabbinic scholars, there were also poets, grammarians, court officials and philosophers. Maimonides was the leading philosopher and rabbinic authority of Medieval Jewry. The central work of Jewish mysticism, the Zohar, was composed in Spain. 1492: Jews' expulsion from Spain. Spanish Inquisition. Marranos (secret Jews).

A WORLD IN TRANSITION (1500-1750 C.E.)

Jews from Spain spread throughout the Mediterranean and to Amsterdam. The Jews from France and Germany settled in Poland and Russia. Rabbinic Judaism continued even as the first signs of the modern world emerged. Spinoza. Isaac Luria and the mystics of Safed. The Shulchan Arukh—code of Jewish law. The Chelmnitzki massacres of 1648. The false messiah Shabbetai Zevi. The first Jews in North America.

MODERN WORLD (1750 C.E. to the present)

Revolution is in the air. Enlightenment and Emancipation. Jews become citizens. In Eastern Europe, Hasidism breaks with rabbinic Judaism and with earlier Jewish mysticism. Moses Mendelssohn. Reform Judaism. Conservative Judaism. Modern Orthodoxy. Secular Judaism. Wissenschaft—Jewish scholarship. Political Judaism. Jewish fiction and poetry. Sholem Aleichem. Zionism. Emigration to America. Aliyah to Israel. Martin Buber. Mordecai Kaplan. Franz Rosenzweig.

Holocaust. Founding of the State of Israel. Federations. The Six-Day War. Jewish counter-culture. Elie Wiesel. Abraham Joshua Heschel. Soviet Jewry.

Glossary

Aliyah (aliyot-pl.): being called up for a portion of Torah read in synagogue. Also, to emigrate to Israel.

Amidah: central prayer of every service (lit. standing)

Berakhah: a blessing recited before eating food or performing a ritual

Ein sof: a mystical description of God as infinite (lit. without end)

Ethics of Our Ancestors (Pirkei Avot): a section of the Talmud composed of wise sayings

Halakha: the system of Jewish law

Hasid: follower of Hasidism

Hasidism: a pietistic mystical movement begun in the 18th century

Havdalah: ceremony that marks the end of Shabbat (lit. separation)

Havurah: intentional fellowship/community

Havurat Shalom: intentional community of the Jewish counter-culture

Hol: the everyday or the ordinary. Opposite of holy/Kadosh

Kabbalah: Jewish mysticism (lit. tradition)

Kabbalists: Jewish mystics

Kadosh: holy

Kavanah: intention, mindfulness

Kohanim: priests who officiated in the Temple, descendants of Aaron

Kosher/Kashrut: dietary laws (also can mean acceptable)

Maimonides (Rambam): 12th-century Jewish philosopher and rabbinic authority

Makom: one of God's names (lit. place)

Mensch: a kind and ethical person

Midah: ethical quality

Midrash/Midrashim (pl.): commonly used for non-legal rabbinic material, e.g., imaginative stories, theology. (In fact, there are also legal midrashim.)

Mikvah:ritual bath

Minhag: custom in distinction to law

Minyan: the quorum of ten Jews necessary for a complete service

Mishkan: the portable sanctuary the Israelites built and used for the 40 years in the desert

Mitzvah/Mitzvot(pl.): commandment/s. Traditionally there are 613 commandments in the Torah

Mussar: a focus on cultivating inner qualities such as patience or gratitude

Nachmanides (Ramban): 13th-century Bible commentator

Neshama: soul

Niggun: a wordless melody
Pareve: food that is neither milk nor meat, has come to mean "neutral"
Rashi: 11th-century Bible and Talmud commentator
Rebbe: a Hasidic spiritual master
Sefirot: aspects/qualities. In Jewish mysticism there are 10 sefirot of God
Shabbat: the sabbath, day of rest
Shabbaton: gathering over Shabbat
Shalom: peace
Shema: Hear O Israel, the central prayer of Jewish liturgy
Shiva: the period of mourning following a death (lit. the number seven)
Shulchan Arukh: code of Jewish law (16th century) (lit. the set table)
Taharah: ritual purity. Opposite of Tum'ah
Talmud: the many volumes text of Rabbinic Judaism also known as the Oral
   Law (composed 200-600 C.E.)
Teshuvah: repentance or change
Tikkun Olam: social justice (lit. repair of the world)
Torah: The Five Books of Moses, or the whole Bible or Jewish tradition
Tov: goodness. How God describes each day of creation
Treif: non-kosher
Tum'ah: ritual impurity
Tzedakah: charity; or *Tzedakah u-mishpat*—to do righteousness and justice
Tzimtzum: mystical doctrine that God contracted God's self to make room for
   a finite world
Yeshiva: school of Jewish learning with an emphasis on studying Talmud
Yoztei: to fulfill a commandment/mitzvah
Zohar: central text of Jewish mysticism. Composed by Moses de Leon in 13th-
   century Spain.

Acknowledgements

Although I have been actively working on this book for seven years—longer than any of my other books— its ideas have taken most of my adult life to fully articulate. I am grateful to the day school education I received at Maimonides in Boston for giving me a love for Judaism and the foundation for all of my work. My years at Havurat Shalom, where I engaged in community, spiritual learning and spirited prayer enabled me to immerse myself in the practice of Judaism and introduced me to lifelong teachers and friends. I became a rabbi at the age of 41, and was fortunate to find my way to the Reconstructionist Rabbinical College, where the central notion that Judaism is evolving, calling on each generation of Jews to reimagine Judaism is the core understanding of my Jewish life. My years as the rabbi of the SAJ, a leading Reconstructionist synagogue in Manhattan, provided me with a living laboratory for many of the ideas in this book. I am indebted to my dear friend Rachel Cowan, of blessed memory, who invited me to be part of the founding of the Institute of Jewish Spirituality, providing a lens on the inner life through which I see Judaism. I want to thank my long time hevruta partners Jonathan Slater with whom I study Hasidic texts and Roly Matalon with whom I study Talmud.

For many years, a group of friends have gathered in an Upper West Side living rooms (and for a few years online) once a month on Shabbat to form what we lovingly call the non-minyan. I feel blessed for this hevre, who have joined me to explore ideas of prayer and Torah study: Martha Ackelsberg, Shifra Bonznick, David Ellenson, Jackie Ellenson, Elan Ezrachi, Barry Holtz, Bethamie Horowitz, Tobi Kahn, Naamah Kelman, Dana Kurzweil, Andrew Lachman, Ace Leveen, Diane Levitt, Lisa Messinger, Ruth Messinger, Samuel Norich, Judith Plaskow, Nessa Rapaport, Debbie Ugoretz, Levi Weimen-Kelman, and Paula Weiman-Kelman. Jane Eisner and Mark Berger, also members of the non-minyan, graciously agreed to read an earlier version of the book and provided valuable feedback. I had many conversations with Irwin Kula, another member of the non-minyan, whose ideas and thought-provoking questions have helped shape my thinking. I want to thank Benjamin Belfer, Steve M. Cohen, Michelle Friedman, and Adam Mintz who read the manuscript at various stages and offered a variety of useful criticisms and suggestions.

My wife, Joy Levitt, used an earlier version of the manuscript with a group of people in a Torah study group at the Marlene Meyerson JCC Manhattan, where many comments and questions made their way into the final book.

From the time I sat in silence in Barre, Massachusetts with a group of rabbis first learning how to bring spirituality into Jewish practice, Sylvia Boorstein has been my guide and friend. I am grateful to her for all that she has done to bring deeper awareness to Jewish life.

Special thanks to Harold Grinspoon for his support and to the following people who helped me with specific ideas and comments: Julie Barer, Amy Bernstein, Aryeh Cohen, Laura Geller, David Kaplan, David Rosenn, Drorah Setel, Larry Schwartz, and Dan Woods. I want to thank Larry Yudelson, my publisher, Laura Logan, my editor, and Brian Feinblum, my publicist; without their talents this book would not be in your hands.

My wife, Joy Levitt, is not only my in-house editor, but my life partner, who brings me joy and holds my hand as we journey together through life. This book is an articulation of our lives together.

For those who wish to continue walking with me on the journey, please subscribe to my free weekly newsletter about the Torah portion from a spiritual perspective. You can find it at my website: michaelstrassfeld.com. For those who are interested in using the book in a class or to study with a partner, I have created a study guide with many of the texts in the book and questions to think about. You can find it with the following link to Sefaria: https://www.sefaria.org/sheets/457706

About the Author

Michael Strassfeld grew up in a Modern Orthodox home. He received a BA and MA in Jewish Studies from Brandeis. After college, he became a member of Havurat Shalom, an intentional community, and was one of the editors of the *Jewish Catalog* (1973) that sold over 300,000 copies.

He edited the *Second* and *Third Jewish Catalogs* (1975,1979), authored *The Jewish Holidays* (1985), co-authored *A Night of Questions: A Passover Haggadah* (1999), and authored *A Book of Life: Embracing Judaism as a Spiritual Practice* (2002). He recorded *Songs to Open the Heart: Contemplative Niggunim* (2003). He edits a free weekly newsletter about Judaism (subscribe at michaelstrassfeld.com).

He graduated the Reconstructionist Rabbinical College at the age of 41 and served as the rabbi of Congregation Ansche Chesed and then of the Society for the Advancement of Judaism (both in Manhattan) until his retirement in 2015. He was a faculty member of the Institute for Jewish Spirituality (1999-2014). He is married and lives in Manhattan.

An Angel Called Truth and Other Tales from the Torah by Rabbi Jeremy Gordon and Emma Parlons. Funny, engaging micro-tales for each of the portions of the Torah and one for each of the Jewish festivals as well. These tales are told from the perspective of young people who feature in the Biblical narrative, young people who feature in classic Rabbinic commentary on our Biblical narratives an young people just made up for this book.

Torah & Company: The weekly portion of Torah, accompanied by generous helpings of Mishnah and Gemara, served with discussion questions to spice up your Sabbath Table by Rabbi Judith Z. Abrams. Serve up a rich feast of spiritual discussion from an age-old recipe: One part Torah. Two parts classic Jewish texts. Add conversation. Stir... and enjoy! "A valuable guide for the Shabbat table of every Jew."—Rabbi Burton L. Visotzky, author *Reading the Book*

Torah Journeys: The Inner Path to the Promised Land by Rabbi Shefa Gold shows us how to find blessing, challenge and the opportunity for spiritual transformation in each portion of Torah. An inspiring guide to exploring the landscape of Scripture... and recognizing that landscape as the story of your life. "Deep study and contemplation went into the writing of this work. Reading her Torah teachings one becomes attuned to the voice of the Shekhinah, the feminine aspect of God which brings needed healing to our wounded world." —Rabbib Zalman Schachter-Shalomi

American Torah Toons 2: Fifty-Four Illustrated Commentaries by Lawrence Bush. Deeply personal and provocative artworks responding to each weekly Torah portion. Each two-page spread includes a Torah passage, a paragraph of commentary from both traditional and modern Jewish sources, and a photo-collage that responds to the text with humor, ethical conscience, and both social and self awareness. "What a vexing, funny, offensive, insightful, infuriating, thought-provoking book." —Rabbi David Saperstein

The Comic Torah: Reimagining the Very Good Book. Stand-up comic Aaron Freeman and artist Sharon Rosenzweig reimagine the Torah with provocative humor and irreverent reverence in this hilarious, gorgeous, off-beat graphic version of the Bible's first five books! Each weekly portion gets a two-page spread. Like the original, the Comic Torah is not always suitable for children.

we who desire: poems and Torah riffs by Sue Swartz. From Genesis to Deuteronomy, from Bereshit to Zot Haberacha, from Eden to Gaza, from Eve to Emma Goldman, *we who desire* interweaves the mythic and the mundane as it follows the arc of the Torah with carefully chosen words, astute observations, and deep emotion. "Sue Swartz has used a brilliant, fortified, playful, serious, humanely furious moral imagination, and a poet's love of the music of language, to re-tell the saga of the Bible you thought you knew."
—Alicia Ostriker, author, *For the Love of God: The Bible as an Open Book*

Eternal Questions by Rabbi Josh Feigelson. These essays on the weekly Torah portion guide readers on a journey that weaves together Torah, Talmud, Hasidic masters, and a diverse array of writers, poets, musicians, and thinkers. Each essay includes questions for reflection and suggestions for practices to help turn study into more mindful, intentional living. "This is the wisdom that we always need—but maybe particularly now, more than ever, during these turbulent times." —Rabbi Danya Ruttenberg, author, *On Repentance and Repair*

Jewish spirituality and thought from *Ben Yehuda Press*

The Essential Writings of Abraham Isaac Kook. Translated and edited by Rabbi Ben Zion Bokser. This volume of letters, aphorisms and excerpts from essays and other writings provide a wide-ranging perspective on the thought and writing of Rav Kook. With most selections running two or three pages, readers gain a gentle introduction to one of the great Jewish thinkers of the modern era.

Ahron's Heart: Essential Prayers, Teachings and Letters of Ahrele Roth, a Hasidic Reformer. Translated and edited by by Rabbi Zalman Schachter-Shalomi and Rabbi Yair Hillel Goelman. For the first time, the writings of one of the 20th century's most important Hasidic thinkers are made available to a non-Hasidic English audience. Rabbi Ahron "Ahrele" Roth (1894-1944) has a great deal to say to sincere spiritual seekers far beyond his own community.

A Passionate Pacifist: Essential Writings of Aaron Samuel Tamares. Translated and edited by Rabbi Everett Gendler. Rabbi Aaron Samuel Tamares (1869-1931) addresses the timeless issues of ethics, morality, communal morale, and Judaism in relation to the world at large in these essays and sermons, written in Hebrew between 1904 and 1931. "For those who seek a Torah of compassion and pacifism, a Judaism not tied to 19th century political nationalism, and a vision of Jewish spirituality outside of political thinking this book will be essential." –Rabbi Dr. Alan Brill, author, *Thinking God: The Mysticism of Rabbi Zadok of Lublin*

Return to the Place: The Magic, Meditation, and Mystery of Sefer Yetzirah by Rabbi Jill Hammer. A translation of and commentary to an ancient Jewish mystical text that transforms it into a contemporary guide for meditative practice. "A tour de force—at once scholarly, whimsical, deeply poetic, and eminently accessible." —Rabbi Tirzah Firestone, author of *The Receiving: Reclaiming Jewish Women's Wisdom*

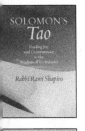

Enlightenment by Trial and Error: Ten Years on the Slippery Slopes of Jewish Mysticism, Postmodern Buddhist Meditation, and Heretical Flexidox Spirituality by Rabbi Jay Michaelson. A unique record of the 21st century spiritual search, from the perspective of someone who made plenty of mistakes along the way.

The Tao of Solomon: Finding Joy and Contentment in the Wisdom of Ecclesiastes by Rabbi Rami Shapiro. Rabbi Rami Shapiro unravels the golden philosophical threads of wisdom in the book of Ecclesiastes, reweaving the vibrant book of the Bible into a 21st century tapestry. Shapiro honors the roots of the ancient writing, explores the timeless truth that we are merely a drop in the endless river of time, and reveals a path to finding personal and spiritual fulfillment even as we embrace our impermanent place in the universe.

Embracing Auschwitz: Forging a Vibrant, Life-Affirming Judaism that Takes the Holocaust Seriously by Rabbi Joshua Hammerman.The Judaism of Sinai and the Judaism of Auschwitz are merging, resulting in new visions of Judaism that are only beginning to take shape. "Should be read by every Jew who cares about Judaism." — Rabbi Dr. Irving "Yitz" Greenberg